THE BIBLE

ANSWER BOOK™

Over 260 of the Most Frequently Asked Questions

JAMES STUART BELL WITH SAM O'NEAL

.
Published by Sourcebooks, Inc.
P.O. Box 4410, Naperville, Illinois 60567-4410
(630) 961-3900
Fax: (630) 961-2168
www.sourcebooks.com

Library of Congress CIP Data is on file with the publisher.

Printed and bound in the United States of America.
VP 10 9 8 7 6 5

Dedication

This book is dedicated to my sister, Cathy Massarelli

Acknowledgments

I'd like to especially thank Peter Lynch for acquiring this title and seeing it fit in this quality series, as well as introducing me to Sourcebooks. Also, appreciation goes to Kelly Bale and Anne Hartman for their fine editorial assistance.

Contents

Introduction

Given that you're reading this book, it's a fairly safe bet that you're interested in the Bible, and you should be! The Bible is the bestselling book of all time, after all, with millions of copies produced every year. (It's the most quoted book of all time, too.) Beyond that, the Bible serves as the foundation of Christianity, Western literature, and modern law. Thousands of people have spent their entire lives studying the Bible, and millions of people base the most important decisions of their lives on what the Bible says.

But if that's true, then why does the world need something called *The Bible Answer Book*? If the Bible is that pervasive, shouldn't everyone have a good understanding of it by now? The answer is no, of course, because popularity does not always lead to understanding. Recognition does not lead to knowledge.

It's kind of like those fancy DVD players that people take home from Best Buy or Target—the kind with all the different bells and whistles. Almost everyone has one at home (some people have several), and a great many people use them regularly, but how often have you encountered someone who has really explored what those DVD players can do? How often have you explored them yourself? Do you know what makes a progressive-scan DVD player different from other kinds? Do you look at digital pictures through your DVD player, or play MP3s? Can you even set the clock to the right time?

No, most of us keep things on the surface. We put a DVD in the slot, use the remote to press Play, and take the DVD out when the movie is over. Anything else just seems too complicated—the rewards don't match the effort involved.

A lot of people feel the same way about the Bible. They take it off the shelf, carry it to church or to a Bible study, and then put it back on the shelf when they are finished. Even when people make an effort to read the Bible regularly on their own, they often feel confused about what it says or unsure about what to do. Or they just feel bored.

These feelings shouldn't be surprising. The Bible was written over a period of two thousand years by more than forty authors. It was written in three separate languages by people from cultures that look nothing like ours, and it has been translated over and over again through the centuries.

In other words, the Bible is a confusing book! It's also a supernatural book, though, a holy book, and a book that can help us change into the people we were meant to be. It's a book that is worth the effort of digging deeper and one that will reward us for our effort.

The Bible Answer Book can help you in that process. The chapter following this introduction will give you a better understanding of the ancient world and the cultural assumptions and expectations of the biblical authors. Chapter 2 will help you answer the question that we all need to address at some point in our spiritual walk: Can the Bible really be trusted?

In the middle chapters of this book, you'll take a whirlwind tour through the pages of scripture that will help you answer fundamental questions about the Bible's authors, main characters, main places, and main events. Those chapters divide the Bible into its various literary genres, as follows:

- **The Pentateuch** The first five books of the Bible, also known as the Books of the Law.
- **The Histories** These historical narratives describe God's continued interaction with the Jewish people and the establishment of Israel as a nation.
- **Wisdom and Poetry** Written much differently from the historical books, this section delves into the heart and emotion of God's interaction with humanity and our interaction with God.
- **The Prophets** Throughout Israel's history, God often spoke to his people and the people of other nations through human representatives. These books contain their words and deeds.
- **The Gospels and Acts** The first four books of the New Testament record the life and ministry of Jesus through the insight and experience of four people. The Book of Acts serves as their sequel and tells the story of the birth of the church.
- **The Letters of Paul** The apostle Paul was a leading figure in the early church, especially among the gentiles. These letters contain fruitful words of warning and instruction for Christians of all ages.
- **The General Epistles** Other leaders of the early church—including Peter, James, and John—contributed instruction for the first Christians, and sometimes correction for harmful practices and beliefs.
- **The Apocalyptic Books** The literature of Apocalypse was a specific genre in the ancient world, with specific rules and structures. The Book of Daniel and the Book of Revelation follow these rules and need to be interpreted accordingly.

The final chapters of this book are focused on application. They explore the Bible's influence in the doctrine of Judaism and Christianity, as well as its contributions to modern ethics. The last chapter will help you learn several ways to use and connect with God's Word every day.

OVERVIEW

The revolutionary words of the Bible seek to change the course of our lives and point us in a new direction. This first section answers some key questions about the origins of the Bible. Where did the Bible come from and can it be trusted?

Chapter 1

THE BIBLE AND ANCIENT CULTURE

- Question 1. Other than the Israelites, what cultures were present in the ancient Middle East during the time of the Old Testament?
- Question 2. What other historical events were occurring around the world during the time of the Israelites?
- Question 3. What was the geography of the Promised Land?
- Question 4. What are some of the main cultural differences between the ancient Middle East and the modern West?
- Question 5. How did the Israelites understand the structure of the world around them?
- Question 6. What was the role of mythology in the ancient world?
- Question 7. Are there connections between the Old Testament and the mythologies of the ancient world?
- Question 8. How did people in the ancient world understand genealogies?
- Question 9. How did the people of the ancient world view religion and worship?

Question 1. Other than the Israelites, what cultures were present in the ancient Middle East during the time of the Old Testament?

The region we now call the Middle East contains a large amount of land, and the time line of the Old Testament spans almost four thousand years, so obviously there isn't room here to discuss all of the cultures that came and went around the Israelites. There were several major groups that interacted with the Israelites in various ways, though, including the following:

- **The Egyptians** No other people or group intersected with the records of the Old Testament more than the Egyptians. Located to the south and west of Palestine along the Mediterranean coast, Egypt remained a dominant power in the Middle East for most of the time period covered by the Old Testament, due largely to the country's advantageous natural resources, especially the Nile River, which gave the Egyptians a consistent source of irrigation for their crops.
- **The Sumerians** Most scholars believe that the Sumerians are the earliest known civilization in the world. They date back to 4500 BC, perhaps beyond, and were influential in the region until around 1700 BC, when they were swallowed up by the Babylonians. Sumer was located in the southeastern corner of Mesopotamia, in what is now the country of Iraq. The Sumerians did not interact much with the Old Testament except that Abraham, obeying a command from God, left the Sumerian city of Ur and settled in what would become the Promised Land.
- **The Canaanites** The land of Canaan is where Abraham settled in obedience to God, probably around 2000 BC. It was a stretch of land extending along the coast of the Mediterranean Sea in what today is called Israel and Palestine. The Israelites began taking control of Canaan under God's direction and the leadership of Joshua around 1400 BC. What was left of the Canaanites was later consumed by the rising empires of Assyria and Babylon. The Philistines were the strongest of the Canaanite tribes and proved to be a thorn in the flesh of the Israelites until the reigns of David and Solomon.
- **The Assyrians** Quickly expanding their empire in 900 BC, the Assyrians were the first culture to rival the Egyptians as a regional power. Their capital was Nineveh, located northeast of Israel along the Tigris River in an area that today we would call the western edge of Iran. Assyria controlled most of the Middle East from 900 to 600 BC, until it was overthrown by the Babylonians. It was the

Assyrians who conquered Judah, the northern kingdom of the Israelites, and took the people into captivity.

• **The Babylonians** The Babylonians may have been the most impressive empire during the Old Testament, at least in terms of military might and ferocity, but they were also the shortest lived. Babylon as a nation was under the thumb of Assyria for many years until finally breaking free in the early 600s BC. The Babylonians expanded quickly, taking even more territory than the Assyrians had held. It was the Babylonians who finally conquered and destroyed Jerusalem, for example, but their dominance was temporary against the scale of history. An alliance of the Medes and the Persians surprised and conquered Babylon in 539 BC, and it was under the Persians that the captive Israelites were allowed to return to Jerusalem.

Question 2. What other historical events were occurring around the world during the time of the Israelites?

As mentioned in the previous question, the earliest record of an ancient civilization is the Sumerians in what we would today call southern Iraq. Those records point to several populations in the Middle East going all the way back to 4500 BC, and maybe even further than that. Most of the historical events in the Old Testament take place centuries later, however, in what historians today call the Bronze Age and the Iron Age.

The Bronze Age occurred from roughly 3100–1200 BC. It is called the Bronze Age because it covers the time when weapons and commercial instruments first started to be cast from bronze instead of being made from stone. (Incidentally, the period of time before the Bronze Age is known as the Stone Age.) The Bronze Age was a time of both technological and cultural advancement for the communities of the ancient Middle East. Written languages were formed, people began to build large architectural structures, and cities began to grow along major trade routes and bodies of water. During this time national identities were first formed, which led to political structures and the rise of nobility and kings.

Looking at the Old Testament, we see that Noah lived during the beginning of the Bronze Age (he was probably born around 2800 BC), and many scholars believe the flood occurred around 2300 BC. As a reference, the ancient Egyptians began building their pyramids in 2600 BC, so their culture was well-established by that time. Moving forward, God established his covenant with Abraham during the

Bronze Age (probably around 1900 BC), and many scholars date the exodus from Egypt and the giving of the law on Mount Sinai at 1446 BC, which means Joshua would have led the Israelites into Canaan right around 1400 BC. To put that in reference, Greece began to develop as a nation and culture around 1600 BC, which was about the same time the Shang Dynasty was established in China.

The Iron Age took place from 1200 BC to about 330 BC, and it was at the beginning of this period that Israel really thrived. The time of the judges ran from 1375–1050 BC, which includes people like Deborah, Gideon, Samson, and Samuel. David was king of Israel from 1010–970 BC, and Solomon reigned from 970–930. That's when things took a turn for the worse, of course, and the nation of Israel quickly dissolved in size and power until the Assyrians conquered the northern kingdom in 722 BC and Babylon destroyed Jerusalem in 586. After the Israelites were freed during the reign of Cyrus the Persian, Jerusalem was rebuilt in 445 BC. The last recorded book of the Old Testament is Malachi, which was written in 430 BC.

To put those events in context, Confucius was born in China in 551 BC, and the Battle of Thermopylae occurred in 480 BC. Moving forward, Alexander the Great died in 323 BC, and the Roman Empire began to take control of the known world around 150 BC.

Question 3. What was the geography of the Promised Land?

The land we call Israel and Palestine today held a prominent location during ancient times, because of several geographical factors. First, the land was very fertile and part of what archaeologists call the "fertile crescent." This was a swath of land that was well-watered by great river systems: the Tigris and Euphrates and the Nile. While much of the Middle East was (and still is) desert, the lands supported by these river systems were capable of providing plentiful amounts of food and resources; thus the Promised Land was famously described by Moses as "flowing with milk and honey" (Exodus 3:8).

The Promised Land also held a strategic position at the intersection of three continents: Africa, Asia, and Europe. This spot made Israel a central location on several major trade routes, which greatly increased the wealth and prestige of the nation during its prime. Israel's central location, however, also made it a battleground between other stronger countries. Clashes between Egypt (to the south) and Assyria and Babylon (to the north) were especially destructive to the people of the Promised Land, who were sandwiched in the middle.

Question 4. What are some of the main cultural differences between the ancient Middle East and the modern West?

The biggest cultural difference is that people in the Western world today find their identities through being an individual, while people of the ancient world found their identities through being part of a community or group. In our culture, for example, we value things like independence and being seen as unique. In the ancient world, people were much more interested in interdependence and conformity. In our culture we are primarily responsible for ourselves—we "look out for number one," as the saying goes. In the ancient world, though, people were primarily responsible for the development and sustainability of the community.

This focus is evident from several biblical texts, including the account of Achan's sin and the Battle of Ai. After the Israelites defeated Jericho upon entering the Promised Land, they were commanded not to plunder. All of the Israelites obeyed this command from God except for one person: Achan. He took several pieces of gold and silver, among other items, and hid them in his tent. Here's what the text says about that event: "But the Israelites acted unfaithfully in regard to the devoted things; Achan son of Carmi, the son of Zimri, the son of Zerah, of the tribe of Judah, took some of them. So the LORD's anger burned against Israel" (Joshua 7:1).

Notice that the Lord's wrath did not burn against Achan alone. God was angry with all of Israel, and as a result, the Israelites were soundly defeated in battle when they confronted the people of Ai. This treatment doesn't seem fair to a person with a Western mind-set; after all, 99.99 percent of the people did the right thing! It was just Achan who sinned, so why should everyone else be punished? But that is not how the Israelites viewed the situation. In their minds, the community had sinned, the community had suffered the consequences, and the community needed to make things right. (Read the rest of Joshua 7 to see what happened next.)

There are other differences between our culture and that of the Israelites. We view status and prestige as something that can be worked for and earned, but for the ancient people, status and honor were mostly inherited at birth. Similarly, we view equality as a fundamental freedom for all people. Not so for the people of the ancient world. They sought to establish a hierarchy—a system where every person had his or her place and knew what was expected of them. For example, here's what the Israelites said to Gideon after his ragtag army had defeated the mighty Midianites: "Rule over us—you, your son and your grandson—because you have saved us out of the hand of Midian" (Judges 8:22).

Question 5. How did the Israelites understand the structure of the world around them?

They thought of the world in a very different way from how we understand it to be today. Geographically, the Middle East has some interesting physical characteristics. For one thing, it is surrounded by several different mountains and mountain ranges, including the mountains of Ararat in the north and the Zagros Mountains in the east. Beyond these mountains are several large bodies of water: the Mediterranean Sea, the Black Sea, the Caspian Sea, the Arabian Sea, and the Red Sea.

Given those realities, the people of the ancient world formed several conclusions about their environment that differ from what we would consider reality. First, the ancients believed the world was made up of a single continent, which was surrounded by mountains. These mountains were where the gods resided, similar to the Greek gods living on Mount Olympus, and beyond the mountains was an endless sea. In addition, the tops of the mountains held up the sky, which was believed to be made of rock. In the people's eyes, the sky literally sat on top of the mountains, and the heavenly bodies (sun, moon, stars) were carved into it or hung down like decorations from a Christmas tree.

Several passages of scripture in the Old Testament reveal this mind-set about the world. In Job 38:22, for example, God asks the following question of Job: "Have you entered the storehouses of the snow or seen the storehouses of the hail?" The ancients believed that anything that fell from the sky—lightning, rain, snow, hail—was physically stored on top of the solid sheet of sky and then dropped down to the earth at different times. Isaiah 34:4 talks about the sky being "rolled up like a scroll." The image of the sky was a physical substance that could be rolled up like a piece of paper in the hands of God.

Question 6. What was the role of mythology in the ancient world?

Mythology was a very important aspect within ancient cultures, but it is an aspect that people from the modern West generally have a difficult time understanding. When we think of mythology, we think of words like *stories*, *fiction*, and even *fairy tales*. We as a culture are most familiar with Greek mythology—Zeus and Hercules and Athena, among several dozen other gods—which we think of as literature. For us, mythology is entertainment.

Mythology had a very different role for the people of the ancient world, including the Israelites, though. Simply put, they viewed mythology in the same way that we view science. Myths were how the ancient Israelites and other groups processed and explained how the world came into being, how it worked, and how it was sustained.

One famous myth was the story called "Enuma Elish," the Babylonian epic of creation. The story revolves around a confrontation between Marduk, the leader of the older gods, and Tiamat, the leader of a younger and wilder group of gods. The conflict between these groups grows until Marduk and Tiamat engage in physical combat, which Marduk wins; thus Marduk becomes the head of the Babylonian pantheon of gods. After his victory, he uses the corpse of Tiamat and the blood of her companions to construct the universe, make people, and order the world.

This concept sounds very strange to people of our day, who rely on the scientific method to figure things out—cause and effect, observation, and experimentation. But those concepts were unknown to the people of the ancient world, and we will never properly understand scripture texts that were written for those people if we interpret those texts based on our modern way of thinking.

Question 7. Are there connections between the Old Testament and the mythologies of the ancient world?

Yes, there are several ways in which the Old Testament intersects with the mythological stories and ideas of ancient cultures. For one thing, the Bible makes use of several themes and images that were common in ancient mythology. One of them is the sea.

To the ancients, any kind of open water was terrifying—it was uncontrollable, unexplored, and often a source of injury and death—and so the sea became a symbol of chaos, confusion, and fear. Darkness inspired similar emotions. The ancients did not have many ways to illuminate the darkness of night as we do, so darkness was another symbol of fear and lack of control. With that in mind, take a look at Genesis 1:2: "Now the earth was formless and empty, darkness was over the surface of the deep, and the Spirit of God was hovering over the waters." There are those two mythological themes, darkness and the deep sea, both of which represent chaos and fear. For the ancient readers of Genesis 1, the meaning of this verse would have been clear. The author is describing the unformed world as a frightening and chaotic place. But then, through the rest of Genesis 1, the author shows how God introduced light into the darkness and drew a functioning world out of the sea.

Now read these words from Revelation 21, which describes the future home of God's followers in heaven: "Then I saw a new heaven and a new earth, for the first heaven and the first earth had passed away, and there was no longer any sea" (v. 1). When God remakes the world into a perfect place once more, there will be no more chaos and confusion, which are represented by the sea, and neither will there be any darkness: "The city does not need the sun or the moon to shine on it, for the glory of God gives it light, and the Lamb is its lamp. The nations will walk by its light, and the kings of the earth will bring their splendor into it. On no day will its gates ever be shut, for there will be no night there" (21:23–25).

The Bible also references myths and stories that were well known to the ancient world. One of them is the Gilgamesh Epic, the story of a warrior king named Gilgamesh who travels over the mountains at the edge of the world and across the endless sea on a quest for immortality. Referencing that story, God says the following in Deuteronomy 30:11–14: "Now what I am commanding you today is not too difficult for you or beyond your reach. It is not up in heaven, so that you have to ask, 'Who will ascend into heaven to get it and proclaim it to us so we may obey it?' Nor is it beyond the sea, so that you have to ask, 'Who will cross the sea to get it and proclaim it to us so we may obey it?' No, the word is very near you; it is in your mouth and in your heart so you may obey it." The lesson from God is clear: The Israelites will not be able to secure eternal life through feats of strength and cunning, as Gilgamesh sought to do. Instead, they just need to obey the will of God.

Question 8. How did people in the ancient world understand genealogies?

They did not understand them as scientifically accurate lists of people and dates, which is what people in the modern West usually assume. For the people of the ancient world, a genealogy was a way to connect major events in time or to trace the lineage of a single family. Genealogies were considered historical records, but those who wrote them were not usually concerned with technical accuracy when it came to dates, and sometimes even when it came to the order of the events or people recorded.

Instead of scientific accuracy, the ancient genealogies focused on being complete in terms of literary structure. We can see this when we compare two distinct genealogies recorded in Genesis. The first is found in 5:1–32, and it traces the connection between Adam and Noah. The second is found in 11:10–27, and it traces the connection between Noah and Abraham. Both of these genealogies contain ten members, and the last person recorded in each has three sons. Does that represent a coincidence—that there were the same number of people between Adam and Noah and Noah and Abraham, and that the last person had three sons? Probably not. The author of those genealogies was intentionally structuring the two records to make them complete and presentable as good literature.

This focus on structure rather than accuracy may strike readers today as strange, maybe even manipulative. We have to remember that our values are different from the values of the ancient world, which was not concerned about scientific accuracy in the same way that we are. Therefore, if we attempt to impose scientific accuracy on what they recorded in order to set historical dates and make statements about when different things happened, we are making a mistake. If someone says, "Brett Favre's interception record won't be broken in a million years," it is understood that the person is using a slang term. It would be a mistake to try to set a date for a new record based on a million years from 2007.

Question 9. How did the people of the ancient world view religion and worship?

As mentioned earlier in the question about mythology, the people of ancient cultures processed the world around them through myths and stories about the gods' creation and maintenance of the universe. They viewed these mythologies in a similar way to how people in the modern West think about science. Therefore, an ancient culture's collection of gods played an important role in all aspects of life.

The first thing that stands out about these ancient gods is that they behaved very much like human beings. They were not distant and impersonal; they experienced emotions, became involved in rivalries, had physical needs, and so on. Sometimes the gods displayed positive characteristics, such as mercy or tenderness, but negative behavior was much more common. They often became angry and violent; they were petty at times, even sulky. Many gods were lazy. For example, the Atrahasis Epic includes a hierarchy of gods, with the more powerful deities forcing the weaker ones to do all the work. When these lower gods become weary, they decide to create human beings to do their work for them. As these humans multiply and go about their lives, though, they create a lot of noise, which irritates both the upper and lower gods. These gods solve the problem by sending plagues and famines and eventually creating a great flood that wipes out most of the human population.

The Atrahasis Epic highlights the second thing that stands out about the gods of the ancient world: They had needs, and they were in some ways dependent on human beings to meet those needs. This point is best seen through the systems of sacrifice that made up worship in ancient days. Simply put, the gods needed food and supplies for their heavenly dwellings, so the people offered sacrifices to keep them happy. In return, the gods were expected to throw down blessings on the people such as good harvests, fertility in bearing children, and so on. The relationship between gods and humans was a "you scratch my back, I'll scratch yours" affair. Worship was viewed as a contract, with both parties expected to fulfill certain obligations, to maintain peace and harmony in the world.

It's important for readers of the Bible to understand the religious worldview of the ancient world, because the Old Testament marks a strikingly different view of God and worship. First and foremost, the scriptures take pains to reject the polytheism of pagan mythologies. Every other religious system of the ancient world contained a large number of gods, each with their own domains, functions, and personalities. But that is not true of the Old Testament. "Hear, O Israel: The LORD our God, the LORD is one" (Deuteronomy 6:4) is a central theme that is repeated over and over throughout the Bible.

In a similar way, the Old Testament seeks to reject the idea that God has any needs. When God makes his covenant with Abraham in Genesis 15, it is a one-sided deal. God offers Abraham the blessing of future descendants forming a mighty nation, but there is nothing Abraham offers in return. And while the Israelites are instructed by God to offer sacrifices, the purpose is not to provide food or sustenance for God; rather, the sacrifices are to cleanse the people from sin so that they could continue to have a relationship with God. "I have no need of a bull from your stall or of goats from your pens," God says in Psalm 57:9–10, "for every animal of the forest is mine, and the cattle on a thousand hills."

Finally, while the gods of pagan mythology are usually cruel, uncaring, and petty, the Old Testament reveals that the true God loves and cares for his people. The following passage from Hosea 11 is a great example of God's tender love for his people, even in the face of their disobedience:

> When Israel was a child, I loved him,
> and out of Egypt I called my son.
> But the more I called Israel,
> the further they went from me.
> They sacrificed to the Baals
> and they burned incense to images.

It was I who taught Ephraim to walk,
taking them by the arms;
but they did not realize
it was I who healed them.

I led them with cords of human kindness,
with ties of love;
I lifted the yoke from their neck
and bent down to feed them.

Will they not return to Egypt
and will not Assyria rule over them
because they refuse to repent?

Swords will flash in their cities,
will destroy the bars of their gates
and put an end to their plans.

My people are determined to turn from me.
Even if they call to the Most High,
he will by no means exalt them.

How can I give you up, Ephraim?
How can I hand you over, Israel?
How can I treat you like Admah?
How can I make you like Zeboiim?
My heart is changed within me;
all my compassion is aroused.

I will not carry out my fierce anger,
nor will I turn and devastate Ephraim.
For I am God, and not man—
the Holy One among you.
I will not come in wrath.

All of these ideas were radical to the ancient world because they painted a picture of a God who should be worshiped based on who he is, not on what he could do for human beings.

Chapter 2

CAN THE BIBLE BE TRUSTED?

Question 10. What is general revelation?

First, we need to understand that the term *revelation* includes the many ways in which God has made himself known (revealed) to humanity. There are two types of revelation, general and specific, and we'll discuss specific revelation in the next question.

General revelation refers to the ways in which God has been revealed in the world around us, including nature, history, time, people, and so on. The Bible specifically notes that people should be able to look at the world around them and conclude from what they see that God exists. For example, Romans 1:20 says, "For since the creation of the world God's invisible qualities—his eternal power and divine nature—have been clearly seen, being understood from what has been made, so that men are without excuse." And Psalm 19:1 says, "The heavens declare the glory of God; the skies proclaim the work of his hands." Practical examples of God's general revelation include the intricacy and complexity of the natural world, the way the universe is perfectly designed to support human life (called the *teleological principle*), the miracle of human self-awareness, and the fact that the universe had a beginning at the Big Bang (and therefore must have something outside that began it).

But general revelation does not give us specific details about God, including how to have a relationship with him and how to participate in his plan for the world. That is why special revelation is necessary for us.

Question 11. What is special revelation?

Special revelation is where God makes known specific details about himself and his work in this world. The best-known example of special revelation is the Bible itself, which 2 Timothy 3:16 refers to as being "God-breathed." This idea gets a little clearer when we read 2 Peter 1:20–21, which says: "Above all, you must understand that no prophecy of scripture came about by the prophet's own interpretation. For prophecy never had its origin in the will of man, but men spoke from God as they were carried along by the Holy Spirit."

The Bible is not the only example of special revelation. Indeed, any time God made himself known to people through supernatural means qualifies as special revelation. Examples include appearances of the Angel of the LORD (Genesis 18:1–15), Moses's encounter with the burning bush (Exodus 3:1–22), and the visions and instructions received from God by the prophets. The most striking example of special revelation is Jesus Christ, God revealed to us in the form of a man.

Question 12. How and when was the modern Bible assembled?

The book that we call the Bible today was assembled gradually over a period of more than two thousand years, so it's hard to get a real definite grasp on the questions of how and when. There are a few major events throughout the history of the Bible's construction that we can focus on to get an overall picture, though.

The Book of Job was probably the earliest piece of literature recorded in the Bible. The cultural and historical setting of the book point to the time period described in Genesis 12–50, or sometime within the second millennium BC. Moses recorded the Pentateuch around 1440 BC, and David wrote all his psalms somewhere around 1000 BC. The last recorded book of the Old Testament was Malachi, written in 460 BC after the temple and walls of Jerusalem had been rebuilt. The books that make up the Old Testament were therefore recorded in a variety of places across the Middle East over a period of 1,000 to 1,400 years. It should be pointed out that we are not sure how the Jewish scribes and scholars separated the thirty-nine books we know as the Old Testament from the rest of Jewish literature, but the fact is astonishing that those books paint a unified picture of God's work in the world without contradicting each other.

We know a good deal more about the formation of the New Testament. After the death and resurrection of Jesus and the coming of the Holy Spirit at Pentecost, the early church expanded rapidly and steadily throughout the known world, which resulted in a rapid expansion of Christian literature and records as well. Mark recorded his record of Jesus's life somewhere around AD 50, and the other Gospel writers followed soon after. The leaders of the early church, called apostles, regularly communicated to churches and people in many regions, and their letters were quickly recognized as being spiritually beneficial.

After a couple of centuries, a great number of books and records claimed to speak authoritatively on Christian history and doctrine, and it became necessary to identify which ones were true revelations from God and which were simply the opinions of people. Starting in AD 325, groups of church leaders began gathering in councils to decide which new pieces of literature should be added to the thirty-nine books of the Jewish scriptures. Over a period of decades, these councils settled on the twenty-seven books we now refer to as the New Testament. They decided that those books were "inspired by God," meaning that God took a direct role in their production through the Holy Spirit. The councils used these three major criteria to determine whether a piece of literature was inspired:

1. The pieces needed to demonstrate apostolic authorship, meaning they had to be written by Jesus's hand-picked followers or the apostles of the early church.
2. They needed to be written in the first century. In other words, they needed to be primary or secondary sources to the work of Jesus as the expansion of the church.
3. They needed to be doctrinally consistent with the message and life of Jesus.

Question 13. Should the Apocrypha be included in the Bible?

The Apocrypha is a collection of fourteen books that were written in Greek from about 200 BC to AD 100. They cover several important events in Jewish history, such as the revolt against Rome led by Maccabeus, as well as religious ideas related to the law. They were not identified as inspired scripture by the early church, nor were they included in most constructions of scripture during the councils of the fourth and fifth centuries. Many people continued to study the books of the Apocrypha throughout the centuries, and during the Council of Trent in 1546, they were officially recognized as scripture by the Catholic Church. This recognition was not adopted by the Protestant churches, which is why the apocryphal books are not present in the Bible today.

And they should not be present. They are worth reading, certainly, and valuable as a supplement to the Bible, but they were rejected as being inspired by God early on in the debates surrounding what should become scripture. As the Thirty-Nine Articles of the Church of England stated in 1562, "The church doth read [them] for example of life and instruction of manners; but yet it doth not apply them to establish any doctrine."

Question 14. What does it mean to say that the Bible is inspired?

To say that the Bible is inspired means that God is the author of every chapter and verse within it. This idea is summed up well in 2 Timothy 3:16–17: "All Scripture is God-breathed and is useful for teaching, rebuking, correcting and training in righteousness, so that the man of God may be thoroughly equipped for every good work." That picture of God breathing the scriptures into life is especially appropriate because the Greek word for breath, *pneuma*, is often used when speaking of the Holy Spirit.

The fact that the Bible is inspired does not mean that human beings were not involved in the process. We know that Moses was the human author of Genesis through Deuteronomy, for example, and that Paul wrote many of the epistles in the New Testament, but to say that the Bible is inspired is to say that God worked through those human authors—through their cultures and languages and personalities—to bring the scriptures into life. You might think of God using the human authors to write the words of the Bible in the same way that we might use a pen or a keyboard.

There is one caveat to add to this discussion that is rarely brought up. When we say that God inspired the writing of the Bible, we are talking about the original document that was written by Moses or Paul or David. We need to understand that the Bible one would purchase in a Christian bookstore today is a couple steps removed from those original documents. First of all, those documents had to be copied many thousands of times through the centuries. While the scribes and copyists who worked on those documents were famously diligent, the potential exists for a few mistakes to be present in our modern Bible. More importantly, though, any Bible written in English has been translated from the original languages of the texts, and the process of translation is not inspired by the Holy Spirit; the possibility for mistakes exists in that process as well.

Does this mean Christians today cannot have confidence in the Bibles they own and read? Certainly not. The caveats mentioned above apply to all documents written before the invention of the printing press, including famous works by Plato, Virgil, Augustine, and countless others, and the historical accuracy of the Bible far surpasses any other written document (see Question 19 for more information).

Through the work of the Holy Spirit, the Bibles we hold in our hands today are extremely accurate copies and translations of God's inspired Word, and we can be confident in using those Bibles to learn more about God and grow closer to him.

Question 15. Can the inspiration of the Bible be proven?

It surprises many people to learn that there is a lot of hard evidence to support the inspiration of the Bible. Christians are usually taught that they need to accept that kind of thing "through faith," and some people think there isn't any real evidence to help people believe, but that's not the case.

The main evidence of the Bible's divine inspiration comes through the fulfillment of biblical prophecy. Some Bible scholars say they have identified more than 2,500 instances of biblical prophecy, and that about 2,000 of those prophecies have already been fulfilled. These numbers are probably a bit inflated. For one thing, some historical events, such as the fall of Babylon or the birth of Jesus, are predicted in numerous places in the Bible, and sometimes what a person claims to be a prophecy is more of a general statement.

Taking those factors into account, however, there are still several hundred prophetic verses of scripture that have legitimately been fulfilled by historical events. One of the most striking examples comes from the Book of Daniel. In two prophetic chapters, Daniel makes several statements about nations that will become world powers after Babylon is destroyed. In doing so, he correctly predicts the rise of the Medes and Persians, followed by Alexander the Great and Greece, followed by the Roman Empire. His predictions are also very detailed. For example, he notes that Alexander the Great's empire would be split into four parts, which happened when the young warrior died suddenly and was succeeded by four tetrarchs. The Book of Daniel was written around 530 BC, and the events described there were fulfilled hundreds of years later. (Go to Daniel chapter 2 and chapter 7 to read the prophecies and see an explanation of their fulfillment in chapter 10 of this book.)

The life of Jesus also represents the dramatic fulfillment of several prophecies. For example, the Book of Micah, written between 750–686 BC, predicted that the Messiah would be born in Bethlehem (see 5:1–2). Jeremiah 23:5, written around 600 BC, predicted that the Messiah would be a descendant of David. In Daniel 9:26, the prophet writes the following: "...the Anointed One will be cut off and will have nothing. The people of the ruler who will come will destroy the city and the sanctuary." Thus he predicted Jesus's death at the hands of men, as well as the destruction of Jerusalem and the sanctuary, which happened in AD 70. Both Isaiah, written around 700 BC, and Zechariah, written in 520 BC, predicted that the Messiah would suffer death and be "pierced."

Taken individually, each of these predictions about Jesus could be considered a coincidence, kind of like a fortune cookie saying you will "experience something interesting today," but taken all together, there is no room for coincidence at all. Indeed, it is statistically impossible that one man could inadvertently confirm the number of past predictions that Jesus did.

Question 16. What does it mean to say that the Bible is inerrant?

To say that the Bible is inerrant means that every chapter, verse, and word contained within the Bible is perfect. It means that we can fully trust what the Bible says to be the truth and to contain no errors. If we accept the Bible to be inerrant, we must also accept it to be authoritative in the areas of which it speaks. In other words, if we believe that the Bible is inerrant (and the Bible itself claims to be so), then we must obey what it says as a whole or reject what it says as a whole. We can't pick and choose which parts we agree with.

Again, as in the previous question, we need to understand that this inerrancy does not apply to the copied and translated Bibles we have in America and around the world today. Those are translated copies of inerrant texts, which means that because of the potential for human error, it is theoretically possible for them to contain errors. We also believe that the same Holy Spirit who wrote the Bible has preserved its integrity over the centuries through the many processes of copying and translation.

One more thing needs to be mentioned. To say that the words of the Bible are inerrant does not mean that our interpretation of those words is also inerrant. In other words, the original text of God's inspired Word is inerrant, but our opinions are not.

Question 17. Can the inerrancy of the Bible be proven?

No, the inerrancy of the Bible cannot be proven in an active way, simply because it addresses events that haven't happened yet, such as the second coming of Jesus as the Messiah. Therefore, we can't say at this time that every word of the Bible is correct, because some of the things the Bible says haven't happened yet.

What we can say, however, is that nothing contained in the Bible has been disproved. In other words, nothing that the Bible says can be proved wrong, which applies throughout the genres and purposes of the Bible. For example, we discussed the topic of prophecy in previous questions, and we can say for sure that nothing predicted or promised in the Bible has been actively wrong. Some predictions have yet to be fulfilled, but nothing has been contradicted. Similarly, none of the historical facts presented in the Bible as truth have been proved false by archaeologists or historical scholars.

Question 18. Is it possible that the New Testament is a work of fiction based on Old Testament prophecies?

Many people have used this theory in an attempt to discredit the New Testament, especially the Gospels. If the Old Testament contains several prophecies about the Messiah, they say, it would have been easy for a writer or group of writers to create a fictional story about a character who fulfills those prophecies. In other words, since the Book of Micah (5:2) predicted that the Messiah would be born in Bethlehem, the authors of the New Testament wrote down that Jesus was born in Bethlehem. Because Isaiah says the Messiah would be born of a virgin (7:14), they wrote that Mary, Jesus's mother, was a virgin; since Zechariah predicted that the Messiah would ride into Jerusalem on a young donkey, they wrote that Jesus entered Jerusalem on a donkey; and so on.

The main problem with this line of thinking is that it ignores the presence of a good deal of evidence about Jesus's life that is outside of the New Testament. Secular historians, both Roman and Jewish, recorded the events of this turbulent time in Jerusalem's history, including the birth of Jesus in Bethlehem and his death by crucifixion on a Roman cross. Josephus is the most famous of these historians, and there are also several others. Therefore, for a group of writers to "invent" a fictional Messiah and write him into the New Testament, they would have needed to find a man born in Bethlehem (a town of a few hundred people) who led a religious movement and was crucified by the Romans. The idea of all those criteria being met by coincidence is nearly impossible.

Question 19. How can we measure the Bible's accuracy?

Yes, we can measure the accuracy of the Bible, just like we can measure the historical accuracy of any ancient book. It is actually an important process that scholars use all the time to determine which ancient manuscripts are reliable and which are not, not just the Bible, but any manuscript produced before the invention of the printing press.

There are three methods that scholars use to test the historical accuracy of ancient manuscripts: the number of extant copies, the agreement between known copies, and the gap of time between the original manuscript and the earliest copy that still exists. In all three categories, the Bible stands out as the most historically accurate book on earth, especially the New Testament.

First, let's look at the number of extant copies, or ancient copies of a manuscript that are not the original. Obviously none of the original manuscripts of the Bible are around today, and even if they were, we wouldn't be able to identify them as such, so one thing scholars look at is the total number of the same ancient manuscript that are known to exist. For example, Julius Caesar wrote a book called *The Gallic Wars*, and there are currently ten ancient copies of that book known to be in existence. That sounds like a small number, but it's actually large in terms of ancient manuscripts. No scholar would suggest that *The Gallic Wars* is not a reliable book because of that number.

For the Bible, however, the number of extant copies is astounding. There are several thousand ancient copies of the Old Testament, and there are more than twenty-five thousand known copies of the New Testament. It should be pointed out that some scholars claim these numbers to be inflated, and a large percentage of the ancient manuscripts, especially of the Old Testament, are fragments instead of complete texts. Still, the number of reliable extant copies is in the thousands, a number that dwarfs every other ancient manuscript in existence.

Second, scholars who study ancient manuscripts look at the agreement between ancient copies as another measurement of accuracy. They study the earliest known copies of a book and compare them to the most recent manuscripts that were around before the printing press was invented around AD 1450. It's commonsense, really—if several things have been changed between the earliest copy and the most recent pre–printing press copy, then the book is not very reliable. That's because we don't know how much was changed between the original manuscript and the earliest copy we have today. Looking at another example from history, we have 643 extant copies of *The Iliad* by Homer, which is the second-highest number of extant copies for an ancient manuscript behind the Bible, but there are 764 disputed lines within those manuscripts. In other words, there are 764 differences between the earliest manuscripts we can find and the most recent ones. For the New Testament, there are less than forty disputed lines.

Finally, the third test that scholars use to determine the accuracy of an ancient manuscript is the number of years between the date of the original manuscript and the date of the earliest copy that still exists. The larger the gap between those two manuscripts, the more likely it is that errors were made in the copying. For example, *The Gallic Wars* was written by Caesar a few decades before the birth of Christ, but the earliest known copy still in existence was written almost one thousand years later. Again, that seems like a large number, but it is within an acceptable range for ancient manuscripts. The gap between the original manuscript of Tacitus's *Annals* and the earliest surviving copy is also about one thousand years.

For the Bible, the gaps are much, much smaller. For example, scholars today have fragments of the Gospel of John that are dated before AD 100, and whole copies of New Testament books exist today that were written only one hundred years or so after the original manuscript. For the books of the Old Testament, the gaps are consistent with other ancient manuscripts of their eras.

Question 20. If there are inaccuracies between the manuscripts of the Bible, does it mean the Bible isn't inspired or inerrant?

In the previous question we explored the consistency between copies of ancient manuscripts as one way that historians judge the accuracy of an ancient book. Homer's *The Iliad*, for example, has a total of around 15,600 lines, with 764 lines that are different between the earliest known manuscript and the most recent one. That's about five percent. For the New Testament, there are forty disputed lines from more than 20,000 total lines, which represents less than a quarter of a percent of the total text.

Still, doesn't the fact that there are forty inaccuracies prove that the Bible isn't inerrant? And if the Bible isn't inerrant, doesn't it prove that it's not inspired? And if the Bible isn't inspired or inerrant, isn't it useless?

The answer to all of those questions is no. Remember that the books of the Bible were copied by hand for hundreds (and in some cases thousands) of years before the invention of the printing press around AD 1450. The scribes who did this work had very strict rules and were exacting about every letter, but human error is still a reality, and yet none of the discrepancies we are aware of changes or affects any point of doctrine or theology. They are all inconsequential. For example, here's how 1 Kings 4:26 is translated in the King James Version: "And Solomon had forty thousand stalls of horses for his chariots, and twelve thousand horsemen." But 2 Chronicles 9:25 says this: "And Solomon had four thousand stalls for horses and chariots, and twelve thousand horsemen." After a great deal of research, Bible scholars have concluded that the passage from 1 Kings contains a scribal error, and should actually read "four thousand." Forty thousand stalls of horses for a kingdom of Israel's size in that time period would have been a bit outrageous. Those are the kinds of transcribing discrepancies found in the Bible—minor glitches of numbers, names, and places, but nothing major involving the core beliefs of the Christian faith.

We can therefore say that the Bibles we use today are extremely accurate copies of original manuscripts that were inspired by God and contained no error, and that makes our Bibles extremely useful.

Question 21. How are the books of today's Bible organized?

The Bible we use today was organized into its sections and parts using three steps. First, there is the division between the Old Testament and the New Testament. The Old Testament contains books that were written before the time of Jesus Christ, while the New Testament books were written after Jesus's life, ministry, death, and resurrection.

The books are divided a second way within each testament, this time by literary genre. For example, there are thirty-nine books in the Old Testament, and they are divided between four genres: the Pentateuch (the first five books, which contain the Law), historical literature, wisdom literature, and the records of the prophets. The New Testament contains twenty-seven books, which are divided into three genres: the Gospels, the epistles, and one book of prophecy (Revelation).

Third, the books within each genre are arranged by chronology and size. For example, the historical books follow the chronological history of the Israelites from the conquest of the Promised Land, Joshua, to the rebuilding of Jerusalem, Nehemiah. In the prophets, the books follow a general chronological order but are also divided by size, with the larger books (Isaiah, Jeremiah, Ezekiel, and Daniel) appearing first. While the Book of Job is probably the oldest recorded piece of literature in scripture, it appears in the middle of the Old Testament because it is a wisdom book. In the New Testament, the Gospels are basically chronological, although they overlap, and the Book of Acts serves as a sequel to Luke. The epistles are arranged by author (Paul, Peter, John) and size, from the largest (Romans) to the smallest (Jude).

THE BOOKS OF THE BIBLE

Although the Bible was written by more than forty authors over a period of two thousand years, it is not just a disconnected bundle of letters, histories, poems, and guidelines. This section reveals how the disparate pieces and parts of Scripture fit together into a unified, life-changing message.

Chapter 3

THE PENTATEUCH

- Question 22. Does the Bible explain how old the earth and the universe are?
- Question 23. Did creation happen in seven twenty-four-hour days?
- Question 24. Why does God speak of himself as a plural when he says, "Let us make man in our image"?
- Question 25. What would have happened if Adam and Eve had not sinned in the Garden of Eden?
- Question 26. Where did Cain's wife come from?
- Question 27. Did Noah's flood cover the entire earth?
- Question 28. What was so bad about building the Tower of Babel?
- Question 29. What was the purpose of circumcision?
- Question 30. Was it cruel of God to ask Abraham to sacrifice Isaac?
- Question 31. Who did Jacob have a wrestling match with?
- Question 32. How did the Israelites become slaves in Egypt?
- Question 33. Who was Moses?
- Question 34. Why were the Egyptians attacked by ten plagues?
- Question 35. Was there a literal parting of the Red Sea as the Israelites fled Egypt?
- Question 36. Are Christians today required to obey the Ten Commandments?
- Question 37. What was the tabernacle, and why was it important?
- Question 38. Why did God require his people to sacrifice animals?
- Question 39. What were the main differences among the sacrifices of the Old Testament?
- Question 40. Who was Aaron?
- Question 41. Why were the Israelites forbidden from eating certain types of food?
- Question 42. What was the purpose of each Israelite feast?
- Question 43. Who wrote the Book of Numbers?
- Question 44. Why is there so much repetition in the Old Testament?
- Question 45. Did God break his promise by making the Israelites wander for forty years?
- Question 46. What did it mean to be clean or unclean?
- Question 47. Was it really necessary for the Israelites to destroy all the people living in Canaan?
- Question 48. Why does Deuteronomy retell several events that were recorded earlier in the Bible?
- Question 49. How does the Israelite calendar connect with our modern calendar?
- Question 50. If the New Testament says that God is love, why is he so severe at times in the Old Testament?

GENESIS
Question 22. Does the Bible explain how old the earth and the universe are?

There are many very smart people who have answered those questions in very different ways for a very long time. Some scholars believe that by studying the genealogies in Matthew 1 and Luke 3, we can say for certain that earth is less than ten thousand years old. Others claim that earth is much older, noting that Genesis 1 may leave a gap of time between the creation of the universe and the story of Adam and Eve, and that genealogies from the ancient Near East are famous for being unconcerned with accurate numbers.

Fortunately, there is one important thing we can say for certain: There is no contradiction between the Bible and the world around us. God the Creator is perfect, and that means there is no inconsistency between the world he created (general revelation) and the Bible he inspired (special revelation). They match perfectly because they are both the products of a perfect Creator.

The problem of the age of earth and the universe is a human problem. When imperfect human beings study the world around us, we call it science. When we study the Bible, we call it theology. The clash between science and theology has caused much fuss about the age of all things—the clash between human interpretation of the world and human interpretation of the Bible.

So does the Bible explain how old the universe and earth are? The most honest answer is that we do not know for sure.

Question 23. Did Creation happen in seven twenty-four-hour days?

This is another question that is difficult to answer and that many scholars disagree about. On the one hand, Genesis 1 regularly mentions a daily cycle, as in v. 13: "And there was evening, and there was morning—the third day." This seems to be strong evidence that these are literal days, along with other scriptural texts that reference seven days of creation, such as Exodus 20:11: "For in six days the LORD made the heavens and the earth, the sea, and all that is in them, but he rested on the seventh day."

But there are just as many pieces of evidence that suggest Genesis 1 does not describe seven literal days. For example, the Hebrew word translated as *day* is used in three separate ways throughout Genesis 1 and 2. It describes twelve hours of daylight (1:5); a period of twenty-four hours (1:14); and a period of time involving the whole creative period, from day one to day seven (in 2:4, the word translated as *when* is the same one translated as *day* in other places).

In addition, there are breakdowns in logic that occur when the seven days of creation are viewed as literal, twenty-four-hour periods. For example, the sun and moon are not created until the fourth day, even though they are the agents for tracking a twenty-four-hour day, and the second day of creation doesn't see anything new actually being created, only an expanse between the waters that marks the distinction between sky and sea. But where did the waters come from?

The best way to approach this question is to focus on what the Bible is attempting to communicate. We can say for sure that Genesis 1 is focused on answering the questions of *who* and *what*. The text stresses that God alone is the Creator, and it emphasizes the phases of creation: Light is created in day one and the sun, moon, and stars are created in day four; water and sky are created in day two, while fish and birds are created in day five; land and vegetation are created in day three, and animals and people are created in day six. The text also seems to answer the question of why God created these things, because of the repetition of "And God saw that it was good."

Does Genesis 1 also attempt to answer questions such as when, where, and how? Probably not. The first chapter of the Bible certainly serves as a theological and philosophical guide to the rest of God's Word, but there is little evidence that it is also trying to highlight scientific facts and theories as they are understood today.

Question 24. Why does God speak of himself as a plural when he says, "Let us make man in our image"?

Many people believe this is a reference to the Trinity, to the fact that God exists as three separate persons in one being. These persons are God the Father, God the Son (Jesus), and God the Holy Spirit. How they work and exist together as three parts of a single being is a mystery to human minds, but it is clear from other parts of the Bible that God is not a plural being. One example is Deuteronomy 6:4: "Hear, O Israel: the Lord our God, the Lord is one."

There is a more likely reason for God referring to himself as "us," however. In the ancient world, kings often spoke in the plural when referring to themselves. It was a common figure of speech for referencing the king, his advisors, and his court; the king spoke for everyone, so the "us" and "our" in the Bible is likely God as the divine King speaking for himself and his court of heavenly angels.

Question 25. What would have happened if Adam and Eve had not sinned in the Garden of Eden?

The technically correct answer is, "God only knows," but the logical answer is that sin would have entered the world at a later time. Starting with Adam and Eve, God created all human beings with what we call free will—the ability to choose between right and wrong. It is what makes us capable of loving and obeying God.

If the Tree of the Knowledge of Good and Evil had not been in the garden, Adam and Eve would not have had the chance to obey or disobey God; they would have been no better than robots created to sow and reap and talk and reproduce. With the ability to love and obey God, though, also comes the ability to disobey and reject him, which is what it means to be human. That being the case, it is safe to assume that had Adam and Eve not sinned, some human would have eventually made a poor choice and brought sin into the world.

Question 26. Where did Cain's wife come from?

If we understand Adam and Eve to be the first human beings ever created and the ancestors of all humanity, then Cain's wife had to have been a daughter of Adam and Eve—one of Cain's sisters. Genesis 5:4 makes it clear that Adam and Eve had both "sons and daughters," although only the sons are mentioned by name.

Marriages between these sons and daughters would have been necessary at the beginning of creation for the human race to grow and spread. It wasn't until much later that marriage between close family members was prohibited (see Leviticus 18:6–18, for example).

There are scholars, however, who believe that Adam and Eve and their offspring were not the only people on the earth at that time. In that view, Adam and Eve were created by God as human beings destined to have a special relationship with him, the first ancestors of God's covenant people, the Jews.

So it is possible that Cain took his wife from other clusters of people living at the time who were outside of the new relationship with God. Such a view does solve some of the practical problems surrounding Cain and his wife, although it certainly creates several theological questions at the same time.

Question 27. Did Noah's flood cover the entire earth?

This is another question that seems to pit science and theology against each other as enemies. There is a great deal of scientific evidence that large, regional floods have occurred throughout the world in various places and different times, but there is very little scientific evidence to support a flood that covered the whole earth at the same time. There are also several practical questions that are difficult to answer in support of a global flood, such as these: Where did the water come from that covered the whole earth, and where has it gone since?

On the other hand, many people view the Bible's position on a global flood to be cut and dry. Genesis 7:20–23 says the following:

The waters rose and covered the mountains to a depth of more than twenty feet. Every living thing that moved on the earth perished—birds, livestock, wild animals, all the creatures that swarm over the earth, and all mankind. Everything on dry land that had the breath of life in its nostrils died. Every living thing on the face of the earth was wiped out; men and animals and the creatures that move along the ground and the birds of the air were wiped from the earth. Only Noah was left, and those with him in the ark.

A more detailed look at the text raises some interesting points, however. First of all, the writer of Genesis does not use the most common word translated as *world*, meaning the entire world. Instead, the Hebrew term translated *earth* can also be translated as *land* or *country*. Indeed, the same word pops up again in Genesis 41:57, where a famine is described as affecting "all the world." In that case, we can say for sure that the writer of Genesis did not mean that a famine in Egypt had also affected Australia and South America. Rather, the phrase applies only to the local world known to the writer. Might the same be true in connection with the Genesis flood?

Verse 20 is also troublesome: "The waters rose and covered the mountains to a depth of more than twenty feet." The Hebrew here could also be translated as "the waters rose more than twenty feet, and the mountains were covered," meaning the waters of the flood rose twenty feet up the side of the mountains rather than completely covering them. This however would still have been an immense flood and devastating to the people, animals, and buildings consumed by it.

Question 28. What was so bad about building the Tower of Babel?

It was an attempt to contain God in a comfortable box, and by doing so to control him. In the ancient Near East, worshipers often built large towers, called ziggurats, as part of their religious customs. There is a great deal of archaeological evidence concerning these towers, and some even remain standing today.

Ziggurats were not built to help men climb up into heaven, as is often supposed. Rather, ziggurats provided a way for a god to come down from heaven and enter his temple to be worshiped; thus everything was nice and tidy in the minds of the worshipers—they built a tower and a temple, the god came down and received offerings, and then the god was expected to provide blessings of fertility, rain, and good harvests.

In the Bible account of Genesis 11, God understands what the people are attempting by building the tower. He even seems to accommodate their wishes, saying "Come, let us go down..." (v. 7). God's arrival does not go the way the people expected, though. God is holy, mysterious, and all powerful. He does not fit into the comfortable box set up by the ziggurat and the temple; he cannot be controlled by rituals and customs. Instead, he reveals his power and control by scattering the people and confusing their language.

Question 29. What was the purpose of circumcision?

God set up a covenant, a promise, with Abram that he would bless Abram's descendents, even changing Abram's name to Abraham, which means father of a multitude. God included the Promised Land as part of this blessing, and also promised that all nations would be blessed through Abraham. This was the launching point of the Jewish nation as God's chosen people.

In response, all male descendants of Abraham were required to become circumcised as an act of obedience to the covenant. For each Jewish man, it was public recognition, right at the beginning of life, that he was set apart for God. It was also a permanent reminder of the terms of God's covenant, as well as the blessings God had promised. For a Jewish person in the time of Abraham and beyond, to turn your back on the practice of circumcision was to turn your back on God.

Circumcision no longer has this covenant significance for Christians today. We interact with God under the terms of a new covenant, which was initiated and paid for by the sacrifice of Jesus on the cross. For Christians today, baptism has replaced circumcision as a public expression of our relationship with God.

Question 30. Was it cruel of God to ask Abraham to sacrifice Isaac?

It certainly seems that way to us. Even knowing that God never intended Abraham to carry out the act and actually kill Isaac, it still seems unnecessary for God to put Abraham through the pain he must have experienced on the journey toward Moriah, not to mention how horrific it must have been for him to bind up his son and sharpen the knife.

We can learn from the example of Abraham himself, though. Hebrews 11:17–19 looks back at the incident and says, "By faith Abraham, when God tested him, offered Isaac as a sacrifice.... Abraham reasoned that God could raise the dead, and figuratively speaking, he did receive Isaac back from death." It is certain that Abraham felt anger and fear when he understood that God was asking him to sacrifice his son, but those weren't the strongest emotions inside him. More than anything else, he possessed an overwhelming faith in the goodness of God.

Indeed, we have an even better understanding of God's goodness than Abraham did. Many scholars believe that the mountain to which Abraham brought Isaac was the same region outside Jerusalem where Jesus was crucified. Far from being cruel, God was setting up a tremendous picture of his love for Abraham and all of his descendants. The same God who spared Isaac allowed himself to be sacrificed on that mountain hundreds of years later, so that the whole world could experience eternal life.

Question 31. Who did Jacob have a wrestling match with?

Most scholars believe Jacob's mysterious opponent was none other than God himself. It certainly was a supernatural being, as he dislocates Jacob's hip with only a touch (Genesis 32:25). The man also gave a blessing that only God could give: "Your name will no longer be Jacob, but Israel, because you have struggled with God and with men and have overcome" (Israel means "he struggles with God"). Jacob also certainly believed the man to be God when he named the region Peniel and said, "It is because I saw God face to face, and yet my life was spared" (v. 30).

Jacob recognized the experience to be an act of mercy, where he struggled with God and yet his life was spared. Indeed, his new name and his new limp reminded him for the rest of his life of his encounter with God, who is both powerful and merciful. This strange event was a keen foreshadowing of the relationship between God and Jacob's descendants, the Israelites, who often struggled with

God, sometimes against God, even forcing God to damage them at times, but God remained, and still remains, merciful.

Question 32. How did the Israelites become slaves in Egypt?

The first thing to remember is that it didn't happen all at once. The first seven verses of Exodus cover a span of about four hundred years, so there was plenty of time for the honor of Joseph and his family to fade.

As the Israelites grew in number, the Egyptians began to fear the military and economic consequences of allowing them to remain free. The pharaoh mentioned in verse 8 may have been worried that the Israelites would make an alliance with one of Egypt's enemies and go to war against him, or the pharaoh may have just been concerned that the Israelites would leave Egypt if a war did start up, which would have damaged Egypt's economy.

The actual enslavement of the Israelites was most likely a military move. Egypt had a trained and established army, which the Israelites did not.

Question 33. Who was Moses?

Moses began his life as the firstborn son of an Israelite family, but his history took a dramatic turn because of an Egyptian law requiring all male Israelite babies to be drowned in the Nile River. (The Egyptian leaders were attempting to prevent the Israelite nation from growing any larger and becoming a threat.)

Moses's mother refused to sacrifice her son, however. Instead, she hid him in a basket floating on the Nile. Moses's older sister followed the basket until it was discovered by Pharaoh's daughter, who adopted him, so after being nursed and raised by his natural mother, Moses became educated with Egyptian nobility. He was later given a place of leadership. After killing an Egyptian taskmaster who had been abusing an Israelite slave, Moses fled to the wilderness of Midian, which was east of Egypt. There he lived for several years, married, and started a family, but there he also met God at the burning bush.

This encounter launched a new phase of Moses's life, and he returned to Egypt with a new mission: to lead the Israelites out of Egypt and into the land of Canaan, which God had promised to Abraham more than four hundred years earlier. Moses was successful in his task, although he never entered the Promised Land.

Moses was an early prophet of God and one of the most revered men of the Old Testament. In the course of his journey with the Israelites, Moses developed an extremely intimate relationship with God. He spoke with God in a physical way on several occasions, including the receiving of the Ten Commandments. He was even given a special revelation of God's glory. In spite of these accomplishments, though, Moses is still described as *more humble than anyone else on the face of the earth* (Numbers 12:3).

Question 34. Why were the Egyptians attacked by ten plagues?

These were not random events or coincidences of nature. The ten plagues that God brought down upon the Egyptians constituted a systematic attack on the false gods the Egyptians worshiped. For example, the Egyptians worshiped the god Hapi as a deification of the Nile River, and irrigation from the Nile helped provide much of Egypt's food resources, so Hapi was an important god in their pantheon. When Moses turned the water of the Nile to blood through the power of Yahweh, the true God, it was a direct attack against Hapi.

The same is true of several other plagues. The plague of frogs attacked the goddess Heqt, who had the head of a frog and was supposed to help Egyptian women give birth. The fifth plague, which affected Egypt's livestock, was an assault on the cow god Hathor and the bull gods Apis and Mnevis. Isis and Min were Egyptian gods associated with harvests and productivity, and God targeted them directly through the plagues of hail and locusts. Most dramatically, God showed his dominion over the Egyptian sun god, Ra, by filling the land with darkness for three straight days.

In addition to showing Yahweh's supremacy over false gods, the ten plagues also attacked the Egyptian way of life. Dust was a symbol for mortality and death in Egypt, so when God raised gnats out of the dust for the third plague, he showed his dominion over those elements. His use of flies for the fourth plague showed that God was in control of the air as well as the land and water.

The tenth plague was most important, however, as can be seen by the pharaoh's reaction. The Egyptians believed in divine succession—the idea that each pharaoh was really a god in human form, and that his divinity was passed down to his sons—but this belief was shattered by the death of all the firstborn sons in Egypt, including the son of the pharaoh himself.

This event, along with all of the other plagues, was a dramatic statement that Yahweh alone was God.

Question 35. Was there a literal parting of the Red Sea as the Israelites fled Egypt?

As far as the Bible goes, there is no evidence in the text that would suggest this event was metaphorical; rather, the opposite was true. The author wrote the account as historical fact, the same way he wrote about other events, like the exodus from Egypt and the giving of the Ten Commandments.

Some critics point out that there is no evidence in Egyptian historical records that supports the Bible's claims, but that isn't surprising. It was very common for Egyptian leaders to rewrite history, even so far as wiping out all mention of political enemies, so it's unlikely that any official record would have been made of the Egyptian army being devastated while chasing a bunch of slaves.

Finally, while some Christian scholars have attempted to present differing scientific scenarios that could account for the parting of the Red Sea—including earthquakes or sandbars or extreme evaporation—such explanations aren't necessary. Simply put, an event on the scale described in Exodus could not have happened through a series of natural coincidences. It would have taken a direct intervention from God, which is exactly what the text recorded as having happened.

Question 36. Are Christians today required to obey the Ten Commandments?

Christians today are not required to obey these commandments because of any social obligations, since they are not part of the Israelite nation or culture. That's why Christians don't have to worry about laws that prohibit tattoos (Leviticus 19:28) or wearing clothes made of different materials (Leviticus 19:19).

They do not have to obey the Ten Commandments out of covenant obligation to God, either, since Christians aren't bound to God's covenant with Abraham. That's why circumcision is no longer viewed as a necessary step to forming a relationship with God (Genesis 17:10).

The Ten Commandments, however, still remain extremely relevant to all followers of God—past, present, and future—because they are a revelation of who God is and what he expects from those who follow him. They are a snapshot of God's holiness and of how Christians can live in ways that are set apart from the world around them.

Question 37. What was the tabernacle, and why was it important?

The tabernacle was a temporary structure on earth where God made his presence known to his people. Structurally, it was basically a large tent that could be carried, assembled, and disassembled regularly as the Israelites journeyed toward the Promised Land. The tent was divided into three sections: the outer courtyard, the holy place, and the Holy of Holies. Only priests were allowed in the holy place, and only the high priest was allowed, once a year, into the Holy of Holies, where God's presence rested.

The tabernacle was important because it represented God's commitment to restoring a relationship with his people. Back in the Garden of Eden, God had walked and talked with Adam and Eve in physical form, but sin separated humanity from God, and people were forced to leave his presence.

God did not abandon us, however. He still spoke to a few select men, like Noah and Abraham. The exodus from Egypt was a turning point in the Israelites' relationship with God because of the pillars of fire and smoke, which represented God's presence. That was the first time he had appeared to all the Israelites instead of only a select few. God was bringing his people one step closer to a restored relationship with him.

The tabernacle was another step. The pillars of fire and smoke appeared and disappeared, but the tabernacle was always present in the Israelite camp. It was a more permanent manifestation of God's presence. It was also a constant reminder that God was journeying with his people and that they could trust him to fulfill his promises.

LEVITICUS
Question 38. Why did God require his people to sacrifice animals?

To fully understand the answer to this question, we need to pull away from our modern, Western culture. Few Americans today witness the killing of animals, even those consumed as food, but that was not the case in the ancient world. For the Israelites, there were no grocery stores, no freezers. Killing animals for food was an everyday occurrence in the community. It was more than accepted; it was necessary.

Still, we might think it unfair that innocent animals had to die because of sins committed by human beings, but again, it's important to realize that the animal was not wasted after such sacrifices. The choicest portions of the meat were burned as an offering to God, but the majority was eaten by people, sometimes by the priests as payment for their labors and sometimes by the family who brought the offering.

More importantly, though, we cannot ignore the seriousness of sin. When human beings rebel against God, there are consequences. There is a debt created that needs to be repaid in order for us to remain in relationship with God, and the Bible repeatedly says that a sacrifice is the only way to pay those debts. Hebrews 9:22 says that "Without the shedding of blood there is no forgiveness." Fortunately for human beings, God allowed us to sacrifice animals to pay atonement for our sin, rather than demanding our own blood. The Bible clearly states that "without the shedding of blood there is no forgiveness" (Hebrews 9:22). And lest we begin to think that God acted cruelly by requiring that blood from animals, who do not sin, we need to remember that God gave his own blood for the same purpose. Jesus Christ died on the cross as a sacrifice for the sins of all people, and it is through his blood that we receive forgiveness from our sins today.

Question 39. What were the main differences among the sacrifices of the Old Testament?

The various passages in Leviticus may seem like a lot of the same thing, but each sacrifice had a specific and defined purpose.

Interestingly, several types of sacrifices were voluntary. The "burnt offering" was a voluntary act of worship that was intended to atone for unintentional sin, but also to express devotion and dedication to God. As an example, Mary and Joseph sacrificed a pair of birds as a burnt offering when they consecrated Jesus at the temple in Jerusalem. The "grain offering" was similar to the burnt offering, except it involved certain portions of grain and produce instead of meat. The "fellowship offering" was a voluntary sacrifice designed as an act of thanksgiving; it usually included a communal meal.

The two sacrifices that were not voluntary were connected to the atonement of sin. For the sin offering, a person sacrificed a specific animal according to the person's standing in society. It was designed to cleanse a person from specific sins committed intentionally or unintentionally or from ritual defilement.

The guilt offering was something different. It involved a ram, and the ritual was performed once a year by the high priest for the mandatory atonement of unintentional sins committed by the entire community.

Question 40. Who was Aaron?

Aaron was the brother of Moses, although he was not raised with Egyptian nobility. He was a leader among the Israelites before Moses returned from the wilderness and also served as Moses's spokesman and mouthpiece during their confrontations with the pharaoh and the Egyptian leaders.

After the exodus, Aaron was given an important role by God. He became the first high priest, and his descendents alone served as priests before God for hundreds of years. These priests were mediators between God and humanity, representing God to the people and the people to God. As such, they did the daily work of preparing and offering sacrifices. As high priest, Aaron alone could enter the Holy of Holies and stand in God's presence once a year to make atonement for the entire nation.

Question 41. Why were the Israelites forbidden from eating certain types of food?

The dietary restrictions that God laid out for his people are often puzzling today, because they were so specific. For example, God said "You may eat any animal that has a split hoof completely divided and that chews the cud" (Leviticus 11:3). This description meant that cows and sheep were permissible to eat, but not pigs.

That issue seems simple enough, but then we read something like this: "All flying insects that walk on all fours are to be detestable to you. There are, however, some winged creatures that walk on all fours that you may eat: those that have jointed legs for hopping on the ground. Of these you may eat any kind of locust, katydid, cricket or grasshopper. But all other winged creatures that have four legs you are to detest" (Leviticus 4:20–23).

Why so specific? The answer lies in God's desire for the Israelites to be set apart from the pagan nations that surrounded them. The Israelites were intimately connected with God; therefore, they were supposed to stand out as holy and pure, just as God is holy and pure.

With that in mind, many of the dietary restrictions become clearer. Most of the forbidden animals don't fit into the original ideals of creation described in Genesis 1: birds that fly in the air, fish that swim in the sea, and animals that walk on the land. Anything that was mixed—like creatures that lived in the water but didn't have fins or scales—was considered unclean. Sheep and goats were apparently considered to be the "pure" land animal (possibly as a foreshadowing of Jesus as the perfect lamb), and any other creatures that walked or ate differently were considered unclean.

While all of this detail may seem oppressive—even a bit silly—there's no indication that it bothered the Israelites. They understood their mission to be set apart from the nations around them, and they understood that what they ate was one area where they were to be different.

Question 42. What was the purpose of each Israelite feast?

Each of the feasts had its own unique history and customs, but all the feasts had the same two purposes: to celebrate and to remember.

God had been good to the Israelites, and the feasts were designed to help people rejoice in that goodness and express thanksgiving to God because of it. During the Feast of Firstfruits, the Israelites celebrated the coming of the harvest and God's provision of food for his people. The Feast of Unleavened Bread commemorated the Israelites' exodus from Egypt and journey into the Promised Land.

The feasts were also designed as teaching tools to help the people remember what God had done for them and what they were supposed to do for him. During the Feast of the Passover, the people ate lamb and bitter herbs, which reminded them of the lamb's blood sprinkled on the doorposts as a signal for the Angel of Death to pass over the house and of the bitterness of the night when so many people perished in Egypt.

NUMBERS
Question 43. Who wrote the Book of Numbers?

Both Jewish and Christian tradition has identified Moses as the author of the first five books of the Bible: Genesis, Exodus, Leviticus, Numbers, and Deuteronomy. These books are known as the Pentateuch. Most scholars today would agree that Moses wrote these books, and that the likeliest time for him to do so would have been about forty years after the exodus from Egypt, just as the Israelites were about to enter the Promised Land.

It is also clear, however, that an unknown editor (or editors) added to these books later, after Moses passed away. The main reason we know this is because Moses's death is recorded in Deuteronomy, but there is also a repeated phrase, "to this day," that points to someone editing the text after the Israelites had entered the Promised Land. For example, Deuteronomy 3:14 says the following: "Jair, a descendant of Manasseh, took the whole region of Argob as far as the border of the Geshurites and the Maacathites; it was named after him, so that to this day Bashan is called Havvoth Jair." It wouldn't make sense for Moses to have added this nugget of information because he never entered the Promised Land and thus never saw Havvoth Jair.

Question 44. Why is there so much repetition in the Old Testament?

This question is another that needs to be answered through the cultural lens of the ancient Israelites. Remember that their culture was almost completely illiterate— nobody could read except for the priests and scribes. For that reason, the words of God's law were read out loud weekly on the Sabbath and also in larger chunks during feast days. Repetition was a good way to help people remember what was being read.

Repetition was also a way of showing importance in the ancient Middle East. Think of the Psalms, for example, and how often you find phrases like "holy, holy, holy." Repeating the word several times draws attention to it as something worth hearing again.

Question 45. Did God break his promise by making the Israelites wander for forty years?

No, God absolutely did not break any of the promises he made to Abraham regarding the Promised Land. God brought his people safely to the Promised Land, as he had said in the covenant with Abraham more than four hundred years earlier. It was the Israelites who decided to blatantly disobey God by refusing to enter that land.

This refusal was apparently the last straw for the people of Moses's generation. They had grumbled and complained against God ever since being delivered from Egypt, and they had even participated in outright idolatry while Moses was on Mount Sinai with God, but God had forgiven them.

When they turned their back on God's Promised Land, though, thus turning their back on their covenant with God, they sealed their fate. Even though God later forgave even this sin (Numbers 14:20–35), he did not remove the consequences of their decision not to enter the good land God had prepared for them.

Question 46. What did it mean to be clean or unclean?

God had chosen to set up a special relationship with the nation of Israel, which came with responsibilities in addition to blessings. God wanted to have an impact on the world through the lives and example of his chosen people, which meant that they had to be different, or set apart, from the rest of the world. They had to be holy, because they reflected God, who is holy (Leviticus 11:44).

One way that God chose for his people to be set apart was in the area of purity, or cleanliness. The Israelites were to be pure and without defect, especially when God dwelt among them in the tabernacle.

Several things changed a person's status from clean to unclean. The most prominent was sin—deliberately or accidentally violating God's standards. Other actions that resulted in becoming unclean included touching a dead body, contracting certain diseases, interacting with mildew, and experiencing bodily discharges.

The point was not to label these things as bad. Rather, having a system of uncleanness and cleansing helped the Israelites in their relationship with God on two fronts. First, the fact that their actions could lead to becoming unclean helped the Israelites constantly monitor their behavior in view of their relationship with God. Second, God's laws and standards of purity helped the Israelites—and us—to see that they were incapable of remaining in a relationship with a pure and holy God unless he continually cleared them of their sin and impurity.

DEUTERONOMY
Question 47. Was it really necessary for the Israelites to destroy all the people living in Canaan?

Yes, it really was necessary, but it wasn't a decision God made just so that the Israelites could have a shiny new land, and neither was it a decision God made hastily.

In fact, God gave the Canaanites hundreds of years to repent of their sins. It was more than six hundred years earlier that God first promised Abraham that his descendents would inherit the Promised Land. Why didn't Abraham get to have the land right then and there? Because the sin of the Amorites had net yet "reached its full measure" (Genesis 15:16). In other words, God was being gracious and giving the Canaanite people time to change their ways.

Because the people of Canaan continued in their rebellion, God chose a separate nation to act as instruments of their punishment. He gave their land to the Israelites as a consequence of their sin. It should be noted that when the Israelites turned their backs on God hundreds of years later, the same thing happened to them. God used the Assyrians and Babylonians to conquer the Israelites and drive them away from the land he had given them.

Also, God commanded the Israelites to utterly wipe out the people of Canaan because he knew that the Canaanite false religions would be a distraction to the Israelites. God knew that the Israelites were susceptible to temptation, so he ordered them to remove the promiscuous and self-centered rituals of the Canaanite culture. Unfortunately, the Israelites did not completely obey, and they were indeed eventually turned aside from God by the wicked practices of the Canaanites.

Question 48. Why does Deuteronomy retell several events that were recorded earlier in the Bible?

If we understand Moses to be the primary author of Deuteronomy, which is the conventional wisdom, then a look back at the history of the Israelites makes perfect sense, given the situation.

Remember that Moses has just led God's people on a forty-year journey through the wilderness because of their disobedience the previous time they approached the Promised Land. Remember also that God has already told Moses that he would not enter the Promised Land with the rest of the Israelites, so he wrote the Book of Deuteronomy knowing that he was about to die and wanted to help his people remember their mistakes from the past so they would not repeat them in the future.

Deuteronomy is a collection of a few songs and poems as well as speeches Moses delivered to the Israelites before his passing. They are gathered into three sections. The first section looks back over the history of the Israelites as a reminder of God's faithfulness despite their many mistakes. The second section looks up toward God and reiterates the laws and rituals he has instructed the Israelites to follow. It is another reminder to be holy, because God is holy. The third section looks forward to the future. In it, God clearly and specifically recites all the blessings the Israelites will receive if they faithfully follow and obey him. At the same time, he clearly and specifically recites all the curses that will come upon the Israelites if they turn away.

Question 49. How does the Israelite calendar connect with our modern calendar?

In the word of the ancient Middle East, time was always marked by the phases of the sun and moon. For the Israelites, months were delineated by the lunar cycle, with each cycle lasting about twenty-eight days. The passing of time from month to month was similar to what we experience today, as was the separation of four seasons.

The Israelite new year began in the month of Tishri, though—about mid-September in our calendar—in honor of the exodus from Egypt. The months then proceeded in the following order: Cheshvan, Kislev, Tevet, Shevat, Adar, Nissan, Iyar, Sivan, Tammuz, Av, and Elul.

Question 50. If the New Testament says that God is love, why is he so severe at times in the Old Testament?

The first thing that needs to be stated in response to this question is that God does not change. He is the same yesterday, today, and forever (Hebrews 13:8).

Why, then, does he seem to behave so differently in separate sections of the Bible? The punishments he lays out in Deuteronomy in case the Israelites disobey are extremely violent and somewhat disturbing. "The LORD will send on you curses, confusion and rebuke in everything you put your hand to," the text says in 28:20. Later it gets worse: "Your carcasses will be food for all the birds of the air and the beasts of the earth, and there will be no one to frighten them away" (v. 26); "You will be pledged to be married to a woman, but another will take her and ravish her" (v. 30); and "The sights you see will drive you mad" (v. 34). How can this be the same God who said "Peace I leave with you; my peace I give you" (John 14:27) and "But I tell you, Do not resist an evil person. If someone strikes you on the right cheek, turn to him the other also" (Matthew 5:39).

The answer is much more practical than we might think. Simply put, things aren't nearly as different as they may first appear. In both the Old and New Testaments, God seems to be especially vigilant that the beginnings of his covenant relationships are marked by pure and unblemished obedience. The passages mentioned above in Deuteronomy were written as the Israelites were just about to inherit the Promised Land, ushering in the fullness of God's original covenant with Abraham. Look at early church, though, and we see that God is also vigilant to protect the purity of the new covenant provided through Jesus's death and resurrection. Thus, when Ananias and Sapphira lie to the apostles and grieve the Holy Spirit in Acts 5, they are both stricken dead on the spot.

In addition, the Old and New Testaments have differing goals and writing styles. The New Testament covers only a few decades and focuses mainly on the new and blooming relationship between God and his bride, the church. On the other hand, the Old Testament is a sweeping narrative covering thousands of years of history. It's like a summer blockbuster, filled with the rise and fall of nations, as well as the most dramatic stories of rebellion, grace, and redemption. As such, it makes sense that the Old Testament is a little more violent at times, and even a little more cruel, yet there are tender moments as well. Indeed, few passages of scripture can match the pathos of Hosea 11:1–11.

Chapter 4

THE HISTORIES

- Question 51. Who wrote the Book of Joshua?
- Question 52. Did the miraculous events that led to the Israelites' victories in the Promised Land actually occur?
- Question 53. Why does the Book of Joshua spend so much time detailing how the Promised Land was divided?
- Question 54. What was the purpose of the Israelite cities of refuge?
- Question 55. Who wrote the Book of Judges, and when was it written?
- Question 56. How many judges ruled over Israel?
- Question 57. Was Samson a positive figure?
- Question 58. Who wrote the Book of Ruth, and when was it written?
- Question 59. What are the main themes of the Book of Ruth?
- Question 60. What is gleaning, and how did it work?
- Question 61. Who was Samuel, and what role did he play in Israel?
- Question 62. Why do several men in the Old Testament have more than one wife?
- Question 63. What were the Urim and Thummim?
- Question 64. Should Christians use casting lots as a method of identifying God's will today?
- Question 65. What was significant about the Ark of the Covenant?
- Question 66. Why did the Israelites establish kings?
- Question 67. Why was Jerusalem chosen as the capital city?
- Question 68. What lessons can be learned from David's life and decisions?
- Question 69. Why do some of the Bible's books come in two parts?
- Question 70. What lessons can be learned from Solomon's life and decisions?
- Question 71. What was the purpose of the temple Solomon built?
- Question 72. Why did Israel split into two nations?
- Question 73. Who was Elijah, and what was his role in Israel?
- Question 74. Who was Elisha, and what was his role in Israel?
- Question 75. Who wrote 1 and 2 Chronicles, and why are they so similar to 1 and 2 Kings?
- Question 76. How accurate are the numbers described in these books?
- Question 77. Who were the Assyrians?
- Question 78. What is the importance of the Book of Ezra?

- Question 79. What is the importance of the Book of Nehemiah?
- Question 80. Did Nehemiah spark a revival of faith and obedience in Jerusalem?
- Question 81. Who wrote the Book of Esther, and when was it written?
- Question 82. Why isn't God mentioned in the entire Book of Esther?

JOSHUA

Question 51. Who wrote the Book of Joshua?

Tradition says that Joshua is the author of the book that bears his name, but scholars are less certain of this fact than they are of Moses's being the author of the five previous books.

Joshua had been an apprentice to Moses for a long time, and he had seen much of how Moses interacted with both God and the Israelites. Eventually Joshua became the leader of Israel's armies, and even went up onto Mount Sinai when Moses met with God (Exodus 24:13). It is interesting that God spoke directly to Joshua at the beginning of this book, and it is certainly a strong possibility that God led Joshua to record his history in the same way that Moses did.

Others believe that the priests or scholars around Joshua were responsible for recording what happened during his leadership of Israel. Eleazar, or Phinehas in particular, could have been the author, if not Joshua. Regardless of who penned the words of Joshua, it was likely written around 1390 BC, which was between ten and twenty years after the death of Moses.

Question 52. Did the miraculous events that led to the Israelites' victories in the Promised Land actually occur?

The conquest of Canaan is recorded as a historical event in the Bible, as are each of the battles listed in Joshua and other books, but some have questioned whether the miraculous circumstances surrounding individual battles really happened, or if they may have been embellishments on the part of the Bible's authors.

Let's take a look at some of the battles in question:

The siege of Jericho God instructed the Israelites to march around the city of Jericho, blowing trumpets for six days. On the seventh day, they marched again with the trumpets, and then all the Israelites gave a great shout, which resulted in the walls of the city falling down, giving the Israelites an easy victory.

Marching around a city was a common practice when laying a siege in those days, as was blowing the trumpets and shouting, but the collapse of Jericho's wall had to be a supernatural event; there is no explanation other than God intervened in a unique way to bring victory for his people. This supernatural intervention was foreshadowed by the presence of an angelic being called the "commander of the armies of the Lord" (Joshua 5:14).

The battle of Ai The two battles surrounding Ai were not miraculous in and of themselves, but there was the strange circumstance of Israel being soundly defeated during the first battle but then routing the defenders of Ai during the second battle. The reason for the different results is that one of the Israelites, Achan, had taken plunder from Jericho, against God's specific command. As a result, the Israelites were defeated. After Achan confessed his sin and was stoned by the whole community, the Israelites were able to conquer Ai and continue their march through the Promised Land. Although God did not intervene supernaturally, it is clear that he was the cause of Israel's amazing string of military successes.

The victory at Gibeon There were two unusual events surrounding this battle, in which the five kings of the Amorites were routed by Joshua and the Israelites. After Joshua surprised the Amorites and threw them into confusion, they attempted to retreat and flee the army of Israel, but the Bible says "the LORD hurled large hailstones down on them from the sky, and more of them died from the hailstones than were killed by the swords of the Israelites" (Joshua 10:11). The timing of these hailstones seems more than coincidental, especially since none of the Israelites seemed to be harmed by them. Again, God stepped into the natural world to assist the Israelites in the battle.

The second miraculous event is harder to figure out. While the Amorites were running away, the text says the following: "Joshua said to the LORD in the presence of Israel: 'O sun, stand still over Gibeon, O moon, over the Valley of Aijalon.' So the sun stood still, and the moon stopped, till the nation avenged itself on its enemies" (Joshua 10:12–13). What happened there? Did God actually stop the planet from rotating on its axis or from orbiting the sun? That seems unlikely. It's important to note that these words are written as a poem, which is different from the historical structure of the rest of the chapter, so while it's possible God supernaturally extended the daylight on that particular day so that Israel could continue fighting, it's more likely that another explanation is more accurate. Many scholars believe this was a way of saying that the day remained cool (perhaps overcast with clouds), allowing the fighting to continue all afternoon.

So yes, these events all happened. The Israelites won definitive battles at Jericho, Ai, and Gibeon, and the details of those battles are presented as historical facts, not legends or embellished tales. The only possible exception is the sun standing still at Gibeon, which is probably a poetic phrase or figure of speech that we have difficulty translating today.

Question 53. Why does the Book of Joshua spend so much time detailing how the Promised Land was divided?

The Israelites' conquest and possession of the Promised Land was intimately tied to God's original covenant with Abraham, which had occurred more than six hundred years earlier. This event was therefore a major one in Israelite history, on the same level as the Revolutionary War for the United States. That being the case, it's no surprise that the historical records surrounding it go into great detail about what might seem like minor details.

They weren't minor details. When God promised Abraham that his descendants would inhabit the land of Canaan, he gave specific details about the future borders of that land (Genesis 15:18–20); therefore, the territorial details of the Israelites in Joshua's days give us hope. They show that God keeps his promises.

Question 54. What was the purpose of the Israelite cities of refuge?

As the land was being divided among the tribes of Israel, God instructed that six separate cities be set apart as "cities of refuge," three on the east side of the Jordan River and three on the west side. They operated similarly to Israel's other cities in terms of everyday life, but they had one unique function that related to the judicial process for murder cases.

When a person was killed in the ancient world, one of his close family members was designated the "avenger of blood." It was the avenger's job to kill the person responsible for his family member's death. Vengeance was not necessarily fueled by anger, but was a way of maintaining balance and justice, "an eye for an eye."

The cities of refuge were a new addition to this system. Anyone accused of murdering another person could flee to a city of refuge to escape the avenger of blood. That person would then remain in the city until a judge reviewed the evidence and declared him innocent or guilty. If he was innocent, he could remain in the city of refuge safely until the death of the high priest, and then he could return to his home. If the accused was found guilty, he was given over to the avenger of blood.

The cities of refuge thus were a forerunner of a judicial principle that we now hold dear: innocent until proven guilty.

JUDGES
Question 55. Who wrote the Book of Judges, and when was it written?

Scholars aren't certain who wrote the Book of Judges, although tradition says it was Samuel, the prophet. Other options include one of Samuel's associates, or perhaps a prophet who lived after Samuel. There simply isn't enough evidence to say for certain.

The book covers a span of about 350 years, but we can be reasonably sure from historical data and church tradition that it was written after the birth of Samuel, which was in 1105 BC. If Samuel was the author of the bulk of the material in Judges, then it was probably written around 1000 BC. If someone else wrote it, the date could be decades later.

Question 56. How many judges ruled over Israel?

Fourteen judges ruled over Israel between the death of Joshua and the crowning of Saul as the nation's first king. They were Othniel, Ehud, Shamgar, Deborah, Gideon, Tola, Jair, Jephthah, Ibzan, Elon, Abdon, Samson, Eli, and Samuel.

Scholars have divided these judges into three distinct types. The warrior judges led Israel through times of military conflict with surrounding nations—most often the Philistines. The most famous warrior judges were Gideon and Samson. There were also judges who served as priests, such as Eli. Some judges were also prophets, including Deborah and Samuel.

The length of time that each judge ruled is not known for certain, although the total span of their influence is believed to be around 350 years. It should be noted that the judges did not come one after another in succession, as kings do. Rather, judges were probably lifted up in different parts of the nation at different times as they were needed. It is also likely that their times of influence overlapped on occasion.

Question 57. Was Samson a positive figure?

Samson was a judge of Israel—a man specifically raised up by God to free the Israelites from the oppression of the Philistines (Judges 13:3–5). Samson certainly did make his mark in history as a military leader, routing the Philistines in several battles and even eliminating many of their rulers with his final feat of strength.

The main part of Samson's life represented disobedience and wasted potential, though. Samson was a Nazirite from birth, meaning he was specially set apart to serve God with his life. Nazirites took several vows to symbolize their consecration to God, including abstaining from wine and non-kosher foods, not cutting their hair, and not touching dead bodies. Samson violated all of these vows, however, displaying his lack of commitment both to God and to his special calling against the Philistines. His lack of commitment ultimately cost Samson his life after his famous tryst with Delilah. More importantly, however, it represented a wasted opportunity for the people of God to break free from oppression and turn back to God with their whole hearts.

RUTH

Question 58. Who wrote the Book of Ruth, and when was it written?

Jewish tradition credits Samuel as the author of this book, as with Judges. There is not enough evidence to confirm this fact, however, and many scholars today believe that Ruth's story was written by an unknown author many decades after Samuel passed away.

Since we know that Ruth was the great-grandmother of King David (Ruth 4:17), we can make a good guess as to when the events of her life took place. Most likely it was between 1200 and 1100 BC. As to when Ruth's story was written down, scholars are unsure of the exact date. Most likely it was after 1000 BC, especially if someone other than Samuel was the author.

Question 59. What are the main themes of the Book of Ruth?

Ruth's story reflects ideas of grace, sacrificial love, and redemption. Ruth was a Moabitess, a foreigner married to an Israelite, which was an act of disobedience on behalf of Ruth's husband (see Deuteronomy 7:1–4), yet Ruth ultimately became the grandmother of David, Israel's greatest king. Even more, she is an ancestor of

Jesus. Thus, her life is a wonderful picture of God's grace to his people, as well as a foreshadowing of the redemption we can all receive through Christ.

The Book of Ruth is also filled with examples of sacrificial love. Ruth abandoned both her family and her country to remain with her mother-in-law, Naomi. Ruth worked hard on Naomi's behalf and was herself the recipient of sacrificial love from Boaz, a kind and godly man who took Ruth as his wife and worked to restore Naomi's place of honor in society. In a final act of sacrificial love—one that again foreshadows the work of Jesus—Ruth and Boaz legally gave their firstborn son to Naomi so that her husband's lineage would not die out and her family line could be restored.

Question 60. What is gleaning, and how did it work?

Gleaning was basically a social program designed to make sure that all members of God's people had access to food. Here is what God commanded of the Israelites in Deuteronomy 24:19–22: "When you are harvesting in your field and you overlook a sheaf, do not go back to get it. Leave it for the alien, the fatherless and the widow, so that the LORD your God may bless you in all the work of your hands. When you beat the olives from your trees, do not go over the branches a second time. Leave what remains for the alien, the fatherless and the widow. When you harvest the grapes in your vineyard, do not go over the vines again. Leave what remains for the alien, the fatherless and the widow. Remember that you were slaves in Egypt. That is why I command you to do this."

When farmers or their hired workers gathered harvests from their crops, they were commanded not to be meticulous about making sure that every last branch or stalk was picked clean. Whatever was left after the harvest was completed became available to people who did not have fields and crops of their own, usually widows and orphans whose families had lost their primary breadwinners (like Ruth and Naomi). It should be noted that the word *alien* referred to people who were cultural outsiders living amongst the Israelites.

It is interesting to note that Ruth made a bold request when she asked permission to glean "among the sheaves behind the harvesters" (2:7). Usually people gleaned along the corners and edges of a field, where the harvesters did the least amount of work, but because Ruth had promised to take care of her mother-in-law, she asked permission to follow right behind the harvesters, a plan that was both productive and risky, because it put Ruth in direct contact with the male harvesters.

Fortunately, when Boaz saw how Ruth was willing to put herself at risk for Naomi, he reciprocated with generosity and sacrifice of his own.

1 AND 2 SAMUEL
Question 61. Who was Samuel, and what role did he play in Israel?

We first see Samuel as a child after his mother, Hannah, prayed fervently to be given a son and was blessed by Eli, the high priest. Because Hannah promised to dedicate her son to God, Samuel served Eli in the tabernacle at a young age and even heard directly from God that Eli's family would not continue in the priesthood because of the wickedness of his sons. Eventually, Samuel replaced Eli as the spiritual leader of God's people.

As an adult, Samuel played a variety of roles during a pivotal time in Israel's history. Like Moses, he led the Israelite army to victory, routing the Philistines and securing their freedom as a replacement for Samson (chapter 7). Also like Moses, Samuel served as a primary judge for the people of Israel. He traveled a yearly circuit from his home base in Ramah to Bethel, Gilgal, Mizpah, and then back to Ramah.

Samuel also had the distinction of crowning the first kings of Israel, even though he continually warned the Israelites against pining for a king instead of concentrating on God as their leader. It was Samuel who crowned Saul and served as a spiritual advisor to the king for most of his reign. When Saul began to go off track, as Samuel had warned, it was Samuel again who anointed David as the next king.

Spiritually, Samuel's life was marked by consistent and powerful prayer. He was conceived on the wings of his mother's desperate plea before God. He prayed for victory against the Philistines, and God responded. He responded to the people's request for a king by praying, and his prayers yielded a wealth of wise advice for that king and the entire nation.

Question 62. Why do several men in the Old Testament have more than one wife?

It is clear from Genesis that God's original plan for marriage involved one man being joined to one woman: "For this reason a man will leave his father and mother and be united to his wife, and they will become one flesh" (Genesis 2:24). Jesus confirmed this ideal during his time on earth (see Matthew 19:4–6).

So why doesn't God speak out against the practice of polygamy, which seems to have been common in ancient Israel? His silence is somewhat of a mystery, although there are several possible answers.

First, there are times when God does remind the Israelites that a man should have only one wife. This point is most notable in his instructions for the future kings of Israel: "The king, moreover, must not acquire great numbers of horses for himself or make the people return to Egypt to get more of them…. He must not take many wives, or his heart will be led astray" (Deuteronomy 17:16–17). The king was the representative of the entire people in the ancient world, so a restriction for the king was a restriction for all the people. Still, we would expect God to speak out more strongly against polygamy, given the clear instruction in Genesis 2.

The best explanation for God's silence is that he chose for the Israelites to figure this issue out on their own through negative experience. Indeed, most families recorded as having multiple wives in the Old Testament include a great deal of strife. Examples include Abraham (Genesis 16), Jacob (Genesis 29–30), Solomon (1 Kings 11), and others. Indeed, it does seem that the Israelites eventually learned their lesson on this particular issue. After they returned from the captivity of the Babylonians and Assyrians—a wake-up call for the people on many levels—polygamy seems to have been eliminated from Jewish culture and God's original plan lifted up as the standard.

Question 63. What were the Urim and Thummim?

The Urim and Thummim were a set of tools used to communicate with God about his will. Although we don't know for sure what they looked like, they were probably a set of marked stones stored in the breast piece of the high priest. The priest would present a question to God and then roll the stones along the ground, similar to casting lots or throwing dice. The priest would then "read" how the stones fell, to determine a yes or no answer from God.

Someone from today's culture might view this practice as random, maybe even a little silly, but the Israelites took it very seriously, and it seems that God did, too. Proverbs 16:33 says, "The lot is cast into the lap, but its every decision is from the LORD." The idea was that God directed how the Urim and Thummim fell to make his will known to the high priest.

It's hard to argue with the results from the Old Testament. Joshua probably used the Urim and Thummim to identify Achan as the man who stole the devoted items from the ruins of Jericho (Joshua 7:10–21), and David used them to continually avoid Saul in the wilderness (1 Samuel 23:9–12).

Question 64. Should Christians use casting lots as a method of identifying God's will today?

The short answer is no, but first a point of history. It isn't known how or when the Urim and Thummim were lost, but it seems they were discarded during the years when God's people were split into two nations: Israel and Judah. (This schism occurred during the reign of King Rehoboam, who was Solomon's son.) It coincides with the emergence of the prophets as the primary mouthpiece for God's will, and the fact that God never commanded anyone to create a new Urim and Thummim seems to indicate that they had served their purpose.

Today, God makes his will known to us in two primary ways: through the Bible and through the guidance of the Holy Spirit. To reach back to methods like casting lots and "putting out a fleece" is an attempt to circumvent the communication system that God has set up for us; it's an attempt to make God speak to us on our terms instead of his terms.

Question 65. What was significant about the Ark of the Covenant?

In terms of its physical structure, there was nothing especially significant about the ark. It was a large rectangular box made of wood and overlaid with gold and other decorations. The ark had rings and poles with which it was carried, and on top of the lid it had two cherubim who faced each other with their wings spread upward.

The real significance of the ark came from what it represented: the presence of God. In a way that the Israelites didn't really understand, God's presence remained inside the ark, making it holy.

In some ways it was an accommodation of the ancient culture, where people were used to the idea of gods supposedly living in idols or carved images. God made sure that his people, and the cultures around the Israelites, knew that the ark was different from a wooden idol. The Philistines actually captured the ark during a battle recorded in the Book of 1 Samuel, but the people were tormented with boils and plagued with rats so much that they eventually sent the ark back to the Israelites, to be rid of it.

Looking back, we can now see that the Ark of the Covenant was yet another foreshadowing of salvation through Jesus Christ and the coming of the Holy Spirit. Just like God's presence dwelt in the ark, making it holy, so the Holy Spirit dwells in us when we accept Jesus's free gift of salvation.

Question 66. Why did the Israelites establish kings?

The Israelites of Samuel's day wanted a king for two main reasons. Samuel's sons were lazy and wicked, and the people did not want them to become the nation's leaders, and all the other nations surrounding Israel had kings, which made them seem more fierce and stable to the Israelites.

God had been very clear from the beginning of his relationship with the Israelites that he would bless them and they were to be set apart from the surrounding nations. They were to be different, so that all the people could see that God was blessing and protecting them; therefore, the Israelites of Samuel's day showed a lack of faith in God by clamoring for a human king to provide them with a sense of safety, instead of relying on God.

Much good did eventually come from Israelite kings, though. The nation came to the peak of its influence, power, and wealth under the leadership of David and Solomon—both men who followed God for most of their reigns. It is clear that God adopted the Israelite kings into his purpose and used them for good. It is also clear that obeying God and relying on him for leadership would have been best, a fact that became clear when the nation of Israel split and eventually collapsed under poor leadership after Solomon.

Question 67. Why was Jerusalem chosen as the capital city?

In terms of the ancient world, one of the best things about Jerusalem was its value as a military stronghold. The city of Jerusalem was built on top of Mount Zion, which meant it was very easy to defend and difficult to attack. Indeed, from the time of Joshua all the way up to the reign of David (about four hundred years), Jerusalem had remained in Canaanite hands because it was such an impregnable fortress, probably the main reason why David chose it as his capital after officially taking his place as king.

Jerusalem was also located roughly in the center of Israel's territory, making it accessible for both the northern and southern tribes. Even more, Jerusalem was surrounded by fertile fields and valleys, making it a great place for farming and raising livestock.

Question 68. What lessons can be learned from David's life and decisions?

The best phrase to describe the life of David comes from Samuel's rebuke of Saul in 1 Samuel 13:14: "But now your kingdom will not endure; the LORD has sought out a man after his own heart and appointed him leader of his people, because you have not kept the LORD's command."

A man after God's own heart; that's the phrase that is often used to describe David and his life, and it's a good description. In many ways, David's story represents the best of what a person can become in this life. He was dedicated to God from his youth, and even as a young man he was used by God to do mighty things. As he became older, he experienced hardship and trial while on the run from Saul, and yet he remained faithful to God. In the prime of his life he became king, and under his leadership the nation of Israel blossomed in wealth and power, in prime position to have an impact on the rest of the world, as God originally intended.

Yet David was still a man, and the best of men are still only human. That being the case, David made some terrible mistakes that marred not only his own life, but the entire nation as well. David's adulterous relationship with Bathsheba was inexcusable. His decision to cover up his sin by arranging the murder of Bathsheba's husband was even worse. These decisions caused strife in his family for decades, and they reduced David to a shell of his former self during the later years of his reign.

What can we learn from David's life and decisions? There are at least two lessons: God has made us for a purpose and given us gifts to be a blessing in this world, and we can make good on that purpose and those gifts only when our human hearts remain connected to God.

1 AND 2 KINGS
Question 69. Why do some of the Bible's books come in two parts?

In the case of books like 1 and 2 Samuel, 1 and 2 Kings, and 1 and 2 Chronicles, size was the major issue. Each of these was originally one book, but they were split into two segments by scribes in order to make them easier to record, store, and access.

The story is different for books like 1 and 2 Timothy and 1, 2, and 3 John in the New Testament. These books were originally letters written by one of the apostles to a church in a specific region. In those cases, each book represents a separate letter that was written and sent at a separate date.

Question 70. What lessons can be learned from Solomon's life and decisions?

In many ways, Solomon's life was similar to that of his father, David. From the very beginning, Solomon's life was marked by God's grace. He was the child of David and Bathsheba, who had been married under a cloud of adultery and murder—proof that God can take even our worst mistakes and transform them into something good in his time and power. Like his father, Solomon grew close to God at a young age and was blessed.

Specifically, Solomon was blessed with wisdom. As a young man, God told Solomon to ask him for anything he wanted, and Solomon said: "Give your servant a discerning heart to govern your people and to distinguish between right and wrong. For who is able to govern this great people of yours?" As his answer shows, Solomon already had a good amount of wisdom, but God granted his request by giving Solomon a capacity to learn a great store of information and to process things quickly. As king, the Bible describes him as "wiser than any other man" (1 Kings 4:31), and Solomon's counsel was sought by kings and rulers from all over the known world. As a result, the power and influence of Israel increased, as it had done under David.

Like his father, though, Solomon began to wander from God as he grew older and more distracted by his royal privileges. Specifically, Solomon ignored the commands God had given concerning Israel's kings way back in Deuteronomy 17: "The king, moreover, must not acquire great numbers of horses for himself or make the people return to Egypt to get more of them…. He must not take many wives, or his heart will be led astray. He must not accumulate large amounts of silver and gold" (vv. 16–17).

The Book of 1 Kings specifically notes that, throughout the course of his reign, Solomon acquired twelve thousand horses (4:26), large amounts of gold and silver (chapter 10), and over one thousand wives and concubines (chapter 11). In other words, Solomon had a problem with obedience, and like his father, David, his disobedience had grave consequences for both himself and the entire nation.

Solomon teaches us that wisdom is a valuable treasure that is worth seeking after, but also teaches us that knowing the right thing to do is not enough; we must take the next step and act on what we know, which is obedience.

Question 71. What was the purpose of the temple Solomon built?

The primary purpose of the temple was to worship God. The structure of the temple was similar to the tabernacle: an outer court, an inner area for the priests and Levites, and a "Holy of Holies" where the Ark of the Covenant rested, containing the presence of God. The temple was a central location for the offerings and sacrifices of the Israelite community, as the tabernacle had been. As such, it was filled with many symbols and artifacts that revealed the character of God and also had practical functions. The "bronze sea," for example, was a huge basin of water used for ritual cleansing, which reminded the people of God's holiness.

If the temple served the same function as the tabernacle, why not just keep the tabernacle? The immediate reason for David and Solomon was a desire to express gratitude to God for the newfound wealth and power of Israel. As their fortunes and fame grew, they felt a desire to upgrade God's dwelling place and give him a house filled with splendor.

There was another reason God encouraged David to plan out the details of the temple and encouraged Solomon to build it. God desired to take another step closer to his people. Remember, he started by walking and talking with Adam and Eve in the Garden of Eden, but because of sin, God had to withdraw himself from the world lest human beings be overcome by his holiness.

From that point on, God began a step-by-step plan designed to restore the relationship that had been lost. He started by appearing as spirit to only a select group of men—as a smoking pot to Abraham, as a burning bush to Moses. He then appeared as pillars of cloud and fire to the entire Israelite community. He next took another step and began to dwell permanently with the Israelites through the tabernacle, a temporary structure. Through the temple, God moved his presence to a permanent structure, a sign that he meant to dwell with his people forever in their new home.

Question 72. Why did Israel split into two nations?

The actual split of the kingdom took place largely because of poor leadership on the part of Rehoboam, Solomon's son and the next king after him. In reality, though, the division of the kingdom began during the later years of Solomon's reign, when he wandered away from God and began serving the various idols of his wives:

> *So the LORD said to Solomon, "Since this is your attitude and you have not kept my covenant and my decrees, which I commanded you, I will most certainly tear the kingdom away from you and give it to one of your subordinates. Nevertheless, for the sake of David your father, I will not do it during your lifetime. I will tear it out of the hand of your son. Yet I will not tear the whole kingdom from him, but will give him one tribe for the sake of David my servant and for the sake of Jerusalem, which I have chosen" (1 Kings 11:11–13).*

That is exactly what happened after Solomon died and Rehoboam became king. It all started when a man named Jeroboam, one of Solomon's officials, rebelled against the king and attempted to seize the throne. Solomon thwarted the attempt, and Jeroboam was forced to flee to Egypt. Years later, when Rehoboam was king, the people grew tired of the high taxes and other burdens that Solomon had imposed on them. When they complained to the king, though, he told them to get used to it; in fact, he told them he would make his father look like a lenient puppy.

The people didn't like that, and the major part of the nation rose up against Rehoboam, bringing Jeroboam back out of Egypt and proclaiming him as their new king. Only the tribes of Judah and Benjamin stayed loyal to Rehoboam. For his part, Jeroboam believed that if he kept the status quo and people continued going to Jerusalem to worship God, the kingship would eventually return to David's bloodline, so he set up his own nation, with its own system of worship and altars for sacrifices.

The people of God thus were divided in two. Jeroboam was king of the northern half, which retained the name Israel. Rehoboam ruled the southern portion, which was called Judah from then on.

Question 73. Who was Elijah, and what was his role in Israel?

Elijah was a prophet who spent most of his time in the northern kingdom of Israel. His ministry spanned about twenty-five years, from 875 BC to 848 BC, and mostly coincided with the rule of Ahab as king of Israel.

The way Elijah burst onto the scene in 1 Kings 17 is interesting. He appeared in the first verse of that chapter and said, "As the LORD, the God of Israel, lives, whom I serve, there will be neither dew nor rain in the next few years except at my word." This is interesting because it marks another shift in the focus on these historical books in the Bible. The Book of Judges ended with the prophet Samuel and his counsel and criticism of King Saul, but then the story shifted away from the prophets and settled on Israel's most famous kings: David and Solomon. After those two, however, the kings of Israel took a turn for the worse and the focus returned to the prophets, like Elijah.

As a prophet, Elijah was a mouthpiece for the will and counsel of God. He spoke what God told him to speak (as in the verse mentioned above) and he did what God told him to do. It's appropriate, then, that the name Elijah means "Jehovah is my God."

Elijah's main task was to highlight the wickedness of Ahab and the nation of Israel, especially their worship of the false god Baal, led by Ahab's wife, Jezebel. Elijah is perhaps most famous for his confrontation with the 450 prophets of Baal on Mount Carmel, where they spent the entire day begging Baal to send fire and consume a bull that had been prepared on an altar. When Baal was silent, Elijah had the altar doused with buckets of water and then prayed a simple prayer to God. Fire immediately came down from heaven and consumed the offering, proving Jehovah to be the true God in Israel.

Elijah is also famous for how his story ended. Instead of dying a physical death, he was carried into heaven by God's angels as a sign of great favor (2 Kings 2:11).

Question 74. Who was Elisha, and what was his role in Israel?

Elisha was another prophet, and he actually began as the apprentice of Elijah. It is notable that when Elijah called the younger man to be his apprentice, Elisha burned the yoke and farming equipment (the tools of his former job) and sacrificed the oxen he had been plowing with, an emphatic sign that he was starting a new life as a prophet of God, with no thought of turning back.

Elisha had the privilege of seeing Elijah taken up to heaven by the fiery angels of God, a transition that left Elisha as the primary prophet in the region of Israel. He ministered for about fifty years, from 848 BC to 797 BC. While Elijah was brash and powerful in his role as God's mouthpiece, his younger apprentice was more beneficent. Most of his miracles were acts of kindness and mercy, such as healing tainted wells (2 Kings 2:19–22), providing food for a starving widow and her son (2 Kings 4:1–7), and bringing a Shunammite woman's son back to life (2 Kings 4:8–37).

1 AND 2 CHRONICLES

Question 75. Who wrote 1 and 2 Chronicles, and why are they so similar to 1 and 2 Kings?

Both Jewish tradition and church history identify Ezra as the author of both 1 and 2 Chronicles—originally one manuscript—although it is possible that an unknown priest or Levite could have been the author instead. The original text was probably first recorded around 530 BC.

At first glance, the similarities between the books of Kings and Chronicles are striking. Both books cover roughly the same period of time, and both books focus on many of the same main characters, including Saul, David, Solomon, and other kings and prophets. But there is one very important difference in focus between the two books: 1 and 2 Kings emphasize the negative events in the histories of Judah and Israel, while the Chronicles highlight the positive people and events of those times.

The reason for this shift in focus has to do with when the books were written. Both the books of Samuel and the books of Kings were written while the people of Israel and Judah were in exile. The people had been taken from their Promised Land, and they needed answers as to why God had allowed such a thing to happen, so Samuel and Kings clearly show the disobedience and rebellion of the people, resulting in their punishment.

The books of Chronicles, however, were written after the people of Israel and Judah returned from exile and were attempting to re-establish their nation and identity. Thus, the Chronicles answer the question: Who are we? That explains why 1 Chronicles features an extended genealogy throughout the first nine chapters. It also explains why the Chronicles focus more on the godly kings and positive steps. It was an attempt to show the people from which direction they had wandered and how they could regain their place as God's chosen people.

Question 76. How accurate are the numbers described in these books?

In general, the Bible is said to be completely accurate, in that it correctly describes what it intends to describe. In other words, it is not expected that the Bible be accurate when the authors are writing in a literary style, such as poetry, that is not intended for technical accuracy. For example, when David says in Psalm 90 that "a thousand years in your sight are like a day that has just gone by," it is understood that he is not literally saying that God's perspective on time brings a ratio of 1:1000 when compared to ours. David is speaking poetically. But when the Bible is describing historical events and presenting factual records of people and places, we can be confident in its accuracy, as when Luke claims that "about three thousand" people joined the early church on the Day of Pentecost (Acts 2:41). We understand that number to be historically accurate.

There are some exceptions that cause confusion, however, most notably the large numbers of people recorded in different historical books of the Old Testament. For example, 2 Chronicles 13:17 says the following: "Abijah and his men inflicted heavy losses on them, so that there were five hundred thousand casualties among Israel's able men." That's an extraordinarily large number for the ancient world. Remember that most historians estimate the size of Pharaoh's army to have been about 20,000 men during the time of the exodus. Remember also that the total number of U.S. deaths during World War II was 405,000. Could there really have been 500,000 men slain during the one battle in ancient Israel, and if not, does that mean the Bible is false?

A couple of explanations can clear up this confusion. The first is that scribes and scholars over the centuries have had a difficult time with the Hebrew system of numbers. The reality is that the ancient world just wasn't as concerned about the accuracy of numbers as we are, a fact that is supported in many sources outside of the Bible. This often resulted in scribal errors, which has made it difficult to say for sure exactly how to translate various sets of numbers. In the verse mentioned above, for example, it's possible the phrase from Chronicles could be translated as "five hundred chiefs" or even five hundred military "troops."

The other explanation is that the author of Chronicles was simply using a figure of speech to show that "many people were killed." This is perhaps a use of hyperbole—the same as a modern writer saying something along the lines of "the hero walked a million miles." Again, such wording would not fly in a modern historical document, but the ancient historians weren't as concerned with recording accurate numbers as we are today.

Question 77. Who were the Assyrians?

The Assyrian empire was founded by a ruler named Tiglath-Pileser I, who lived from 1116–1078 BC. The Assyrians remained a minor power in the world through the reigns of David and Solomon and did not begin gaining their full strength until the nation was well over two hundred years old.

Around 745 BC, a ruler naming himself Tiglath-Pileser III united the Assyrian empire and began a string of military conquests that included Babylon and Samaria. At the height of its power, the Assyrian empire spread across the Persian Gulf north to Arminea and west to the Mediterranean Sea and into Egypt. Its capital was Nineveh, which was located in modern-day country of Iraq.

During this time period, the Assyrians also conquered the ten tribes making up the kingdom of Israel. It happened gradually, with Israel's kings being made to pay tribute and sometimes rebelling. The Assyrians eventually took most of the Israelites into captivity, thus removing them from the Promised Land and fulfilling God's judgment against Israel's rebellion and sins.

The Assyrians were eventually drowned out by the rise of the Babylonian empire, which had broken free from Assyrian control in 626 BC and laid waste to Nineveh in 612 BC.

EZRA AND NEHEMIAH
Question 78. What is the importance of the Book of Ezra?

The books of Ezra and Nehemiah were originally one document when they were first written, similar to the books of Samuel, Kings, and Chronicles, and they tell the story of the Israelites' return from exile. Many believe that Ezra was the author of both books, but it is not known for sure. Historians are also unsure of the exact date the book was written, but do know it was written after 440 BC, which is when the last events of Nehemiah took place.

The Israelites' return to the Promised Land was made possible when Cyrus the Mede defeated Babylon. Cyrus had a history of allowing exiled people to return home, which is what he did for the Israelites. He even went so far as to help the Israelites rebuild their temple, a political move that was aimed at keeping his subjects happy and also appeasing the different "gods" of his realm. (Remarkably, the words of Isaiah 44:28 and 45:1–4 prophesied this event, even naming Cyrus, but they were written more than two hundred years before it happened.)

The return to the Promised Land happened in waves, as groups of people from various lands decided to make the hard journey back to Jerusalem. Ezra was a leader in the second wave, at least sixty years after the first fifty thousand or so Jews returned. Ezra was a scribe, and much of the Book of Ezra recounts his efforts to bring the residents of Jerusalem back into a proper relationship with God.

Question 79. What is the importance of the Book of Nehemiah?

The Book of Nehemiah continues the story of the Jewish people returned from exile but takes a specific look at several key events after the return to Jerusalem. Nehemiah is also unique in that it sticks closely to the perspective, thoughts, and opinions of Nehemiah, instead of giving a broader view.

Originally employed as the cup bearer to Artaxerxes—an important and trusted position in the royal court—Nehemiah felt God's leading to return to Jerusalem and aid in the rebuilding of the city. The first wave of returning Israelites had settled back into Jerusalem in 538 BC, with the second wave led by Ezra in 458 BC. Nehemiah led a third return in 445 BC, and what he found in Jerusalem was not encouraging. Though under Ezra's leadership the temple had been rebuilt and the people had begun their return to a spiritual life with Jehovah, the city itself was in bad shape economically and politically. Worst of all was the ruined state of Jerusalem's walls, which left the city weak and vulnerable to outside forces.

The first half of Nehemiah details the inspiring rebuilding of that wall, including the many obstacles that could have derailed the project, save for God's provision and Nehemiah's leadership. The later sections of the book detail the rebuilding of Israel's moral character and continued return to God.

Question 80. Did Nehemiah spark a revival of faith and obedience in Jerusalem?

Yes, although it may be more accurate to say that God sparked a revival in his people through Nehemiah. Ezra had been teaching the people about God's law for thirteen years when Nehemiah arrived, but something seems to have clicked in the people of Jerusalem when they participated in the rebuilding of the city wall. It was a miraculous accomplishment in only fifty-two days, and it seemed to remind people in a real way that God was still with them.

As a result, revival broke out across the whole city. The people yearned to hear God's law, and Ezra the scribe read them portions of Genesis through Deuteronomy for six straight hours (Nehemiah 8:1–3). They grieved over their sin and wept before God (8:9–11). Released of their guilt and filled with a new desire to follow God again as their ancestors had done in days before, the people of Jerusalem threw a tremendous party and celebrated all that God had done for them, and they continued celebrating for seven days (8:9–18).

Of course, the Israelites were still human, and this revival did not fix all of their spiritual troubles in one swoop. Indeed, after returning to King Artaxerxes for a time, Nehemiah came back to Jerusalem to find several disturbing practices taking place regarding the temple and the Sabbath (chapter 13). But in general, the revival was a much-needed step for the Israelites as they began to accept their sin of previous centuries and re-establish both their nation and their relationship with God.

ESTHER
Question 81. Who wrote the Book of Esther, and when was it written?

Scholars do not know for certain who wrote the Book of Esther, although possibilities include Mordecai, Ezra, Nehemiah, or one of their contemporaries. The story of Esther and Mordecai was written down mainly to establish the history of the Feast of Purim.

The date of the book is also difficult to determine, although there are a few markers to help narrow the possible time line. Esther likely became queen around 479 BC, which means her story would not have been written down before that time. Specific dates for the book have ranged from 460 to 350 BC. It is interesting to note that Esther would have been queen during the time when many Jews began returning to the Promised Land, which makes her a contemporary of people like Ezra and Nehemiah.

Question 82. Why isn't God mentioned in the entire Book of Esther?

It is true that the author of Esther does not use any word that could be translated *God*, which has been a point of controversy regarding the book for many centuries, with some early scholars even questioning whether it belonged in the Bible. There are explanations, of course. Some believe the author was using the literary technique of understatement—deliberately leaving God's name out of the book so that we notice its absence and immediately think of him. Or it may have been that the book was written in Persia and a reference to Jehovah, a foreign deity, could have caused problems.

Regardless of the reason for the absence of God's name, the presence of God is not absent from the book at all. First, there are the string of "coincidences" that make up the main plot of the story: Esther being chosen as queen, Mordecai accidentally discovering a plot against the king, the king re-reading the account of that discovery when he couldn't fall asleep, Esther braving the king's wrath to accuse Haman, and then Mordecai being given Haman's position of honor, allowing him to save the Jewish people in the land. To any person familiar with the stories of Joseph, David, Ruth, and many others in scripture, the hand of God in these events is clear.

In addition, several characters make offhand references that are targeted at the person of God. For example, Mordecai's speech to Esther when she is unsure about going to the king hints at God's hand guiding events: "For if you remain silent at this time, relief and deliverance for the Jews will arise from another place, but you and your father's family will perish. And who knows but that you have come to royal position for such a time as this?" (Esther 4:14). When Esther does decide to visit the king, she requests that Mordecai "gather together all the Jews who are in Susa, and fast for me. Do not eat or drink for three days, night or day. I and my maids will fast as you do" (v. 16). This is clearly an appeal to God for help.

Chapter 5

WISDOM AND POETRY

JOB
Question 83. What is the importance of the Book of Job?

The author of this book is unknown, as is the exact date when the story was written down, since it was probably passed down from generation to generation as an oral tale. Taking cues from the culture and history found in the story, many scholars believe that the events of Job took place around the time of Genesis 12–50, which means that this book may very well have been the earliest recorded piece of scripture.

What is understood for sure is that Job is a unique and powerful book, and though it may be the oldest book of the Bible, the main themes explored through the interaction of Job, his friends, and God are extremely relevant in today's culture. Why is there pain and suffering in the world? Why does God allow evil to remain? Where can we turn when everything goes wrong? These are the questions that make up the story of Job.

Question 84. What is Satan's role in the Book of Job?

The most important thing to realize about Satan is that he is a created being. It is a common misconception that Satan is the opposite of God, as darkness is the opposite of light. Satan was made by God, and therefore he is not equal to God. In reality, Satan is the opposite of Michael, the archangel and servant of God.

Because Satan is a created being, he has the limits of a created being. He cannot be in multiple places at once, for example, as God can, nor does Satan know everything. He is a fallen creation of God who has been allowed to influence the world for reasons known only to God. The same is true for demons, who are also fallen created beings.

When it comes to Satan and his influence in the story of Job, scholars are divided. The translated term *satan* literally means *accuser*, which does not necessarily connect the being described in Job as the "prince of this world" mentioned elsewhere in scripture. After all, if sin cannot exist in the presence of God, how could Satan walk multiple times into the councils of heaven?

One thing to keep in mind regarding this question is that Job is not a historical book along the lines of Esther or 1 and 2 Kings. Rather, Job is a large poem. Most scholars do believe that Job was an actual person who lived in history and who was afflicted in a terrible way; however, there is a good chance that Job's story was modified and adapted as it was sung from ear to ear until it became a teaching tool to demonstrate the sovereignty of God and the proper response to suffering in the world. In such a situation, the presence of the "accuser" may have been added to emphasize the sovereignty of God and explain the initial fall of Job's fortunes.

Question 85. Why isn't Job considered to be a historical book?

The basic answer is because Job isn't written as historical literature. It's actually a long and elaborate poem. This kind of literary work has been common throughout many cultures over the years, including famous masterpieces like *The Odyssey*, *Beowulf*, and Dante's *Inferno*.

Does that mean the people and events in Job weren't real? That is a question that cannot be answered for sure. Most likely the narrative was based on the life of a real person, but the story was probably embellished and shaped into a song over years of oral repetition. It is likely that the author of the book found in the Bible then crafted Job's story into the structured and complex poem we know today, one that follows the traditional rules of this kind of literature.

It's especially important to notice how structured the story is. The story begins with Job being stripped of everything he owns and loves and then ends with a double restoration of his family and all possessions. It involves three friends, each of whom give long speeches one at a time and are each answered by Job. A fourth friend heightens the intensity in anticipation of the crux of the story: God's appearance in answer to Job's charges.

This is a literary structure, not a historical one, and yet such structure does not mean that the Book of Job has no value. Quite the contrary. The poem is finely crafted to address and answer one overriding question: Why do good people still suffer? That is certainly a question that has had value in all cultures over the years.

Question 86. Does the Book of Job explain why good people suffer?

Yes and no. One of the main goals behind the Book of Job is to correct a mistaken way of thinking: the idea that suffering always occurs because a person has done something wrong, and blessing always occurs because a person has done something right. These were very common beliefs in the ancient world, as the different speeches from Job's "friends" show. But the story of Job reveals that suffering and blessing are both part of God's plan, no matter how good or evil a person may be.

Regarding the specific question of why bad things happen to good people, the Book of Job does give at least two explanations. The first is that we live in a broken world. Our world has been impacted by sin and evil and death. We can't escape it while we are here. The good news, of course, is that God has something better planned for us that is beyond this world. Heaven is our true home and the suffering we experience here will not be present there. As Job says: "I know that my Redeemer lives and that in the end he will stand upon the earth. And after my skin has been destroyed, yet in my flesh I will see God" (19.25–26).

The second explanation is that suffering often produces growth. Indeed, Christians most often experience maturity and development in their relationship with God after enduring different trials and coming out stronger on the other side. Job's life is an example of this. He was a good man to begin with and as a result he was praised by God. But not until Job endured tremendous suffering did he have the opportunity to speak with God, and the result of that encounter was deeper spiritual understanding for both Job and the people around him.

Question 87. Does the Book of Job include descriptions of dinosaurs?

Probably not. Some people believe that God's description of the behemoth and leviathan in Job 40–41 refers to dinosaurs. The behemoth has a tail that "sways like a cedar" and bones that are "tubes of bronze." Leviathan has a mouth "ringed about with fearsome teeth" and a back with "rows of shields tightly sealed together." Those who interpret these animals as dinosaurs almost always do so to gather evidence for the theory of young-earth creationism. In other words, they are shoehorning interpretations into the text to support an alternate agenda.

In reality, there is no real evidence to connect these descriptions with dinosaurs. Both the behemoth and leviathan are used in the poem to represent the power of nature; they are animals that fear no person and cannot be tamed by man. An elephant or rhinoceros would fit that description for behemoth, and a crocodile or whale fits well for leviathan. Still, the point of the author was not to identify literal creatures, which can be seen in the fact that leviathan has "flames dart from his mouth." The point is to emphasize that man is powerless against the forces of nature and is therefore even more powerless in comparison to the Creator of nature.

PSALMS
Question 88. Who wrote the Book of Psalms?

Psalms is a collection of 150 poetic works from several authors. The most famous and most prolific of these authors was David, who is connected with seventy-three separate Psalms. He wrote these poems at different times over the course of his life, and they give us a valuable window into his thoughts as both king and servant of God.

A man named Asaph is credited with writing twelve more of the psalms. He was appointed by King David as the worship leader for the nation of Israel. Another group of musicians called the Sons of Korah wrote several more psalms. These were descendants of Korah, a grandson of Levi, whom David appointed to serve as worshipers in the temple. Other psalmists include Solomon (David's son and heir as king), Moses, and other anonymous authors.

Question 89. Why are the psalms divided into five books?

The divisions are an imitation of the Torah, which are also known as the Pentateuch (the first five books of the Bible), done by the editors who compiled all these psalms into one book, and the purpose seems to have been to lend some credibility and authority to the collection. It was their way of saying, "Just as the Torah has authority from God, so do these prayers and songs from God's people. They are also the Word of God."

Question 90. What can be learned from the thoughts and prayers of ancient poets?

There is much to learn indeed, but learning is not necessarily the point. The psalms are more about experiencing powerful emotions, questions, and feelings than about transmitting information from one source to another.

The men who wrote these poems and songs were spiritual leaders in their communities, but they also experienced the ups and downs of life. They felt joy and pain, excitement and dread, confidence and confusion. In their minds, all these realities of life were connected to and influenced by their deep relationship with God. Their recorded prayers and cries offer a great model for communicating with God in the middle of our own up-and-down lives.

For example, Psalm 22 is a poignant lament from David at a time when he felt cut off from the presence of God. He cries, "My God, my God, why have you forsaken me?"—words later repeated by Jesus while he died on the cross. In Psalm 48, the

Sons of Korah rejoice in the power and protection of God. Psalm 51 is a confession of guilt and shame after David's affair with Bathsheba. Psalm 90 is a prayer and request from Moses that God would guide his people to "number our days aright" and to have compassion on their failures.

Question 91. What are the types of psalms?

There are several kinds, including the following:

1. **Historical** These psalms summarize important people or events in history. Psalm 106 is a good example, detailing the continued rebellion of the Israelites after the exodus and the continued grace of God toward them.
2. **Hymns of praise** These songs were used for worship in the temple. Psalm 89 is a good example, written by Ethan the Ezrahite.
3. **Complaints** Several of the psalms are honest expressions of frustration and confusion about what God is doing in the world. In most circumstances, though, these psalms do include a confession of God's sovereignty near the end. Psalm 79 is one of these.
4. **Curses** Just like some of the psalms honestly deal with disappointment toward God, others deal with anger and frustration directed at people. These are often called "imprecatory psalms," and they can be quite violent in their imagery. David's words in Psalm 58 demonstrate this: "Break the teeth in their mouths, O God; tear out, O LORD, the fangs of the lions!"
5. **The Songs of Ascents** These include Psalm 120–134, and were written to be sung by pilgrims returning to Jerusalem for festivals. They are called the "songs of ascents" because they would be sung as people climbed Mount Zion toward Jerusalem.
6. **Wisdom** These psalms are similar to the Proverbs in that they highlight the differences between wisdom and folly. Psalm 127 is a psalm of Wisdom and was written by Solomon.

Question 92. Why are several of the Psalms so repetitive?

Repetition and parallelism are two techniques that were important to ancient poets, including David and the other psalmists. Parallelism is when two or more verses express the same thought or idea, but use different words. The first verse of Psalm 1 is a good example: "Blessed is the man who does not walk in the counsel of the wicked or stand in the way of sinners or sit in the seat of mockers." The verse includes three ways of saying the same thing, and the result is to emphasize that idea, to highlight how much David wishes to avoid behaving in an ungodly way. The parallel structure also builds up the tension before the next verse: "But his delight is in the law of the LORD, and on his law he meditates day and night." It gets the reader prepared for the main point.

Repetition is the technique of recording the same words two or more times in a row. Sometimes it happens in the same verse, as in Psalm 22:1: "My God, my God, why have you forsaken me?" Other times the psalm repeats entire verses or sections, as in Psalm 118:1–4: "Give thanks to the LORD, for he is good; his love endures forever. Let Israel say: 'His love endures forever.' Let the house of Aaron say: 'His love endures forever.' Let those who fear the LORD say: 'His love endures forever.'" As with parallelism, the goal behind this repetition is to emphasize the theme or emotion being expressed, to call attention to it. Remember, most of the Psalms were originally meant to be sung out loud.

Question 93. Why is David so vicious in some of his writing?

David was an emotional man, and his emotions—both positive and negative—spilled out freely when he wrote his psalms and poems. For example, Psalm 58 includes several suggestions that David gives to God concerning his enemies, including these: "Break the teeth in their mouths, O God; tear out, O LORD, the fangs of the lions! Let them vanish like water that flows away; when they draw the bow, let their arrows be blunted. Like a slug melting away as it moves along, like a stillborn child, may they not see the sun." Not very nice!

Again, the reason that David wrote this way is that he expressed real and genuine emotions after he had experienced a betrayal. He was angry, he wanted revenge, and he went to God with his feelings, which is entirely appropriate. David didn't say that he was going to make his enemies pay; he came to God, instead, and cast his emotions at the feet of the one who brings justice.

Question 94. Is it okay for Christians to meditate?

The Bible seems to say that it's okay, especially in the Psalms. "I meditate on your precepts and consider your ways," David writes. "I delight in your decrees; I will not neglect your word" (Psalm 119:15–16). And Psalm 1 says: "Blessed is the man who does not walk in the counsel of the wicked.... But his delight is in the law of the LORD, and on his law he meditates day and night" (vv. 1–2).

The word *meditate* causes some problems for Christians today because it can be confused with the kind of meditation practiced in Eastern religions. Meditation in that context is different from meditating on scripture, however. In Eastern meditation, the goal is to empty the mind and allow other forces to speak to us—the universe, other gods, ancestors, and so on. When meditating on scripture, however, the goal is to fill the mind with God's truth, rather than empty it. When meditating, Christians seek to focus on God, who is inside of them, rather than outside forces or influences.

PROVERBS
Question 95. What is the purpose behind the Book of Proverbs?

The main purpose behind this book is to give advice for living a full and successful life. People who give good counsel have always been a hot commodity, and it's no different in today's culture of advice columnists and talk-show hosts. Solomon was widely considered to be the wisest person of his day, and so it makes sense that his musings and observations were recorded and distributed. Indeed, we learn from 1 Kings 4:31–32 that Solomon was the source for more than three thousand proverbs of wisdom.

The value of these proverbs becomes especially clear when they are juxtaposed with the Book of Psalms. The two volumes complement each other in many ways. Whereas the psalms specialize in emotions and the inner workings of people's hearts and minds, Proverbs is extremely practical and focused on everyday life; thus the two books make a great team.

Question 96. How much can Christians depend on the promises of the Bible's wisdom literature?

We can always depend on the promises of God, but we must be very careful about discerning which passages of scripture actually include such promises.

Much of this has to do with the genre of literature in which a statement is made. For example, some of the best examples of God's promises to his people occur in the historical records of the Pentateuch. God's promise that he will bless Abraham is iron-clad because it is given in the form of a covenant, a legal contract. God promised to bless Abraham with numerous descendants (Genesis 17), and that is exactly what happened. In the same way, God promised that he would punish the Israelites if they turned from him and served other gods instead (Deuteronomy 28), and that is exactly what happened.

It is a mistake to try to hold the same standard to "promises" delivered through the vehicle of poetry and proverbs. For the most part, proverbs are perceptive observations about how life usually works. They are usually true, but they are not meant to be universally applied.

Take Proverbs 22:6, for example: "Train a child in the way he should go, and when he is old he will not depart from it." This is a good saying and generally holds true, but those who try to claim this statement as a covenant promise from God are loading more weight onto the proverb than it was meant to carry. The same is true for those who attempt to claim proverbial promises about health and wealth. Proverbs 3:1–2 says: "My son, do not forget my teaching, but keep my commands in your heart, for they will prolong your life many years and bring you prosperity." This statement is general, not a lever we can use to twist God's arm into giving us what we want.

Question 97. Does the Book of Proverbs advise against cosigning on a loan?

Through one of his many proverbs, Solomon does warn parents against cosigning on loans for other people, yes. The specific passage in question is 6:1–3: "My son, if you have put up security for your neighbor, if you have struck hands in pledge for another, if you have been trapped by what you said, ensnared by the words of your mouth, then do this, my son, to free yourself, since you have fallen into your neighbor's hands: Go and humble yourself; press your plea with your neighbor!"

The important thing to note is that this is not a command. Solomon is saying that it's unwise to burden yourself with bad debt. This is advice that Solomon is giving in the form of a Proverb, rather a universal command from God.

Question 98. Who were Lemuel and Agur?

These two men authored a few of the wise sayings that are included in the Book of Proverbs, along with the wisdom of Solomon. Scholars today do not know much about these two men other than what is included in Proverbs 30 and 31, nor do we know when their sayings were written down. Most experts believe the final Book of Proverbs was compiled by editors around 700 BC, which was more than two hundred years after the death of Solomon.

Agur's words are mostly concerned with the glory of God contrasted with several negative aspects of human behavior. Lemuel was apparently a foreign king, although we don't know what country he ruled. His words in chapter 31 were inspired by his mother.

ECCLESIASTES
Question 99. What is the main purpose behind Ecclesiastes?

In many ways, this book is set up as an experiment that explores the meaning of life. Jewish and Christian tradition both credit Solomon as the author of this book and conductor of the experiment, and he makes his conclusion clear from the very first sentence: "'Meaningless! Meaningless!' says the Teacher. 'Utterly meaningless! Everything is meaningless.'"

This exclamation describes a life lived outside the purpose and plan of God. To support this conclusion, Solomon spends the next several chapters detailing the pursuits of his life, wisdom, pleasure, creative energy, stoicism, ritualism, and wealth. All these things were at Solomon's fingertips, and yet they all failed to bring any meaning to his life.

Chapter 8 presents a turning point as the Teacher makes his first nod toward the influence God can have in our lives: "Although a wicked man commits a hundred crimes and still lives a long time, I know that it will go better with God-fearing men, who are reverent before God" (v. 12). This theme meanders through the remaining chapters until a surprising conclusion is given in 12:13–14: "Now all has been heard; here is the conclusion of the matter: Fear God and keep his commandments, for this is the whole duty of man. For God will bring every deed into judgment, including every hidden thing, whether it is good or evil."

That is the result of the comparison: Life outside of God's plan is meaningless, so don't even bother with it. Follow God and reap your reward in the life that truly matters.

Question 100. Do the words of Ecclesiastes fit with the rest of the Bible?

Surprisingly, the answer to this question is both yes and no. Ecclesiastes fits in well with the other books of wisdom literature in that it explores different paths that one can take in life and ultimately recommends following whatever path God has laid out, but there are some surprising statements along the way.

Perhaps most surprising are these words from chapter 9: "This is the evil in every-thing that happens under the sun: The same destiny overtakes all. The hearts of men, moreover, are full of evil and there is madness in their hearts while they live, and afterward they join the dead. Anyone who is among the living has hope—even a live dog is better off than a dead lion!" For Christians today who define their relationship with God in large part as a ticket to heaven, such words are near blasphemy.

We must understand two things to gain a proper perspective on these words. First, we don't know how the ancient followers of God viewed the afterlife. On one hand, there are brief passages that seem to indicate God's people had some kind of hope for heaven. One example comes from Job 19:25–26: "I know that my Redeemer lives, and that in the end he will stand upon the earth. And after my skin has been destroyed, yet in my flesh I will see God." On the other hand, plenty of godly men in the Old Testament seem to have a negative view of life after death. The word almost always used for the afterlife in the Old Testament is *Sheol*, often translated as *the pit* or *the grave*. This was the place of the dead, and it was thought to be a very different place from the golden streets and pearly gates described in the New Testament.

The other thing we have to remember is that the author of Ecclesiastes intentionally sets his words apart from the conventional ideas in scripture. He is experimenting with all the facets of life except for God's plan and purpose, which means it is no surprise that he would rather remain alive than perish and be subject to the judgment or mercy of God.

SONG OF SONGS
Question 101. What is Song of Songs about?

It's mostly about sex; at least that was how the original Jewish audience read it. Young boys were prevented from reading this portion of the scriptures until they reached a proper age.

Really, given the amount of influence that sex and human relationships have had in all societies, is it a surprise that God's Word would spend an entire book addressing the issue? It shouldn't be. After all, God is the creator of romance, sex, and relationships, just as he is the creator of faith and hope and love.

Still, many readers throughout the centuries have had a tough time reconciling the sensuous, even steamy imagery and descriptions of this book with a "proper" and holy God; therefore, it is often reported that the Song of Songs is an extended allegory about Christ's love for Israel and later for his church. Certainly there are some connections and foreshadowing in the Song of Songs that reflect passages like Revelation 21, which describes the church as the bride of Christ.

Question 102. What is the plot of Song of Songs?

Since this book is poetic, the author takes quite a bit of license with the chronology of the events he describes, causing the story to jump back and forth between times and situations. Still, as a whole it reflects a blossoming love and relationship between the king (Solomon) and his future bride.

The story is told from three perspectives: the Beloved is the woman, the Lover is Solomon, and the Friends are the witnesses of their blossoming love. The woman is described as a Shulammite—which indicates the town or region where she was raised—and was not of noble birth. It is likely that her brothers were charged with tending some of Solomon's vineyards (8:11), which is how Solomon came across her in the first place. Evidently she was ashamed of her appearance during that meeting, noting that she was darkened by the sun because of working in the vineyard, a stigma in a culture where fair skin was prized (1:6).

Solomon still loved her and pursued her as a gentleman. Their compliments and words of love are sometimes startling, as when Solomon refers to his beloved's nose as "the tower of Lebanon looking toward Damascus" (7:4). These expressions had value and poignancy in their culture, though, just like a husband today might compliment his wife by calling her "hot." The imagery and poetic structure of the Song of Solomon make it clear that God really does care about our view of romance, relationships, and sex.

The couple's growing love includes both sexual tension (2:6–7) and restraint (4:12). When they finally join as husband and wife, the text celebrates their physical union instead of turning away (see chapters 4 and 5). The story also seems to include a disagreement between the couple after their wedding, as well as their reconciliation (5:2–16).

Chapter 6

THE PROPHETS

- Question 103. What was the role and function of a prophet?
- Question 104. Who was Isaiah?
- Question 105. Why does Isaiah switch back and forth between poetry and prose?
- Question 106. How accurate were Isaiah's prophecies about the Messiah?
- Question 107. Who wrote the Book of Jeremiah, and when was it written?
- Question 108. What was Jeremiah's primary message?
- Question 109. Why didn't the people of Jerusalem listen to Jeremiah's warning?
- Question 110. Why do people in the Bible tear their clothes?
- Question 111. Was it fair for God to punish the Israelites for their wickedness with the forces of Assyria and Babylon?
- Question 112. Who wrote Lamentations, and why was it written?
- Question 113. What is the primary message of Lamentations?
- Question 114. Who was Ezekiel?
- Question 115. What is the primary message of the Book of Ezekiel?
- Question 116. Why did God assign Ezekiel to perform such strange object lessons?
- Question 117. What is the difference between the minor prophets and the major prophets?
- Question 118. Did God really command Hosea to marry a prostitute?
- Question 119. What is the primary message of the Book of Joel?
- Question 120. Who was Amos?
- Question 121. What is the primary message of the Book of Amos?
- Question 122. What is the primary message of the Book of Obadiah?
- Question 123. Why was Jonah unwilling to obey God?
- Question 124. Was Jonah really swallowed by a whale?
- Question 125. Who was Micah?
- Question 126. What are the primary messages of the Book of Micah?
- Question 127. What is the primary message of the Book of Nahum?
- Question 128. What was happening in the world during Habakkuk's time?
- Question 129. What is the primary message of the Book of Habakkuk?
- Question 130. Who was Zephaniah?
- Question 131. What is the primary message of the Book of Zephaniah?

Question 103. What was the role and function of a prophet?

The primary role of prophets was to be a mouthpiece for the words and will of God, which was their first and foremost concern, even while they took on other roles throughout Israel's history and circumstances. This role was announced by God at the beginning of Israel's history: "I will raise up for them a prophet like you from among their brothers; I will put my words in his mouth, and he will tell them everything I command him. If anyone does not listen to my words that the prophet speaks in my name, I myself will call him to account" (Deuteronomy 18:18–19).

During the glory days of the nation of Israel, from the exodus of Egypt to the reigns of David and Solomon, prophets provided subtle guidance to the nation's leaders in addition to specific commands and proclamations from God. When the nation began to collapse after Solomon died and the people were split between Jeroboam and Rehoboam, God elevated the role of the prophets to include spiritual leadership and moral guidance, even to the point of confronting kings and warning the people of consequences to come for continued disobedience.

Each of the prophets ministered to specific regions. For example, of the prophets who authored books now found in the Bible, three—Amos, Hosea, and Ezekiel—spoke to the northern kingdom of Israel. Nine prophets—Joel, Isaiah, Micah, Jeremiah, Habakkuk, Zephaniah, Haggai, Zechariah, and Malachi—spoke to Judah, the southern kingdom. In addition, Daniel spoke to the Jews who had been taken captive in Babylon, Jonah and Nahum spoke to the Assyrians in Nineveh, and Obadiah spoke primarily to the people of Edom.

The prophets after the time of Solomon mainly preached a message of repentance and coming judgment, and they were often unpopular, especially in the minds of the nobility and other leaders who so often caused the Israelites to turn away from God. Indeed, many of the prophets were thrown into prison or harassed by the kings and queens of Israel and Judah. As the people moved further away from God, many prophets were put to death.

ISAIAH
Question 104. Who was Isaiah?

Isaiah was a prophet to the southern kingdom of Judah, and his ministry extended from 740 to 681 BC. Tradition holds that the evil king Manasseh killed him as a martyr.

Isaiah was a man of royal blood and had been highly trained as a leader in the courts of Judah. His nation was in need of leadership. For one thing, the political climate surrounding Judah was extremely unstable. Assyria was a dominant power in the north during Isaiah's time and had even destroyed the northern kingdom of Israel while he ministered. At the same time, Egypt was still a world power on the south, which meant that Judah was caught in the middle of two violent and aggressive enemies.

At the same time, the moral fiber of Judah was degenerating as the nation's leaders moved deeper into worshiping idols and foreign gods, as the northern kingdom had done. Because of all this, a majority of Isaiah's message addressed the folly of the Israelites' attempt to appease foreign leaders and foreign gods. He urged the people instead to repent of their sin and turn back to the one true God, who alone cared for them and could protect them. As his ministry progressed and the people refused to abandon their rebellion, Isaiah's message shifted to the future destruction of Judah and removal of God's people from the Promised Land.

Isaiah also carried another message, one that becomes especially prominent in the later chapters of his book. In the middle of the degradation and collapse of Israel and Judah, Isaiah prophesied about the coming Messiah, who would redeem God's people and restore the nation of Israel.

Question 105. Why does Isaiah switch back and forth between poetry and prose?

It seems that God spoke to Isaiah primarily through visions—supernatural insights and messages that were communicated to Isaiah's mind, a common way for God to communicate to his messengers. "When a prophet of the LORD is among you, I reveal myself to him in visions, I speak to him in dreams" (Numbers 12:6).

These images and sensations were evidently very powerful, and Isaiah chose the genre of poetry to convey them in written form, which allowed him to communicate God's message in a more powerful way, using imagery and intense language, rather than a straight narration of what God had shown him. In other words, poetry allowed Isaiah to communicate the force of his visions from God, along with their literal meanings. At other times, when Isaiah's goal was to communicate information more quickly and efficiently, he wrote with straight prose.

Question 106. How accurate were Isaiah's prophecies about the Messiah?

They were very accurate, although it's important to understand that biblical prophecies contain several layers and can refer to multiple events that occur years apart.

Consider Isaiah's prophecy concerning Jesus's being born of a virgin: "Therefore the Lord himself will give you a sign: The virgin will be with child and will give birth to a son, and will call him Immanuel. He will eat curds and honey when he knows enough to reject the wrong and choose the right. But before the boy knows enough to reject the wrong and choose the right, the land of the two kings you dread will be laid waste" (7:14). This prophecy applies to two periods of time. The phrase "two kings you dread" refers to Rezin and Pekah, who were kings of Aram and Israel, respectively, enemies that were threatening to attack Judah. On one level, the prophecy is saying that in only a short time, the people of Judah would have no reason to fear those nations, and indeed, they were conquered by the Assyrians. On a second level, however, the prophecy also points to the Messiah, born of a virgin, as a sign that God would not abandon his people.

Isaiah also prophesied about the Messiah's sacrifice on behalf of the world: "But he was pierced for our transgressions, he was crushed for our iniquities; the punishment that brought us peace was upon him, and by his wounds we are healed" (53:5). If it were that plain, why were so many people of Jesus's day convinced that the Messiah would be a conquering hero? Because of Isaiah's words in chapter 9, among other places: "Of the increase of his government and peace there will be no end. He will reign on David's throne and over his kingdom, establishing and upholding it with justice and righteousness from that time on and forever. The zeal of the LORD Almighty will accomplish this." Once again, Isaiah's prophecies concerning the Messiah contain layers. He will one day return to earth as a conquering king (which is what the Jews of Jesus's day were expecting, but still hasn't happened) but first he would fulfill his mission to redeem humanity by offering himself as a perfect sacrifice.

JEREMIAH
Question 107. Who wrote the Book of Jeremiah, and when was it written?

Jeremiah is the author of the book, which makes sense because it bears his name, but he didn't actually write the words on paper. Jeremiah's prophecies were recorded and compiled by his aide, Baruch. That being the case, the visions were recorded throughout the span of Jeremiah's ministry, from 626 to 585 BC. Scholars today believe that the book's final verses were added in 561 BC, about twenty-five years after the destruction of Jerusalem.

Here's another important thing to keep in mind: Like Isaiah, the Book of Jeremiah does not follow any kind of chronological order or pattern. Baruch seems to have kept records of Jeremiah's visions and prophecies throughout their time together, but then pieced them together without regard for a time line. Again, this was a normal thing for the culture of the time, but something that should be kept in mind when the book is read today.

Question 108. What was Jeremiah's primary message?

Like Isaiah and the other prophets who ministered before Israel and Judah were taken into exile, Jeremiah's main message was a warning of coming judgment and a call for nationwide repentance.

Jeremiah was a Levite and priest by birth but was called by God to serve as a prophet at a young age, probably in his late teens or early twenties. He prophesied for more than forty years in the southern kingdom of Judah and saw five kings ascend to the throne in Jerusalem: Josiah, Jehoahaz, Jehoiakim, Jehoiachin, and Zedekiah. While Josiah was a king who followed God and attempted to reform the nation, his early death began a downward spiral for Jerusalem and the surrounding land. The kings that succeeded Josiah all focused more on appeasing foreign kings and gods than Jehovah.

Through it all, Jeremiah faithfully proclaimed the message he had been given by God as a young man: "I will pronounce my judgments on my people because of their wickedness in forsaking me, in burning incense to other gods and in worshiping what their hands have made" (1:16).

Like Isaiah, Jeremiah was also given the chance to speak words of hope for the Israelites after their exile from the Promised Land. His prophecies touched on the future return of the Israelites to Jerusalem (30:10), as well as identifying the Messiah as the future savior of Jerusalem (23:6).

Question 109. Why didn't the people of Jerusalem listen to Jeremiah's warning?

Looking back, it seems that the people of Judah should have been in the right frame of mind to heed Jeremiah's warnings about judgment and destruction. After all, the nation of Israel had been destroyed by Assyria almost one hundred years before Jeremiah received his call—a perfect example of the consequences of turning away from God. Plus, Judah was threatened by three world powers during Jeremiah's ministry: Assyria, Egypt, and Babylon. So the possibility of military defeat and ultimate destruction was regularly on the people's minds.

There are several reasons why the people chose to ignore Jeremiah's warnings, and even attempted to kill him when he would not change his message (chapter 26). First, there were several false prophets operating at the same time as Jeremiah. These were men who claimed to speak for God, and their message was one of hope and future blessing. They told the people of Jerusalem that "no sword or famine will touch this land" (14:15) and that Jeremiah's predictions of judgment and doom were off base. Thus, the people had two opposing viewpoints to choose from, and most chose to believe the comfortable message of the false prophets.

In addition, many people who had begun worshiping idols and false gods did so because they wanted to appease the rulers of Assyria, Egypt, and Babylon. This was especially true of Judah's national leaders; they thought they might receive mercy and friendship from those stronger nations if they were worshiping the same gods.

Question 110. Why do people in the Bible tear their clothes?

All cultures have developed specific ways of identifying when a person is in mourning. In America today, for example, we wear black clothes to a funeral or tie a black strip around our upper arm.

In the ancient Middle East, people expressed extreme grief and sorrow by tearing their clothes. Articles of clothing were highly valued in that culture, because they were made by hand and were not easily purchased or replaced. Tearing your clothes was a big deal and was used to show that a person had experienced a deep hurt. Other methods of showing grief in biblical culture include wearing sackcloth, shaving your beard, and pouring ashes on your head.

Question 111. Was it fair for God to punish the Israelites for their wickedness with the forces of Assyria and Babylon?

It doesn't seem fair at first. God was punishing the Israelites because they had rebelled against him and turned toward foreign gods, but the Assyrians (who conquered Israel) and Babylonians (who conquered Judah) were much worse. They were the source of those foreign gods! When we look deeper, we see that God's actions were indeed just and fair, as is always the case.

For one thing, the Israelites had been fairly warned about the consequences of their rebellion. All the way back in Leviticus 26:30–33, God had spelled out exactly what would happen if the Israelites worshiped idols and refused to repent: "I will destroy your high places, cut down your incense altars and pile your dead bodies on the lifeless forms of your idols, and I will abhor you. I will turn your cities into ruins and lay waste your sanctuaries, and I will take no delight in the pleasing aroma of your offerings. I will lay waste the land, so that your enemies who live there will be appalled. I will scatter you among the nations and will draw out my sword and pursue you. Your land will be laid waste, and your cities will lie in ruins."

More importantly, however, God allowed the Assyrians and Babylonians to capture the Israelites as a means of disciplining his people with the end goal of repentance. He was not out to destroy them, but to heal them. Here are the final words of God's warning in Leviticus 26: "But if they will confess their sins and the sins of their fathers…then when their uncircumcised hearts are humbled and they pay for their sin, I will remember my covenant with Jacob and my covenant with Isaac and my covenant with Abraham, and I will remember the land" (vv. 40–42).

In other words, the Israelites were harming themselves, walking away from God and toward destruction; therefore, God allowed the temporary pain of Assyrian and Babylonian captivity, to stop the Israelites from harming themselves. He always had in mind the goal of returning his people to the land. Indeed, that is exactly what happened. What is more, historical records show that the Israelites never again turned to idolatry or worshiped false gods. They learned their lesson, and they grew from their trouble, as God intended.

LAMENTATIONS

Question 112. Who wrote Lamentations, and why was it written?

History has credited the prophet Jeremiah as the author of Lamentations, and most of today's scholars agree. The book consists of five distinct poems that were gathered together in a single document. Jeremiah likely wrote these poems over a period of five to ten years following the destruction of Jerusalem in 586 BC.

For Jeremiah, these words were probably a way to mourn for the loss of his home, his friends, his culture, and his entire way of life prior to the Babylonian attacks. Perhaps they were even an attempt to process his emotions and move on with his life. Like many of the psalms, these poems provide a window into the soul of a man who did not understand why God had allowed such terrible things to happen, but who still felt hope because of his trust in the goodness and sovereignty of God.

Question 113. What is the primary message of Lamentations?

As the name suggests, Lamentations is first and foremost an expression of lament. It is one man's response to the terrible events that led to the loss of almost everything he held dear. In this way, Lamentations serves as a great example for all human beings, because it is inevitable that all human beings will suffer loss. Through the words of Jeremiah, we see a man who was intimate in his relationship with God, but who still experienced sadness, grief, confusion, bitterness, and anger, which is why Jeremiah is often referred to as "the weeping prophet."

Surprisingly, Jeremiah is also called "the prophet of hope," and, surprisingly, hope is a theme that pops up again and again throughout Jeremiah's lament. "Yet this I call to mind and therefore I have hope," he says in 3:21–23, "Because of the LORD's great love we are not consumed, for his compassions never fail. They are new every morning; great is your faithfulness."

Jeremiah's words serve as an example for us in another way. It is natural and acceptable for us to mourn and grieve when we suffer loss in this world, even to cry out to God with our feelings and tell him we don't understand, but we don't have to bear the burden of that loss alone. Like Jeremiah, we can trust that God is good, even when we don't understand, and we can find hope in the knowledge that this world is not our home—we are designed for an eternity with God in heaven.

EZEKIEL
Question 114. Who was Ezekiel?

Ezekiel was a prophet of God who was born around 622 BC. He served as a priest in Jerusalem, and in 597 he was carried into exile by the Babylonians, along with the rest of Jerusalem's upper class. He was twenty-five years old when it happened. It was actually the second time that captives were taken from Jerusalem to Babylon. The first occurred in 605 BC, and the third in 586, when the city was ultimately destroyed.

When Ezekiel was thirty years old, he was commissioned by God to speak as a prophet to the Israelites living in Babylon. It was not an easy job. God himself warned Ezekiel that the people would ignore him: "But the house of Israel is not willing to listen to you because they are not willing to listen to me, for the whole house of Israel is hardened and obstinate" (3:7). Still, God charged Ezekiel to be faithful to his calling as a prophet and gave him a unique defense against the stubbornness of the Israelites: "But I will make you as unyielding and hardened as they are. I will make your forehead like the hardest stone, harder than flint."

Ezekiel was faithful to the messages God commanded him to proclaim. During the first part of his ministry, he mainly prophesied about the coming destruction of Jerusalem through a series of strange object lessons that were designed to both capture the attention of the crowds and warn them of events to come. After the fall of Jerusalem, Ezekiel's prophecies addressed the eventual destruction of Judah's enemies and the eventual restoration and rebuilding of Israel as a nation.

Ezekiel also experienced a series of strange and vivid visions from God, which he recorded in his book. The most famous of these visions was the Valley of Dry Bones, where he was taken to a valley filled with skeletons and asked, "Son of man, can these bones live?" He was then commanded to prophesy to the bones, and after doing so they came to life and were described as "a vast army." This vision pointed to the future spiritual resurrection that would take place for the nation of Israel after the people returned from exile.

Question 115. What is the primary message of the Book of Ezekiel?

This book can be divided into three major sections, each of which focuses on a specific theme. The first division contains chapters 1–24, which concentrate almost entirely on the coming destruction of Jerusalem. Even though the highest members of Jewish society had been taken captive in Babylon, they still retained hope so long as the city of Jerusalem stood. They thought they might still be able to return home someday, but this hope did not translate into changed behavior or a return to God. As a result, Ezekiel's main message at the beginning of his calling was that God would not spare even the city that held his temple in order to bring the people back to repentance. Indeed, Jerusalem was destroyed by Babylon in 586 BC.

The second division of the book contains chapters 25–32, which focus primarily on future judgments against the enemies of Judah. Now that Jerusalem has been destroyed, Ezekiel's message abruptly shifts to a future restoration of the Israelites in that city, but before that could happen, those who had oppressed God's people needed to receive the consequences for their own sins. Thus God pronounces his judgment against Ammon, Moab, Tyre, Sidon, and Egypt.

Chapters 33–348 make up the third and final division, focusing on the future restoration of Jerusalem and Judah after the judgment of the nation's enemies. Part of this theme includes the future coming of the Messiah. The shepherds of Israel had led their flock astray and into great disaster, but God was going to send a shepherd from the line of David to redeem his people once and for all. This restoration was famously pictured in Ezekiel's vision of the valley of dry bones (chapter 37).

Question 116. Why did God assign Ezekiel to perform such strange object lessons?

In the strange actions and symbols of Ezekiel we can see the persistence and tenacity of God. By no means was Ezekiel the first prophet sent to the people of Israel, nor was he the first prophet to speak to the Israelites in captivity, but God's people had ignored the previous warnings of prophets that came in "normal" ways, so God attempted to get their attention through another method.

For that reason, Ezekiel was commanded to perform several series of strange object lessons in view of the people. He spent time lying on his side for 430 days, reminding the Jews of the 430 years they had spent as slaves in Egypt. He carefully measured out a small portion of food each day, cooked over a fire fueled by feces, as a symbol of the coming siege against Jerusalem. He used a sword to shave off his own hair, while still saving a few strands in a separate pouch, a picture that included both God's judgment (the cutting) and his grace (the saving).

In some ways these object lessons and pantomimes worked. At least the people who saw Ezekiel knew that he was different from the numerous false prophets also in their midst: "As for you, son of man, your countrymen are talking together about you by the walls and at the doors of the houses, saying to each other, 'Come and hear the message that has come from the LORD'" (Ezekiel 33:30). It seems, however, the people viewed Ezekiel's actions as nothing more than entertainment: "Indeed, to them you are nothing more than one who sings love songs with a beautiful voice and plays an instrument well, for they hear your words but do not put them into practice" (v. 32). Israelites failed to open their hearts and minds to the message that God was sending them through his unusual prophet.

HOSEA
Question 117. What is the difference between the minor prophets and the major prophets?

The major prophets are Isaiah, Jeremiah, Ezekiel, and Daniel. The minor prophets include Hosea, Joel, Amos, Obadiah, Jonah, Micah, Habakkuk, Zephaniah, Haggai, Zechariah, and Malachi. Some also consider Ezra, Nehemiah, and Esther to be minor prophets.

The distinction between "minor" and "major" is based only on the amount of material that each prophet wrote down. Books like Isaiah and Jeremiah are very long, while Joel, Amos, and the other books of the minor prophets are relatively small. It does not mean that Isaiah was a better prophet than Joel, or that he heard more from God or served God more fully. Being a major prophet just means that he wrote down more of what happened and that more of what he wrote down survived through the centuries, to be included in the Bible.

Question 118. Did God really command Hosea to marry a prostitute?

Yes, he did: "The LORD said to him, 'Go, take to yourself an adulterous wife and children of unfaithfulness, because the land is guilty of the vilest adultery in departing from the LORD.' So he married Gomer daughter of Diblaim, and she conceived and bore him a son" (1:2–3). Later, when Gomer ran away and joined a house of prostitution once again, God commanded Hosea to take her back. Hosea was forced to purchase his own wife back as a slave, and afterwards he begged her to remain in his house and be faithful to him (3:1–2).

God had a specific reason for this command, though. Hosea's life became an object lesson that highlighted the unfaithfulness of the people of Israel. Just as Gomer had broken promises to her husband and went searching for other men, the Israelites had broken their covenant with God and lusted after foreign gods.

For many people who read this book, the situation seems like an intrusion on God's part. After all, it's one thing for God to ask his servants to give up wealth and power or to risk their health and safety by speaking an unpopular message, but how could God sabotage Hosea's family and personal life? The answer is that while God was intruding, he had a right to do so. Hosea committed himself to serving God and so had to offer control of his life to him.

In Hosea's situation, God was desperate to grab the attention of his people. The Israelites of the northern kingdom had been living in rebellion against God for almost two hundred years. They had ignored the more conventional prophets that God had sent to speak to them, including Amos, who had preached repentance and coming judgment for ten years, right before Hosea. God knew that the time of punishment through the power of the Assyrians was getting closer and closer, and through Hosea's life he made one more attempt to grab the attention of his people, whom he loved.

JOEL
Question 119. What is the primary message of the Book of Joel?

Joel was writing to the people of Judah, the southern kingdom, and his message was similar to that of other prophets—repent of your rebellion and turn back to the Lord, or consequences will come soon—but two items stand out as unique concerning Joel's immediate message and situation.

First, Joel's prophecy of coming judgment was attached to a natural disaster—an unprecedented swarm of locusts that would devour all the food in the land and deal a crippling blow to Judah's economy and morale. Joel used military language to describe the plague of insects: "They charge like warriors; they scale walls like soldiers. They all march in line, not swerving from their course. They do not jostle each other; each marches straight ahead. They plunge through defenses without breaking ranks" (2:7–8). Thus, Joel proclaimed the invasion of locusts to be a warning about a more devastating army, the Babylonians, who would later come down from the north and destroy Jerusalem.

The second unique item about Joel's immediate situation was that his prophecies and warnings seemed to actually work—at least for a time. Joel began his ministry as a prophet right around the time when Joash became king of Judah at the tender age of seven. Joash's father and grandmother had been evil rulers who rebelled against God, but Joash had been raised primarily by Jehoiada, the high priest. Because of the influence of Jehoiada and Joel, the young king Joash was able to help the nation of Judah briefly turn back to God in repentance.

Finally, the prophecy of Joel is also unique in its predictions of the future. Like many of the other prophets, Joel's visions and words applied mostly to the present circumstances of the people in Jerusalem, but they also looked forward in the future to a time when God would once again bless his people. Joel was the first Old Testament writer to speak of the coming of the Holy Spirit for all people: "And afterward, I will pour out my Spirit on all people. Your sons and daughters will prophesy, your old men will dream dreams, your young men will see visions. Even on my servants, both men and women, I will pour out my Spirit in those days" (2:28–29). This prophecy was fulfilled on the Day of Pentecost (see Acts 2).

AMOS
Question 120. Who was Amos?

Many of the people God chose to speak as his prophets were from the upper class of Israelite society—priests and nobleman—but not Amos. He was originally a shepherd from the tiny village of Tekoa, about twelve miles south of Jerusalem. Still, Amos was certain of his role as a true prophet, and he identified it with force when confronted by a priest of Bethel who didn't like his words: "I was neither a prophet nor a prophet's son, but I was a shepherd, and I also took care of sycamore-fig trees. But the LORD took me from tending the flock and said to me, 'Go, prophesy to my people Israel.' Now then, hear the word of the LORD" (7:14–16).

Unfortunately for Amos, he ministered from 760 to 750 BC in the northern kingdom of Israel, during the early reign of Jeroboam II, which was a stable and prosperous time for the nation. Assyria had not yet fully risen as a world power, and the armies of both Israel and Judah had experienced success; therefore, Amos's words and warnings were largely ignored.

Question 121. What is the primary message of the Book of Amos?

As with the other prophets, Amos expended a lot of effort highlighting the ways that the people of Israel had turned away from God, but while several other prophets emphasized the Israelites' worship of foreign gods, Amos chose to focus on issues of justice.

He begins his assessment of Israel, "This is what the LORD says: 'For three sins of Israel, even for four, I will not turn back my wrath. They sell the righteous for silver, and the needy for a pair of sandals. They trample on the heads of the poor as upon the dust of the ground and deny justice to the oppressed. Father and son use the same girl and so profane my holy name'" (2:6–7).

The Israelites' of Amos's day enjoyed a time of wealth and prosperity, but the wealthy members of society had increased their own comfort by trampling down the poor and needy. To Amos, and to God, it was unacceptable.

OBADIAH

Question 122. What is the primary message of the Book of Obadiah?

The first half of the book is directed toward the Edomites, aggressive descendents of Esau, who lived in the mountainous regions near the Dead Sea. The Edomites had a long-standing hatred for the people of Israel and often attacked and plundered Jewish settlements, only to retreat to their mountain strongholds when the Israelite armies came out to stop them.

This prophecy was evidently written after the destruction of Jerusalem, when the Edomites helped the Babylonians trap and enslave the fleeing Israelites. Obadiah proclaimed that the Edomites would be wiped out because of their hatred of God's people (vv. 3–4, 10), and his words were fulfilled five years later when the king of Babylon returned to the region and flushed the Edomites out of their mountain cities. Later, the Edomite people were completely wiped out when the Roman Empire conquered Jerusalem (150 BC).

The second half of Obadiah's prophecy applies to the Israelites. Jerusalem had just been destroyed and its people carried off into captivity, but through Obadiah's worlds, God promised to deliver his people and gather them back to Zion.

JONAH
Question 123. Why was Jonah unwilling to obey God?

Jonah was a prophet in Israel, the northern kingdom, during the reign of Jeroboam II. He was a respected statesman in the court of the king, and the nation of Israel was enjoying a comfortable and prosperous stretch of time. It's not hard to imagine why Jonah was unhappy about being called to speak the word of God in Nineveh.

The other reason that Jonah didn't want to obey God was that Nineveh was the capital city of Assyria, one of Israel's greatest enemies. Assyria had been temporarily weakened as a world power during this time, which is one of the main reasons why Israel was experiencing such prosperity. In no way did Jonah want to give Assyria a chance to get back on its feet through reconciliation with God.

Question 124. Was Jonah really swallowed by a whale?

Yes, the Bible seems to say that he was. Jonah is a prophetic book written in the style of history, and there are no hints in the structure or writing of the verses that imply this was a symbolic event instead of a literal one. Of course, the text uses the word *fish*, but the ancient Israelites did not have a modern understanding of whales as mammals.

Still, many people have a hard time getting their minds around a man surviving for three days inside the digestive tract of a whale, and for good reason. Speaking from the viewpoint of science, there is no way that such a thing could happen naturally. There aren't any fish or whales that could accommodate a living human being for that long. But that's exactly the point: This was not a natural event; it was supernatural. If a man were to survive in the belly of a whale, it would take an act of God to make it happen, and that's exactly what the text records.

The important question to ask about the incident is "What is the meaning of it?" Why would God go through such trouble instead of just sending another prophet to Nineveh, or even speaking directly to Jonah in a less strange way?

The answer is that Jonah's journey is a picture of what happens in every human life. Jonah was put on earth with a set of gifts and a purpose to fulfill in God's Kingdom, as we all are. He rebelled against God and tried to make his own way in the world using his own wisdom and his own plans, as we all do. When Jonah's wisdom and plans took him down to the pit of death and the gates of hell, he finally looked up, and God was there waiting for him, as he waits for everyone.

MICAH
Question 125. Who was Micah?

Micah was a prophet to the southern kingdom of Judah. He was a contemporary of Isaiah and Hosea, and he ministered during the reigns of Jotham (750–735 BC), Ahaz (735–715 BC), and Hezekiah (715–686 BC). Micah was not a voice often heard by those kings, though. He was born in the country about twenty miles south of Jerusalem and spent most of his ministry preaching to the common people, rather than the decision makers.

During Micah's time, the Assyrians aggressively expanded their empire westward, eventually conquering the northern kingdom of Israel in 722 BC and taking its people into captivity. The Assyrians did not stop there, however, but pushed south toward Jerusalem. They inflicted a great deal of damage on the land and even took some captives from the people of Judah, but they were stalled when they laid siege to the city of Jerusalem. Hezekiah was king at the time, and the city was spared when he turned to the Lord for help.

Question 126. What are the primary messages of the Book of Micah?

Micah can be divided into three sections, each beginning with the words *Hear ye* and ending with a particular promise. The first section includes chapters 1 and 2, which focus on the coming judgment upon Samaria, the capital of Israel, and Jerusalem, the capital of Judah. Because of the sins of the people and their rebellion against God, both cities would be destroyed and their inhabitants taken into captivity. It did happen, of course, although Jerusalem did repent somewhat and outlasted Samaria by 150 years. The promise at the end of this section was that God would still deliver his people despite the coming judgment against them (2:12–13).

The second section comes in chapters 3–5 and continues highlighting the unfaithfulness of God's people. Micah tackles issues of justice in this section, delivering sharp criticism to those who oppress the poor, bribe judges, and use false weights and balances. Micah also includes a message of hope in the form of prophecies relating to the future Messiah. It is Micah, for example, who records that the Messiah would be born in Bethlehem (5:2–4). This section ends with the promise that the enemies of God's people would one day be overthrown (5:10, 15).

The final section includes chapters 6 and 7, in which God speaks to the people as a lawyer bringing his case against the people of Israel and Judah. He reminds how they have turned their backs on him even though he has remained faithful to his covenant with Abraham. God promises that he will remain faithful to that covenant and "be true to Jacob" (7:20).

Finally, Micah includes one of the most practical and helpful summaries found in all of scripture of what it means to follow God: "He has showed you, O man, what is good. And what does the LORD require of you? To act justly and to love mercy and to walk humbly with your God" (6:8).

NAHUM
Question 127. What is the primary message of the Book of Nahum?

This book is a declaration of judgment against Nineveh, the capital of the Assyrian Empire. This judgment came between 100 and 150 years after God sent Moses to Nineveh with a warning to repent or be judged. The Ninevites responded positively to Jonah's message at first, but then quickly reverted to their violent ways, destroying Samaria decades later and setting a siege around Jerusalem.

When Nahum arrived in Nineveh, he did not announce another opportunity to repent. God's judgment was coming, and there was nothing the Assyrians could do to stop it: "The LORD has given a command concerning you, Nineveh: 'You will have no descendants to bear your name. I will destroy the carved images and cast idols that are in the temple of your gods. I will prepare your grave, for you are vile'" (1:14).

The Book of Nahum wasn't really written for the Assyrians, though; it was written for the people of Judah. The message is that God is not blind or deaf to what is going on in the world. He sees everything, and he is the source of justice for all who oppose his kingdom.

HABAKKUK
Question 128. What was happening in the world during Habakkuk's time?

Habakkuk was a prophet in the southern kingdom of Judah during the years leading up to the destruction of Jerusalem, which means he was a contemporary of Jeremiah. After a brief return to God during the reign of Joash, the people of Jerusalem had once again followed a line of evil kings into idolatry and oppression.

Jehoiakim was the king during Habakkuk's ministry, and he was extremely hostile toward God. Not only did he lead the people in worshiping false gods, but he also actively persecuted the prophets of Jehovah. He had them arrested, burned their writing, and even sentenced some to execution.

Question 129. What is the primary message of the Book of Habakkuk?

Whereas most prophets spent their time writing about what God was saying to the people, Habakkuk took the questions and frustrations of the people back to God. Habakkuk's cry at the beginning of chapter 1 is a succinct introduction to the book: "How long, O LORD, must I call for help, but you do not listen? Or cry out to you, 'Violence!' but you do not save? Why do you make me look at injustice? Why do you tolerate wrong? Destruction and violence are before me; there is strife, and conflict abounds. Therefore the law is paralyzed, and justice never prevails. The wicked hem in the righteous, so that justice is perverted" (1:2–4). In other words, if God is in control, why do the wicked prosper?

Keep in mind that Habakkuk was not crying out against the injustice of other nations persecuting the people of Jerusalem. It was the leaders of Judah who were wicked and oppressing God's people, and Habakkuk wanted to know why God wasn't doing anything about it. Unfortunately for Jerusalem, God had a surprising answer: "I am raising up the Babylonians, that ruthless and impetuous people, who sweep across the whole earth to seize dwelling places not their own" (1:6). God had already prepared the judgment of Jerusalem in the form of conquest by the Babylonians.

Habakkuk was stunned and confused. He couldn't believe that God would punish the wicked leaders of Jerusalem by allowing an even more wicked nation to destroy the holy city. Once again the question was this: Why do evil people have so much success in this world? But God again assured Habakkuk that everything was under control. The violence and pride of the Babylonians would ultimately result in their destruction.

The overarching message of Habakkuk is that God is always in control, even when we don't understand what he is doing, and in those times, the best thing to do is trust in God's goodness and justice.

ZEPHANIAH
Question 130. Who was Zephaniah?

Not much is known about Zephaniah, although there is a bit of information given about him in the following opening verses of the book: "The word of the LORD that came to Zephaniah son of Cushi, the son of Gedaliah, the son of Amariah, the son of Hezekiah, during the reign of Josiah son of Amon king of Judah." Since he was descended from Hezekiah, he was probably a member of the nobility in the court of Jerusalem.

Josiah was a good king who followed after God despite the wicked way of previous kings and generations. As both a spiritual and political leader, Zephaniah had a great influence on Josiah's reign and the reforms aimed at bringing the people of Jerusalem back to God.

Question 131. What is the primary message of the Book of Zephaniah?

Zephaniah had the unfortunate task of proclaiming that the reforms and positive steps taken by King Josiah were too little too late, and as a result, Jerusalem was going to be destroyed (see chapter 1). Zephaniah also spent time proclaiming the doom of idolatrous nations such as Philistia, Ammon, Moab, Ethiopia, and Assyria. The phrase "Day of the LORD" is used often throughout the book, referring both to the short-term judgment against the city of Jerusalem and the day far in the future when God would defeat all his enemies and judge the earth.

Like many of the other prophets, the ending of Zephaniah is filled with hope, even rejoicing, at God's announcement that a remnant of the Israelites would be saved and the nation would eventually be restored.

HAGGAI
Question 132. What is the primary message of the Book of Haggai?

Haggai ministered in Jerusalem in 520 BC, after the first wave of exiles had been allowed to return to the city by Cyrus, the Persian king who had conquered Babylon. Haggai was a contemporary of the prophet Zechariah, and he had one primary goal: to persuade the people of Jerusalem to rebuild the temple.

The Book of Haggai is split into three messages that were spoken to the people over a period of four months. The first message was intended to rebuke the people of Jerusalem and specifically Zerubbabel, the city governor, and Joshua, the high priest, because they had lost interest in restoring the temple. The people had actually started rebuilding it sixteen years before, when they first came back from Babylon, but opposition from neighboring politicians had made them fearful, and the work had stopped.

That's why the second message of Haggai focuses on courage. His simple message was that the people should have no fear of outsiders, because God was on their side: "'But now be strong, O Zerubbabel,' declares the Lord. 'Be strong, O Joshua son of Jehozadak, the high priest. Be strong, all you people of the land,' declares the Lord, 'and work. For I am with you,' declares the Lord Almighty" (2:4).

The final message was one of assurance. Haggai proclaimed this word from God three months after work on the temple had restarted. In it, God reminded the people that they had suffered since their return from exile because they had not turned completely back to him. Their apathy about the temple was a symptom of their apathy toward God, but when they had started to work diligently once more, God proclaimed that he was about to bless them both now and in the future.

ZECHARIAH
Question 133. Who was Zechariah?

Zechariah was a young prophet who initially served as a priest. Zechariah was born in Babylon but returned to Jerusalem when Cyrus the Persian allowed the city to be re-occupied. He was a contemporary of Haggai, and their relationship was an interesting one.

Haggai was blunt and pointed in his words. He spoke to the people for only a few months, but he badgered them enough to move them beyond their fear of outside retaliation to finish rebuilding the temple. Zechariah was more of an encourager. He constantly lifted up the glory and power of God to the people to keep their eyes on the purpose and mission of their work.

Haggai was old, and he proclaimed the word of the Lord for less than half a year. Zechariah was younger, a new face as God's messenger and one who would continue leading the people for several years. Haggai was able to pass the torch of spiritual leadership onto Zechariah once the older man had helped the Israelites come back to their senses and return to God.

Question 134. What was the main message of the Book of Zechariah?

Like Haggai, Zechariah wanted the people of Jerusalem to fully return to God once their exile was over. Like Haggai, Zechariah believed that the first step in that direction was to rebuild the temple. It was a difficult job, mainly because the people had experienced a number of difficulties upon returning to Jerusalem—slander and attacks from neighboring countries, failing crops, and a struggling economy. They did not understand why life wasn't wonderful once they were back in Jerusalem.

Zechariah and Haggai worked tirelessly to remind the people that it took more than just coming back to the Promised Land to restore their place as God's people. Pure hearts and obedience to God's commands were also key elements in their quest.

Zechariah's encouragement was not only for the people of the present day, however. More than any other prophet except Isaiah, Zechariah's messages from God highlighted the coming Messiah, the Savior of God's people. This message did include images of the Christ as a victorious king who would bring Israel's enemies under his feet, but he also predicted the Messiah's suffering before that could be accomplished. It was Zechariah who prophesied that the Messiah would be sold for thirty pieces of silver (11:12–13), would be "pierced" (12:10), and would be struck down (13:7).

MALACHI

Question 135. What are the primary messages of the Book of Malachi?

As the last book of the Old Testament, Malachi is an interesting bridge to the coming of Jesus as the Messiah and all that followed after. The book was written sometime around 460 BC, which was about one hundred years after the people had returned to Jerusalem from Babylon. In that time, the people had rebuilt the temple and started rededicating their lives to God, thanks to prophets such as Haggai, Zechariah, Ezra, and Nehemiah, but something had stalled. The Israelites had once again become apathetic about God.

One of the main themes Malachi hammered home was the failure of the priests in Jerusalem. They were supposed to be shepherds for the people of God, but instead they actively broke God's commandments and used their position as a means to profit financially. For example, they had begun offering blind and disabled animals as sacrifices to God (1:6–8) instead of those without blemish, as was commanded. (Disabled and blemished animals did not sell very well and would not have been used in breeding other animals because of their faults.) All of this was detestable to God and to Malachi.

While the failure of the spiritual leaders certainly had an impact on the citizens of Jerusalem, God also held the rest of the people accountable for their own sins. The people had begun to grumble and complain about God because of a perceived lack of blessing, and they started withholding their tithes (3:8–10) and abandoning issues of justice.

The Book of Malachi highlights the failure of God's people to honor their covenant with God. In response to these failures, God prepared a new way to restore the relationship between himself and humans, which is the story of the New Testament. "See, I will send my messenger, who will prepare the way before me," God says in 3:1, speaking of John the Baptist. "'Surely the day is coming; it will burn like a furnace. All the arrogant and every evildoer will be stubble, and that day that is coming will set them on fire,' says the Lord Almighty. 'Not a root or a branch will be left to them. But for you who revere my name, the sun of righteousness will rise with healing in its wings. And you will go out and leap like calves released from the stall. Then you will trample down the wicked; they will be ashes under the soles of your feet on the day when I do these things,' says the Lord Almighty" (4:1–3).

Chapter 7

THE GOSPELS AND ACTS

■ Question 136. What historical events occurred in Israel between the end of the Old Testament and the start of the New Testament?

■ Question 137. What historical events occurred in the world during the time of Jesus?

■ Question 138. Why does the Bible include four Gospels?

■ Question 139. Why don't all the details match from one Gospel to another?

■ Question 140. Who was Matthew?

■ Question 141. Who was Mark?

■ Question 142. Who was Luke?

■ Question 143. Why is Luke's genealogy different from Matthew's?

■ Question 144. Who was John?

■ Question 145. Why is John so different from the other Gospels?

■ Question 146. What is the "kingdom of heaven"?

■ Question 147. Why did Jesus use parables so often?

■ Question 148. Is it significant when people have their names changed in the Bible?

■ Question 149. Why were the Pharisees and religious leaders so antagonistic toward Jesus?

■ Question 150. Who was John the Baptist?

■ Question 151. Why did Jesus perform miracles?

■ Question 152. Are demons still active in the world today?

■ Question 153. Who were the disciples?

■ Question 154. Who were the apostles?

■ Question 155. What is the purpose of Communion?

■ Question 156. Is there evidence that Jesus really died on the cross?

■ Question 157. What is the role of the Holy Spirit?

■ Question 158. What was happening in the world during the times described by the Book of Acts?

■ Question 159. Why did God strike down Ananias and Sapphira?

■ Question 160. What led to the rapid growth of the church in the ancient world?

THE FOUR GOSPELS

Question 136. What historical events occurred in Israel between the end of the Old Testament and the start of the New Testament?

The last books to provide a historical account of the Israelites are Ezra and Nehemiah, which cover about one hundred years after King Cyrus issued a decree allowing the exiles to return to Jerusalem and rebuild it.

The four hundred years that followed before the birth of Jesus were difficult for the Jewish people. When the Syrian Empire rose to power, cruel Antiochus Epiphanes seized control of Jerusalem and forbade the residents from worshiping God. He even desecrated the temple by sacrificing a pig in the Holy of Holies and later forced the Israelites to eat pork. This persecution led to the revolt of the Maccabees, headed by a man named Mattathias and his son Judas, which won back some political freedoms for the Jewish people.

In 63 BC, the Roman Empire took control of the Promised Land and retained control through the life of Jesus and the beginning of the church. The Romans were not antagonistic toward the Jews, but they demanded strict obedience and levied high taxes.

Question 137. What historical events occurred in the world during the time of Jesus?

The biggest thing happening in the ancient world at this time was the Roman Empire. The centuries leading up to the birth of Christ were violent and unstable. Vast empires had risen and fallen, including Alexander the Great and the Greeks, Egypt, and Syria.

The Romans were the ultimate victors from this period of strife, and as they expanded their borders to cover most of the known world, the result was a time of relative peace for several hundred years. Peace allowed for safe and easy travel, especially as the Romans continued building their famous system of roads. In other words, this particular period of time was a perfect opportunity for God to step into the world and ignite a movement that would change human history forever.

Question 138. Why does the Bible include four Gospels?

Jesus Christ was one of the most important men ever to live on planet Earth, so it makes sense that the events of his life were recorded by many people. It also makes sense that the Holy Spirit inspired multiple authors to record what they experienced of Jesus, because as it says Deuteronomy 19:15, "A matter must be established by the testimony of two or three witnesses."

In addition to adding credibility to the historical record of Jesus's life, each of the four Gospels views Jesus and his actions through a different lens. The Gospel of Matthew was written primarily for a Jewish audience, so it represents Jesus as the coming Messiah, the longed-for King. Mark was written to gentiles (specifically Roman citizens) and highlights Jesus as the suffering servant. Luke was written after a great deal of research and focuses on Jesus as the perfect man. John, written to Christians beginning to undergo persecution, highlights Jesus as God walking in flesh.

Each of these accounts is accurate in its portrayal of Jesus, and together they give followers of Christ a more complete picture of Jesus, his words, and his deeds.

Question 139. Why don't all the details match from one Gospel to another?

There are several differences between the Gospels, and even between Matthew, Mark, and Luke, which are very similar overall. Part of the reason for these differences is that each Gospel was written by a different person. All four Gospels were inspired by the same Holy Spirit, of course, but that spirit chose to work within the different personalities of the authors.

The order in which the books are written also plays a big part in these differences, especially for the Gospel of Mark, which was written first. The Gospels of Matthew and Luke often record the same events as Mark, but they include more information in several places. Since those authors already had the benefit of reading what Mark had written, they were able to fill in some of the gaps and provide extra input. The Gospel of John was written several years after Matthew and Luke and covers a lot of ground that was unexplored in the first three gospels.

Question 140. Who was Matthew?

Matthew is first seen in verse 9 of chapter 9: "As Jesus went on from there, he saw a man named Matthew sitting at the tax collector's booth. 'Follow me,' he told him, and Matthew got up and followed him."

As has been well-documented, tax collectors were not popular people in those days. Tax collectors were employed by the Roman government and often abused their power to levy high taxes on the people without cause or recourse. It isn't known if Matthew (originally known as Levi) abused his power in this way, but he certainly was a strange choice for one of Jesus's earliest disciples.

Matthew followed Jesus faithfully as a disciple, though, and he later wrote his gospel with one main goal in mind: to help his fellow Jews understand that Jesus was indeed their long-awaited Messiah. Notice, for example, how often Matthew quotes passages from the Old Testament. Notice how he almost always refers to Jesus as the "son of David," an attention-grabbing title for anyone of Jewish descent.

In Matthew we see a man once viewed as a traitor by his own people working diligently to serve them and help them see the truth.

Question 141. Who was Mark?

John Mark was his full name, and he was the son of a widow in Jerusalem. He and his wife had used their house as a meeting place for the early church in the city (Acts 12:12), and various sources have credited the top level of this house as the "upper room" where the disciples met after Jesus was crucified and where they received the Holy Spirit on the Day of Pentecost. As a gospel writer, Mark is believed to have recorded these events as he heard them firsthand from the apostle Peter.

It is not clear when Mark became a follower of Jesus, but he pops up in several places throughout the New Testament. The end of his gospel describes a young man in the Garden of Gethsemane who escaped from the guards arresting Jesus by shedding his linen garment and running away naked (14:51–52). Tradition has identified this young man as Mark himself. Mark was also the source of a sharp disagreement between the apostle Paul and Barnabus in the Book of Acts. He had accompanied Paul and Barnabus on a missionary journey to Antioch, but then became afraid and left. He eventually returned with Paul and Barnabus to Jerusalem, but when Paul refused to take him on the next missionary journey, he and Barnabus split and went in different directions (see Acts 15). Later, though, Mark came around, and Paul wrote the following about him in 2 Timothy 4:11: "Get Mark and bring him with you, because he is helpful to me in my ministry."

Given the early failings of Mark as a disciple, it is no wonder that his gospel focuses on the humanity of Jesus.

Question 142. Who was Luke?

Luke was the author of two books in the New Testament, the Gospel that bears his name and the Book of Acts. He was an educated man—most likely a doctor, according to early sources in church tradition—and he writes in the mode of a historian. His books are filled with details and data that establish historical credibility.

For example, here is what Luke writes in chapter 3: "In the fifteenth year of the reign of Tiberius Caesar—when Pontius Pilate was governor of Judea, Herod tetrarch of Galilee, his brother Philip tetrarch of Iturea and Traconitis, and Lysanias tetrarch of Abilene—during the high priesthood of Annas and Caiaphas, the word of God came to John son of Zechariah in the desert" (vv. 1–2). Tiberius Caesar is a historically known figure, verified by several non-biblical sources, as are Pontius Pilate and the tetrarchs. Luke's information helps us date this event at around AD 25.

We know that Luke was a companion of Paul during some of his missionary activity, which means he had access to a primary source when writing the Book of Acts. Some scholars believe that Mary, Jesus's mother, was Luke's primary source for his gospel. Others believe it was Peter or another apostle.

Question 143. Why is Luke's genealogy different from Matthew's?

The genealogy in the Gospel of Matthew is concerned with establishing Jesus as the Messiah and long-awaited King of the Jews; thus Matthew's genealogy traces Jesus's roots back to David and includes names that are significant in that historical line. Luke, on the other hand, is attempting to show that Jesus is the Savior of all mankind; therefore, his genealogy traces Jesus's line all the way back to Adam.

There have been a number of explanations attempting to account for the differences in the two genealogies found in the Gospels. Some scholars believe that Matthew was attempting to trace Joseph's lineage, while Luke was tracing Mary's. Others believe that the variations were caused by one or more "levirate marriages," where a man without sons is still included in a historical record because his widow married his brother and conceived sons in the original husband's name (see Deuteronomy 25:5–10).

What needs to be understood is that the people of the ancient world did not view genealogies and historical records in the same way we do. We are products of the Enlightenment, and our culture expects numbers and dates and facts to be consistent and accurate. That was not true of the Israelites of that day. They viewed genealogies as a way of making significant connections between people and events. They often skipped several generations of people if those names did not have an impact on those connections.

Question 144. Who was John?

John was one of Jesus's original disciples, and he and his brother James were first called by Jesus as they were operating their family's fishing business along the shores of the Sea of Galilee (see Matthew 4). John refers to himself as "the disciple whom Jesus loved" in his gospel, and most scholars believe that John was one of the people Jesus was closest to on earth, along with James and Peter.

After Jesus's death and resurrection, John became a leader in the early church. He remained in Jerusalem for a while, but was banished to the island of Patmos under the persecution of Roman Emperor Domitian. This is where John received the vision that ultimately became the Book of Revelation. In addition to Revelation and the Gospel that bears his name, John also wrote the epistles called 1, 2, and 3 John.

After his release from prison, John returned to the city of Ephesus where he became the main leader and shepherd of the Ephesian church. He lived quite a few years, and many scholars believe he is the only one of the twelve apostles who was not martyred for his faith.

Question 145. Why is John so different from the other Gospels?

Matthew, Mark, and Luke have been termed the "synoptic Gospels" in recent years because they are very similar in terms of the time line and overall flow of events they each record, but John's Gospel is quite different than the other three—so much so that many people have questioned whether John is contradicting the other Gospel writers or if his work should be considered a Gospel at all.

In reality, the Gospel of John does not contradict the synoptic Gospels, nor are the accounts in the four books at cross purposes. One thing to keep in mind is that John's Gospel was written much later than Matthew, Mark, and Luke—possibly as much as thirty or thirty-five years later. That means he had access to the other three Gospels, and John was writing after AD 70, when the city of Jerusalem was destroyed by the Romans.

John was writing in a different world and speaking to a different audience. Specifically, the main heresy of John's time that was spreading rapidly said that Jesus Christ was a man, but was not God; therefore, it was a main goal of John's Gospel to correct those heresies: "But these are written that you may believe that Jesus is the Christ, the Son of God, and that by believing you may have life in his name" (20:31). To achieve this purpose, John focused on seven miracles of Jesus early in the book (chapters 1–12) as he quickly moved through the history of Jesus's public ministry, and then he spent a great deal of time detailing the last week of Jesus's ministry, including his death and resurrection.

As has been mentioned a few times so far in this book, the people of the ancient Middle East were not concerned with accurate chronological time lines. They connected events to make a point rather than to show which happened first and which happened last. That is why some of the events in John's Gospel appear to happen at different times and in a different order than what is recorded in Matthew, Mark, and Luke. John was using the events to show Jesus's divinity, not to give an accurate timeline.

Question 146. What is the "kingdom of heaven"?

This curious phrase is found thirty-one times in the Book of Matthew, but is not mentioned anywhere else in the Bible, although the other Gospel writers do refer to the "kingdom of God" quite a bit. Perhaps Matthew, with his Jewish background, chose not to write down the word "God."

In any case, a "kingdom" in ancient days referred to any area over which a king had particular influence. In other words, a kingdom was anywhere that a king's will would be obeyed and enforced, so the kingdom of heaven refers to anywhere that God is recognized as king and obeyed as such. This concept would have been easily understood by the Jews of Jesus's day, given the history of Israel as a theocracy.

Notice that Jesus uses this phrase most often to introduce his parables: "The kingdom of heaven is like…." And notice, also, that the kingdom he describes is not at all perfect. There are weeds mixed in with the wheat; there is yeast working throughout the dough (a symbol for sin); and there are bad fish mixed in with the good fish.

In other words, the kingdom of heaven describes the life of those who follow God here on our fallen planet, Earth. It also describes the coming kingdom that followers of God will experience one day, what we usually think of as heaven. Matthew 8:11 says: "I say to you that many will come from the easy and the west, and will take their places at the feast with Abraham, Isaac, and Jacob in the kingdom of heaven." The tension between our work here on earth and our future home in heaven is often referred to as "the already and not yet."

Question 147. Why did Jesus use parables so often?

It was a common teaching strategy of rabbis in Jesus's day and after. Parables were a way to condense a spiritual truth into an interesting story that could be easily remembered and easily explained.

Jesus's parables were different, however, in that many people who heard them could not figure out what they meant. After Jesus told many parables in Matthew 13, for example, the scripture records the following: "Jesus spoke all these things to the crowd in parables; he did not say anything to them without using a parable. So was fulfilled what was spoken through the prophet: 'I will open my mouth in parables, I will utter things hidden since the creation of the world'" (vv. 34–35).

Jesus's message was radical and dangerous, and it eventually led to his death on the cross at the hands of both the Jews and the Romans. Jesus knew that he had to communicate the truth gradually so that his confrontation with the Pharisees would not come too soon and he would have time to prepare his disciples for life and ministry without him. Thus, the parables are like puzzles that can be unlocked with a certain key. That key is the knowledge that Jesus was the Messiah—God in the flesh who had come to save all of mankind from its sins. Anyone who believed that and heard one of Jesus's parables could unlock its meaning, but anyone unaware of Jesus's mission and authority would have been confused by his stories.

Question 148. Is it significant when people have their names changed in the Bible?

Yes, it is. In general, names were more important to people of the ancient Middle East than they are in our culture today, because names were closely connected with a person's character or essential being. Names were often chosen based on a character trait or personality that parents wanted their child to grow into. The name Jesus, for example, means "deliverer" or "savior." Names were also chosen in connection with the circumstances around a child's birth. The name Jacob means "he grasps the heel," for example, and was given to Jacob in Genesis because he came out of the womb holding on to his brother's foot. We can see that Jacob's name was also tied to his character, since "he grasps the heel" became a figure of speech referring to deception.

For those reasons, it is a significant when a character in the Bible is given a new name, especially when that new name comes from God. It means that something has changed in that person's character to such a large degree that his or her name no longer fits. When Jacob matured and developed in his relationship with God, for example, "he grasps the heel" no longer described him, as his deceptive nature was gone. Jacob was renamed Israel, meaning "he struggles with God," which connected to Jacob's wrestling match with God in Genesis 23.

Peter's name change in Matthew 16 is also significant. His original name was Simon, but Jesus changed it after Peter professed Jesus to be the Messiah, which demonstrated that he was solid in his faith: "Jesus replied, 'Blessed are you, Simon son of Jonah, for this was not revealed to you by man, but by my Father in heaven. And I tell you that you are Peter, and on this rock I will build my church, and the gates of Hades will not overcome it'" (vv. 17–18). The name Peter means "rock," and Jesus was foreshadowing Peter's future role as leader of the early church. This name change is particularly interesting because Peter still had a lot to learn when it come to maturity and steadfastness (three times before the crucifixion he denied that he even knew Jesus). By changing his name before Peter had fully demonstrated that he deserved it, Jesus was showing faith in Peter's eventual maturity.

Question 149. Why were the Pharisees and religious leaders so antagonistic toward Jesus?

The religious leaders of Jesus's day usually get a bad rap, especially the Pharisees, and in many ways they deserve it; however, they did not start out hating Jesus. When he first burst onto the scene with miracles and powerful teaching, they were curious; some were even excited. After Jesus healed a blind man on the Sabbath: "Some of the Pharisees said, 'This man is not from God, for he does not keep the Sabbath.' But others asked, 'How can a sinner do such miraculous signs?'" The Pharisees were divided on what to make of Jesus. During this time of curiosity, they continually asked Jesus if he was the Messiah, and if he would be willing to prove that he had come from God (see Matthew 9:38 and John 10:24, among other passages).

In some ways that seems reasonable, and we might wonder why Jesus wouldn't simply call down ten thousand angels from heaven and eliminate all doubt about the matter. The reason Jesus preferred a low profile is that the Jews of his day had a false idea in mind about who the Messiah would be and what he would do. They thought the Messiah would come as a conquering king who would drive the Romans out of the Promised Land and restore the glory that Israel had during the reigns of David and Solomon. But Jesus had come to give himself as a sacrifice to restore the relationship between God and people. His time of glory would come later, but he knew the people would not understand, so he kept silent.

What eventually turned the Pharisees and other leaders against Jesus was that he did not fit into the box they had constructed for him, especially when it came to their religious rules. The Old Testament contained around six hundred commands concerning what God's people should and should not do, and it was the job of the Pharisees to interpret these laws and apply them to everyday life. The Pharisees went way out of control, though, transforming those six hundred commands into thousands of rules and regulations that the Jewish people were expected to follow. For example, God commanded his people not to work on the Sabbath, but it raised the question: What is work? The regulations of the Pharisees defined spitting on the ground as work (because it was potentially watering plants), as well as walking more than three-quarters of a mile.

Not surprisingly, Jesus was unimpressed by these rules, and he did not feel compelled to follow them. In fact, he criticized the Pharisees sharply for twisting God's law, which was supposed to help people avoid sin, into a weapon of control. "Woe to you," he told the experts in the law, "because you load people down with burdens they can hardly carry, and you yourselves will not lift one finger to help them" (Luke 11:46). This is where the relationship between Jesus and the Pharisees started breaking down. When Jesus still refused to give them a sign proving that he was the Messiah, they accused him of blasphemy against God, a crime punishable by death (see John 5:18). The rest is history.

Question 150. Who was John the Baptist?

John the Baptist was a relative of Jesus's. John's mother, Elizabeth, was a cousin of Jesus's mother, Mary. As an adult, John was a prophet—the last of the Old Testament–type prophet, in fact. He was the one Malachi had predicted would come to prepare the way for the Messiah: "'See, I will send my messenger, who will prepare the way before me. Then suddenly the Lord you are seeking will come to his temple; the messenger of the covenant, whom you desire, will come,' says the LORD Almighty" (Malachi 3:1). Isaiah also prophesied about John, calling him "a voice of one calling: 'In the desert prepare the way for the LORD; make straight in the wilderness a highway for our God'" (Isaiah 40:3).

It was John's job to call the people of Israel back to repentance in preparation for the coming Messiah. He was such an effective preacher that large numbers of people came to see him in the wilderness and to be baptized—a ritual washing that symbolized the people's repentance and desire to be cleansed of sin. John helped the people understand that being Jewish was not enough to bring them into fellowship with God. Repentance and obedience were vital.

Question 151. Why did Jesus perform miracles?

Jesus's miracles were intended to be a declaration of his title and position as the Messiah. They were proof that he was more than just an ordinary man and that he had control over things like nature, agriculture, and disease. In addition, several of Jesus's miracles fulfilled specific prophecies from the Old Testament that had been tied to the coming Messiah (see Isaiah 61:1–2, for an example).

Just as important, however, in Jesus's decision to perform miracles is that fact that Jesus loved the people he encountered and genuinely desired to help them. Matthew 14:14 says that "when Jesus landed and saw a large crowd, he had compassion on them and healed their sick."

Question 152. Are demons still active in the world today?

Supernatural activity will always be a reality in the world, both for good and for evil. God has made it clear that he will operate on our behalf through his Holy Spirit, and also through angels (see John 14 and Hebrews 13:2). The Bible also warns us that spiritual beings can operate in ways that are intended to harm us (1 Peter 5:8). Romans 8:38–39 is another good passage that strongly indicates a spiritual reality at play in the world around us: "For I am convinced that neither death nor life, neither angels nor demons, neither the present nor the future, nor any powers, neither height nor depth, nor anything else in all creation, will be able to separate us from the love of God that is in Christ Jesus our Lord."

Why aren't there people possessed by demons on street corners in every town and village, as Jesus seemed to encounter in the Gospels? Or is it possible that demons are active and causing many of the diseases that people are afflicted with today, as often happened in the New Testament?

Many scholars believe that the amount of demonic activity in the Bible might not be "normal," but actually elevated because of the presence of Jesus. In other words, knowing that Jesus was present in the world, Satan and his demons may have become more active, to interfere with his work. It's also possible that Jesus directly confronted demons when he encountered them, to show that he had authority in the spiritual realm.

Question 153. Who were the disciples?

In Jesus's time, all male students attended some schooling during their early years, but only the best and brightest received an extended education and became trained in the interpretation and application of the scriptures. Whereas most men in Jewish society joined the family business or became apprentices to tradesmen, these students became disciples to particular rabbis.

Rabbis were the religious teachers of the day and part of the spiritual leadership of the community. Each rabbi had his own particular set of doctrines and interpretations concerning the law called a "yoke" (see Matthew 11:30 where Jesus says "my yoke is easy and my burden is light"). As each rabbi traveled throughout the land or taught in a particular city or village, he was accompanied and assisted by his disciples. The goal of every disciple was to become more and more like his rabbi.

This is the system that Jesus used when he began his teaching ministry around the age of thirty. He gathered a group of disciples around him and traveled the countryside, explaining his particular yoke in regard to what the scriptures taught about salvation and a true relationship with God. Some people are surprised that disciples dropped everything they were doing to follow Jesus (see Matthew 4, for example), but it would not have been particularly strange. Jesus was known as a rabbi and teacher when he began calling the disciples, so it would have been a great honor to be selected.

Here's an interesting thing to note, however: Most of the disciples Jesus selected were already busy in another trade. James and John were fishermen. Matthew was a tax collector. That's important because it shows that Jesus did not select the best of the best. He chose his followers from those who had washed out of schooling when it came to interpreting the law. In other words, Jesus chose the men who were best able to further his purposes for God's kingdom rather than those who were ideal candidates by the conventional wisdom of the day.

Question 154. Who were the apostles?

It isn't known for sure how many disciples Jesus had. The number fluctuated at different times during his ministry, but we do know that it grew as he gained stature and reputation as a man of power. In Luke 9, Jesus gathers twelve of his disciples and sends them out in pairs to "preach the kingdom of God and to heal the sick" (v. 2), but in chapter 10, he sends out seventy-two of his disciples on a similar mission. There were about 120 believers in the Upper Room after Jesus's death and resurrection (Acts 1:15), and 1 Corinthians 15:6 reports that Jesus interacted with more than five hundred people after his resurrection.

What is known is that Jesus selected twelve men from all of his disciples and provided them with extra attention and expectations (see Mark 3). These are the men we usually call the twelve disciples: Peter; John; James; Andrew; Philip; Matthew; Thomas; Bartholomew; James, son of Alphaeus; Simon the Zealot; Judas, son of James; and Judas Iscariot.

Later, after Jesus's death and resurrection, these men became leaders in the early church and acquired the title "apostle." Matthias was chosen as a replacement apostle for Judas in the Upper Room (Acts 1:12–26), and Paul was later given the title "apostle" (1 Corinthians 15:9).

Question 155. What is the purpose of Communion?

Communion is first and foremost a way for Christians to remember what Jesus did on their behalf to provide reconciliation between God and human beings. Luke writes the following about Jesus's starting the practice of Communion during the Last Supper: "And he took bread, gave thanks and broke it, and gave it to them, saying, 'This is my body given for you; do this in remembrance of me.' In the same way, after the supper he took the cup, saying, 'This cup is the new covenant in my blood, which is poured out for you'" (Luke 22:19–20).

This act of remembering and appreciation was not meant to be a somber affair, however. Jesus was encouraging us to eat and drink together in honor of what he was about to do, suffer and die on the cross, yes, but then be raised back to life and gain victory over death. Communion was given to Christians as a way to celebrate the free gift of forgiveness and salvation as well as a way to honor the man who secured that gift with his own body and blood.

Question 156. Is there evidence that Jesus really died on the cross?

Though some argue it, there is nothing to support the theory that Jesus experienced a swoon on the cross and was actually buried alive, only to emerge from the tomb three days later after recovering consciousness. In fact, the evidence supporting Jesus's physical death on the cross is overwhelming.

First and foremost, the amount of punishment that Jesus's body went through was staggering. He was flogged in the public square by Roman guards, which involved thirty-nine lashes from a specially designed whip called a cat-of-nine-tails. The Romans were experts in torture and had calculated that many people died after receiving forty lashes, so they set their limit at thirty-nine, to inflict the most possible damage and still keep the prisoner alive. After this, Jesus was forced to march from the center of the city up a series of rugged hills and then nailed through his wrists into a large beam of wood, the Roman execution method called crucifixion, which has been well-documented throughout history. It was designed to kill slowly while inflicting as much pain as possible.

Jesus hung suspended on that beam for six hours before crying "It is finished!" and passing away (John 19:30). Since it was Friday evening, the Jewish leaders asked the Romans to put an end to the crucifixion so that they would not have to do the work of taking bodies down on the Sabbath (which would have started Friday at sunset), so the guards broke the legs of the prisoners crucified alongside Jesus, but they did not break Jesus's legs because they knew he was already dead. The Gospel of John records that to confirm Jesus's death, one of the guards pierced Jesus's side with a spear, causing "blood and water" to flow" (John 19:34). This detail is important because there is a sack around the heart that contains a clear liquid very similar to water in appearance, meaning Jesus's heart was pierced by the spear as well.

Physically, the evidence is overwhelming that Jesus did literally die that Friday evening on the cross, but there are also other pieces of evidence. The most convincing is the reaction of Jesus's disciples after the resurrection. Those men and women saw Jesus in his resurrected body, and that brief encounter led them to start a worldwide movement that is now called Christianity. While fighting for that movement, most of the original apostles who led the early church were imprisoned and killed because of their faith in Jesus's resurrection. It makes no sense that these men and women would have gone to such lengths if they had robbed Jesus's body in the night, as the Pharisees claimed, or if they had found Jesus barely alive after recovering from a swoon. In other words, there is no way that so many people willingly gave up their lives for what they knew to be a fraud.

Question 157. What is the role of the Holy Spirit?

The Greek word for the Holy Spirit in the New Testament is *paraclete*, which means "one who is called alongside to help." Just as God's presence dwelt in the Holy of Holies in the tabernacle and temple, the Holy Spirit is a helper, the presence of God dwelling within individual people who make up the church. This presence guides us, often interacting with and engaging our consciences, and intercedes with God on our behalf (Romans 8:26).

Contrary to what some believe and teach, the Holy Spirit was not just a New Testament phenomenon. Many people were empowered by the Holy Spirit throughout the Old Testament, including Bezalel (Exodus 31:2–4), Moses (Numbers 11:17), Samson (Judges 15:14), Saul (1 Samuel 10:10), and many others. In fact, the Holy Spirit is present right from the second verse of the Bible: "Now the earth was formless and empty, darkness was over the surface of the deep, and the Spirit of God was hovering over the waters" (Genesis 1:2).

There was a difference, however, between how the Holy Spirit operated in the Old Testament and how he operated after the Day of Pentecost. In the Old Testament, the Holy Spirit often "filled" a person, to assist that person in fulfilling a certain task or mission. This sometimes included blessing that person with specific gifts, such as Bezalel with art and Samson with superhuman strength, but the Old Testament does not refer to the Holy Spirit as dwelling with God's people on a day-to-day basis.

That changes in the New Testament. When Jesus tells his disciples that he will soon be leaving this earth, he comforts them by saying: "And I will ask the Father, and he will give you another Counselor to be with you forever—the Spirit of truth. The world cannot accept him, because it neither sees him nor knows him. But you know him, for he lives with you and will be in you" (John 14:16–17). These words were fulfilled on the Day of Pentecost, when the Holy Spirit indwelt the disciples in the Upper Room during what became the beginning of the church.

ACTS
Question 158. What was happening in the world during the times described by the Book of Acts?

Surprisingly, very little was happening in the rest of the world at the beginning of Acts—at least in terms of Jesus and the early church. Jesus's three years in ministry had caused a lot of waves in Jerusalem and the surrounding areas of Palestine, but they had little effect on the larger world. The Roman Empire continued in its dominance, unaware of Jesus except for the involvement of Pontius Pilate in his story.

In Jerusalem, the Pharisees and other religious leaders were simply trying to recover from the events surrounding Jesus's death and his suddenly missing body. They believed it was a temporary crisis that would eventually blow over. At the beginning of the Book of Acts, the remaining disciples of Jesus weren't giving the Pharisees much to be concerned about. They had all isolated themselves in a single house and were simply waiting, as they had been told (Acts 1:4).

By the end of the book, the Holy Spirit had led those disciples to spread the truth about Jesus and his resurrection throughout the known world, with tens of thousands of believers joining their cause and forming the first glimpses of God's church, the body of Christ on earth.

Question 159. Why did God strike down Ananias and Sapphira?

During this revolutionary period known as the early church, people seemed to be caught up in a whirlwind of generosity. Acts 2:44–45 says: "All the believers were together and had everything in common. Selling their possessions and goods, they gave to anyone as he had need." Barnabus was one of these people who displayed extreme generosity, and he "sold a field he owned and brought the money and put it at the apostles' feet" (Acts 4:37).

Unfortunately, the members of the early church were still human and still sinful. When married couple Ananias and Sapphira saw the attention that Barnabas received for his generous gift, they came up with a plan. They also sold a piece of land that they owned and gave a portion of the sale price to the apostles as a gift, but they claimed that they were giving *all* of the money they received from the sale. This deception did not fool God, however, and Ananias was struck dead after being confronted by Peter. When Sapphira returned later, Peter questioned her about the sale of the property, and she was also struck dead when she gave the same answers as her husband.

Ananias and Sapphira were more than free to keep some or all of the money they earned from selling their property, as nothing was forced on anyone in the early church. It was their deception that caused God's wrath to break out against them.

Isn't it a little cruel on God's part to kill two people simply because they lied? If that standard were applied to everyone, who could survive? Many people believe that God dealt with this situation so seriously because of the newness and purity of the early church. This collection of new believers was very vulnerable, and God may have wanted to protect his work in the church from an early influx of deception and hypocrisy.

Question 160. What led to the rapid growth of the church in the ancient world?

Ironically, one of the main things that helped the Gospel spread into different regions of the world was the persecution of the early Christians in Jerusalem. After Stephen became the church's first martyr, Acts 8:1 records the following: "On that day a great persecution broke out against the church at Jerusalem, and all except the apostles were scattered throughout Judea and Samaria." This must have been very discouraging to the early Christians at the time; however, the hand of God was clearly involved. Remember the words of Jesus back in Acts 1:8, "But you will receive power when the Holy Spirit comes on you; and you will be my witnesses in Jerusalem, and in all Judea and Samaria, and to the ends of the earth."

In a similar vein, another major cause of Christianity's rapid spread throughout the Roman Empire was the destruction of Jerusalem in AD 70. Just like the Assyrians and Babylonians centuries earlier, the Romans scattered many residents of Jerusalem throughout the empire, including the early Christians.

The final cause for the movement of the Gospel throughout the ancient world was the concentrated effort of early evangelists, such as the apostle Paul. These pioneers traveled to different cities with the express intent of planting a Christian Church. They usually started by working with any Jews living in that city, showing them how Jesus was the Messiah. Many Jews became followers of Christ in this way and in turn helped evangelists spread their message to the local gentiles as well.

Chapter 8

THE LETTERS OF PAUL

- Question 161. Who was Paul?
- Question 162. Where did Paul travel during his missionary journeys?
- Question 163. What are the primary themes of the letter to the Romans?
- Question 164. What is Paul referring to when he talks about the "saints"?
- Question 165. Should Christians today still obey the laws of the Old Testament?
- Question 166. Why are there two books for the Corinthians?
- Question 167. What does it mean to be "worldly"?
- Question 168. What was Paul's message to the church in Corinth?
- Question 169. What is the primary theme in the Book of Galatians?
- Question 170. What is grace, and how does it work?
- Question 171. Why was the practice of circumcision so controversial?
- Question 172. What were the circumstances surrounding Paul's letter to the Ephesians?
- Question 173. What are the primary themes of Ephesians?
- Question 174. Does the Bible instruct wives to submit to their husbands?
- Question 175. What is the primary message of Paul's letter to the Philippians?
- Question 176. What is the primary message of Paul's letter to the Colossians?
- Question 177. What was Paul's relationship with the church at Thessalonica?
- Question 178. What is the primary message of 1 Thessalonians?
- Question 179. What is the primary message of 2 Thessalonians?
- Question 180. Who was Timothy?
- Question 181. What are the primary messages of 1 Timothy?
- Question 182. What do the terms *overseer* and *deacon* mean?
- Question 183. What are the primary messages of 2 Timothy?
- Question 184. Who was Titus?
- Question 185. What was Paul's primary message in his letter to Titus?
- Question 186. Who was Philemon?

Question 161. Who was Paul?

Paul (originally named Saul) was born in Tarsus, a city in modern-day Turkey. Although he received training as a tentmaker, Paul excelled in his education and was groomed from a young age to be a religious leader for the Jews. He writes the following of himself in Philippians 3:5: "circumcised on the eighth day, of the people of Israel, of the tribe of Benjamin, a Hebrew of Hebrews; in regard to the law, a Pharisee." We also know that Paul was trained in the law by Gamaliel, who was a famous Pharisee and famous teacher of Pharisees.

Paul was an up-and-coming Pharisee when Jesus and his disciples burst onto the scene somewhere around AD 30. It isn't known if Paul interacted with Jesus in any meaningful way at that time, but Paul was present when Stephen became the first martyr of the early church (Acts 8:1). Afterward, Paul became a leader in the persecution of the early Christians. Acts 8:3 says, "But Saul began to destroy the church. Going from house to house, he dragged off men and women and put them in prison."

All of that changed, however, when Paul encountered Jesus on the road to Damascus. Paul was traveling with several companions when he was knocked to the ground by a flash of light and confronted by the resurrected Christ. From that moment on, Paul was a dedicated servant of God, Christ, and the church. He was harbored for a while by the believers in Damascus, and then sent to Jerusalem. When the religious leaders learned of his conversion—and that he was teaching about Jesus in the synagogues—they began plotting to kill him, so the leaders of the church sent Paul back to Tarsus for a time, where he was eventually sought out by Barnabas, an early evangelist. It was with Barnabas that Paul undertook his first missionary journey and solidified his calling as the "apostle to the gentiles."

Question 162. Where did Paul travel during his missionary journeys?

Paul went on three large-scale missionary journeys—one from AD 46–48, one from AD 50–52, and the final one from AD 53–57. In between these journeys he served as an apostle in Jerusalem.

Paul's first missionary journey started in Seleucia, which is in the modern-day country of Syria. He then traveled to Cyprus, and then across the Mediterranean Sea to Pamphylia, which in today's world is part of Turkey. From there he went to Antioch, Iconium, Lystra, and Derbe (all still in Turkey). When he was ready to return to Jerusalem, he simply reversed his route and visited each city again. Paul's purpose on this journey was to encourage and equip the Christians that had been scattered by Jerusalem and to plant new churches in the cities he visited along the way.

Paul's second missionary journey was more far reaching. Leaving Jerusalem, he traveled up the coast of the Mediterranean to Syria and then to Tarsus, which today is in Turkey. After Tarsus he revisited the churches in Derbe, Lystra, and Iconium. At this point Paul wanted to travel into Asia, but the Holy Spirit prevented it, leading him instead through Troas and into the region of Macedonia (Acts 16:6–10), which is mostly occupied by Greece today. Before returning to Jerusalem, Paul strengthened and established churches in the important coastal cities of Philippi, Thessalonica, Athens, Corinth, and Rhodes.

Paul's third missionary journey followed a very similar path to his second. He revisited the churches in Antioch, Tarsus, Iconium, Troas, Philippi, Thessalonica, Athens, and Corinth. He also visited Ephesus for the first time, as well as several small cities on the coasts of Syria and Turkey. This missionary journey was Paul's longest, lasting four years. On his return voyage to Jerusalem, several of Paul's friends and fellow workers warned him not to enter this city because they feared for his safety, but Paul continued in obedience to the Holy Spirit (see Acts 21:1–16).

Once in Jerusalem, it turned out that Paul was indeed in danger. The Jewish leaders of the city stirred up a riot against him, causing the Roman soldiers there to arrest him. Through a variety of circumstances, Paul was transported to Rome to appeal his case to Caesar, which ended up being a fourth missionary journey, for all practical purposes, except that Paul never returned home to Jerusalem. After visiting Crete and surviving a shipwreck, he eventually made it to Rome and lived there under house arrest for several years, where Paul wrote many of the epistles that are found in the New Testament today.

The exact date of Paul's death is not known. He may have been executed while under house arrest, or he may have been released from Roman guardianship and have traveled to Spain, only to be arrested again and returned to Rome soon thereafter. Either way, he was martyred in Rome after many years of unbending service to God and his fledgling church.

Question 163. What are the primary themes of the letter to the Romans?

Paul wrote the Book of Romans as an epistle—a letter—when he was ministering in the city of Corinth in Greece. Paul had heard about the flourishing church in Rome, which was the capital of the known world at the time, and he was eager to visit there and encourage the believers. "I long to see you so that I may impart to you some spiritual gift to make you strong," he writes in vv. 11–12, "that is, that you and I may be mutually encouraged by each other's faith." One of the main goals of the Book of Romans is for Paul simply to introduce himself to that church.

Paul's letter also contained a theological and practical primer for the fledging church in Rome. We might think of it as a textbook for Christianity 101. Paul covers the basic doctrines of Christianity—faith (chapter 3), righteousness (chapter 4), grace (chapter 5), and justification (chapter 5). Most importantly, he underlines the basic elements of salvation in stages throughout the book, and the key verses explaining the process of salvation are known today as the "Romans Road to Salvation." Those verses are 3:23, 5:8, 6:23, and 10:9–10.

In addition to theology, the latter chapters of Romans also address the practical aspects of living as a Christian and serving God in the everyday world. For example, chapter 13 covers issues such as politics, authority, and taxes, and chapter 12 should be required reading for all Christians, because it explains how to live in a way that is based on love, both for God and other people.

Question 164. What is Paul referring to when he talks about the "saints"?

Paul is referring to everyone who has given control of their lives over to Jesus Christ and is working to advance God's kingdom. In other words, Paul uses the word *saint* in the same way that we use the word *Christian* today. It wasn't just Paul; anytime you see the word *saint* in the Bible, it refers to the everyday people of God.

Question 165. Should Christians today still obey the laws of the Old Testament?

This is a tricky question, and the answer is both yes and no. Paul talks quite a bit in Romans and other books about how the law of the Old Testament was not sufficient for salvation, and how Jesus replaced it. Here's a good example from Romans 10: "Christ is the end of the law so that there may be righteousness for everyone who believes" (v. 4). Jesus himself made it clear that his life and ministry did not make the Old Testament law null and void, though. "Do not think that I have come to abolish the Law or the Prophets," he said. "I have not come to abolish them but to fulfill them" (Matthew 5:17).

Which is it? Did Jesus abolish the law, or did he somehow make it better? Again, the answer is both. There are some parts of the law that Jesus has made obsolete—specifically, the parts that deal with the Levitical system of sacrifices for the forgiveness of sin, and the parts that helped the Israelites separate themselves ("be holy") from neighboring cultures.

Let's take the sacrificial system first. The basic premise of that system still stands: "without the shedding of blood there can be no forgiveness of sin" (Hebrews 9:22), but because Jesus shed his own blood as a sacrifice for all people, Christians no longer need to shed the blood of animals ritually as a symbol of forgiveness. Colossians 1:19–20 says: "For God was pleased to have all his fullness dwell in him, and through him to reconcile to himself all things, whether things on earth or things in heaven, by making peace through his blood, shed on the cross." The old way was that each sin was paid for by the blood of an animal. The new way is that all sins are paid for by the blood of Jesus.

Jesus's death and resurrection also ended the dietary restrictions and other laws that focused on helping the Israelites remember their place as a nation "set apart" from all the others, including restrictions on what food could be eaten, what seeds could be planted, what kind of material could be used to make clothes, and so on (see Leviticus 11 for a good sample). Because Jesus opened the door for salvation to all people, there is no longer a need for a specific nation to set itself apart through dietary rituals and other customs as a promotion of holiness. All nations now have the opportunity to be holy through Jesus Christ, so those laws have been made obsolete.

The laws that express God's standards for righteousness and living in relationship with him—most of which are summarized in the Ten Commandments—remain in force, however. They have been improved by Jesus's death and resurrection because we now have his example to follow and the blessing of the Holy Spirit to help us.

Question 166. Why are there two books for the Corinthians?

These two books represent two separate letters that were written by Paul to the church in the city of Corinth. The first letter was probably written around AD 54, which was two or three years after Paul first visited the city and planted a church there as part of his second missionary journey. The second letter was written about a year later, while Paul was on his third missionary journey.

Question 167. What does it mean to be "worldly"?

To be worldly means to behave in a way that reflects the culture of the world around you, rather than the Kingdom of God. Here's what Paul says in 1 Corinthians 3, for example: "Brothers, I could not address you as spiritual but as worldly—mere infants in Christ. I gave you milk, not solid food, for you were not yet ready for it. Indeed, you are still not ready. You are still worldly" (v. 3).

Notice that Paul is speaking to Christians, here. You would expect people to behave in a worldly way when they haven't experienced salvation in Christ, but it's possible for those who are believers to still behave in a way that is controlled by their old nature, their sinful nature. The process of gradually peeling away our layers of worldliness and becoming more and more like the people God created us to be is called sanctification.

Question 168. What was Paul's message to the church in Corinth?

Because of its central location and calm seas, the city of Corinth was a very important commercial port in the ancient world. Trade in and around the city was always booming, which meant lives of wealth and luxury for most of the city's residents. In turn, this wealth quickly turned Corinth into a hotbed of vice and debauchery.

For all of those reasons and more, Paul believed it was important that Corinth also have a thriving church, and he successfully organized the believers there on his second missionary journey. About three years later, however, Paul heard that the young community was being damaged by conflict and internal strife. The worldliness and skewed priorities of the Corinthian culture had infected the Corinthian church. As a result, Paul's first letter to the Corinthians contained several rebukes and corrections. The members of the church had apparently split into factions. Some aligned themselves with Paul's teaching, others with Apollos, and still others with Cephas (Peter). Paul told them: "What, after all, is Apollos? And what is Paul? Only servants, through whom you came to believe—as the Lord has assigned to each his task" (3:5).

Even worse, many members of the Corinthian church were participating in destructive activities. Many were prideful, for example, and Paul told them, "Has not God made foolish the wisdom of the world?" Some of the believers were filing lawsuits against other Christians. Paul told them: "The very fact that you have lawsuits among you means you have been completely defeated already. Why not rather be wronged? Why not rather be cheated? Instead, you yourselves cheat and do wrong, and you do this to your brothers" (6:7–8). Other Corinthian believers were actively seeking out sexual immorality. Things had gotten so bad that a member of the church was openly carrying on an incestuous affair with his own stepmother. Paul told them: "Do you not know that your body is a temple of the Holy Spirit, who is in you, whom you have received from God? You are not your own; you were bought at a price. Therefore honor God with your body" (6:19–20).

Because of these corrections, Paul was worried that his letter would not be received well by the leaders of the church in Corinth. So, while travelling on his third missionary journey about a year later, he sent Titus to check on things in Corinth. Surprisingly, Titus reported that most of the church had received his letter well. But there was a group of dissenters who became hostile toward Paul, claiming that he was not a friend of the Corinthians, and even going so far as to say that Paul did not have the proper credentials to be an apostle.

Paul wrote a second letter in response to Titus's news, which communicated his joy over how the first letter had been received and also defended his status as an apostle. "Even if I caused you sorrow by my letter, I do not regret it," he told them. "Though I did regret it—I see that my letter hurt you, but only for a little while—yet now I am happy, not because you were made sorry, but because your sorrow led you to repentance. For you became sorrowful as God intended and so were not harmed in any way by us" (7:8–9). When defending his apostleship, Paul reveals more personal details about himself than in any other epistle (see especially chapters 10–12).

Question 169. What is the primary theme in the Book of Galatians?

Paul's main motivation in writing this letter to the church in Galatia (a region found in the country of Turkey today) was to defend the purity of the Gospel. Specifically, Paul was attempting to battle an influx of legalism ("earning" a way into heaven by obeying rules) and a return to Old Testament methods of operating in a relationship with God.

Paul had founded the Galatian church during his second missionary journey, probably around AD 51, but as with the church in Corinth, outside influences and worldviews began to seep into the congregation and distort the message of the Gospel. For the Corinthians, the damage had come from debauchery and worldly behavior. For the Galatians, the problem was religion. False teachers had infiltrated the church and claimed that, despite the sacrifice of Jesus and the coming of the Holy Spirit, it was necessary to observe the ceremonies and rituals of the Old Testament Law to maintain a relationship with God. These ceremonies included circumcision, offering sacrifices, and observing feasts and traditions.

Paul saw the danger in this false teaching right away. The Israelites had attempted to follow the law for centuries, but their efforts always devolved into apathy or legalism. Some haphazardly observed the traditions and sacrifices while their hearts were far from God, while others strictly followed the law to "earn" their way closer to God. Both those paths proved destructive, which is why God provided a new covenant through the death and resurrection of Jesus Christ, one that is based on grace instead of the strict observation of rituals.

Through his letter, Paul implores the Galatians to remain faithful to the pure Gospel of Jesus Christ and salvation by grace, instead of trying to mix in rituals and legalism. "It is for freedom that Christ has set us free," he wrote. "Stand firm, then, and do not let yourselves be burdened again by a yoke of slavery" (5:1).

Question 170. What is grace, and how does it work?

The concept of grace has been defined in many ways over the years, but one of the most popular definitions is the idea of unmerited favor. Grace means that we receive something positive that we don't deserve. In this way it is tied to mercy, which is not receiving something negative that we do deserve.

In the Bible, and especially for Paul, the concept of grace is almost always tied to salvation. In the ancient world, most religious systems revolved around cause and effect. If a family offered up sacrifices to a god, that god was supposed to recip-rocate with blessings of fertility, good harvests, and so on, so human beings could "earn" good things in life by being religious. This idea infected and twisted the law given to the Jewish people in the Old Testament. The law was originally written to help people understand what behaviors were sinful so that they could avoid them and also provided a means for the people to cleanse themselves if they did sin. But over time, the Jews began to focus solely on the ceremonies and sacrifices (the "letter of the law") instead of the ultimate goal of maintaining a relationship with God (the "spirit of the law").

That's why the concept of grace was so revolutionary for the believers in the early church. Salvation was not something that could be earned. It was a free gift from God that was paid for by the sacrifice of Jesus Christ. In fact, one of the best definitions of grace is an acronym: "God's Riches at Christ's Expense."

Question 171. Why was the practice of circumcision so controversial?

The dispute in the early church over circumcision went back to God's covenant with Abraham in Genesis 17: "This is my covenant with you and your descendants after you, the covenant you are to keep: Every male among you shall be circumcised. You are to undergo circumcision, and it will be the sign of the covenant between me and you.... Any uncircumcised male, who has not been circumcised in the flesh, will be cut off from his people; he has broken my covenant" (vv. 9–14).

Because of this covenant, the Israelites had always connected circumcision with salvation. If a man was not circumcised, he had no relationship with God. As a result, the false teachers in Galatia attempted to persuade the church to make circumcision mandatory for gentile Christians as well as Jews. They wanted to push the Galatian Christians back toward God's covenant with Abraham.

Paul knew that God had established a new covenant with his church, though, one that was based on grace. As an expert in the scriptures, he was certainly aware of these words from Jeremiah 31:31: "'The time is coming,' declares the LORD, 'when I will make a new covenant with the house of Israel and with the house of Judah.'" Jesus was the instigator of this new covenant, which he confirmed during the Last Supper: "In the same way, after the supper he took the cup, saying, 'This cup is the new covenant in my blood, which is poured out for you'" (Luke 22:20).

Therefore, Paul warned the gentile believers in Galatia of the risks of adopting the practice of circumcision. He knew it would be the first step on a dangerous path toward legalism and told them, "Mark my words! I, Paul, tell you that if you let yourselves be circumcised, Christ will be of no value to you at all. Again I declare to every man who lets himself be circumcised that he is obligated to obey the whole law. You who are trying to be justified by law have been alienated from Christ; you have fallen away from grace" (5:2–4).

Question 172. What were the circumstances surrounding Paul's letter to the Ephesians?

The city of Ephesus was one of the largest metropolises of the ancient world, and Paul had spent a great deal of time there on his third missionary journey (from AD 53–57). In fact, Ephesus operated as his home base for many years as he traveled to and from the surrounding cities in Galatia and Macedonia; thus Paul became very close with the members of the Ephesian church (see Acts 20:36–37).

That's why it's strange that Paul's letter to the Ephesians is unusually impersonal. In most of Paul's other epistles, he includes personal greetings and mentions the names of specific individuals. That's not the case with Ephesians. In addition, the themes addressed in the letter are universal (key theological concepts and principles that are applicable for all believers) rather than specific to the people of Ephesus. The reason for this departure from Paul's other letters is likely that the Book of Ephesians was written by Paul as a circuit letter. It was probably delivered first in Ephesus, but then passed around to the cities and churches in the surrounding area, including Smyrna, Laodicea, Philadelphia, and others. Some scholars believe the letter may have been a speech or sermon that was to be delivered in each of the churches that received it.

In any case, Paul wrote this letter while he was imprisoned in Rome, probably around AD 61 or 62, which would mean Paul had been away from Ephesus for about five years.

Question 173. What are the primary themes of Ephesians?

Paul's letter to the Ephesians tackles several important elements of God's kingdom and work in this world, but the most important is the idea that God's "glorious grace" was given as a gift to sinful human beings. Chapter 1 speaks of Christ's exalted place in all the workings of creation, "far above all rule and authority, power and dominion, and every title that can be given, not only in the present age but also in the one to come" (v. 21). Paul rejoices that, because of the grace of God, human beings are able to participate in the riches of this kingdom. We have been redeemed (v. 7) by Christ's blood and given an inheritance (v. 14) as members of God's family.

The second theme Paul tackles in this letter is the importance and purpose of the church. The believers in Ephesus were an ethnically diverse group of Jews and gentiles living and working together. Paul celebrates this fact and urges them to preserve their unity as members of God's family (2:11–22; 4:1–6). The church is lifted up as the Body of Christ that can accomplish God's work in this world because Christ is the head (4:15–16).

The first half of Ephesians focuses on the position that those who believe in God's kingdom have; Christians are heirs in God's family and members of God's functional body on earth, the church. The second half of Ephesians talks about how Christians are supposed to live and behave because of their position in the church.

In the second half of chapter 4, Paul gives instructions on showing love to neighbors, while the next chapter advises believers to avoid sin and the deeds of darkness common in the rest of the world. "Be very careful, then, how you live," he advises, "not as unwise but as wise, making the most of every opportunity, because the days are evil" (vv. 15–16). Chapter 5 also explains how Christians should behave toward the members of their family, and chapter 6 speaks about living as a follower of Christ in the complex relationships and interactions of the workplace. Chapter 6 concludes with several famous verses describing the armor of God, with which believers can stand firm against the forces of evil.

Question 174. Does the Bible instruct wives to submit to their husbands?

Yes, that is certainly a command given in the Bible. Here's what Paul writes in Ephesians 5:22–24: "Wives, submit to your husbands as to the Lord. For the husband is the head of the wife as Christ is the head of the church, his body, of which he is the Savior. Now as the church submits to Christ, so also wives should submit to their husbands in everything." This verse is the one most commonly used by people who believe that wives should submit to their husbands because the Bible tells them to. Peter seems to echo Paul's words, as well: "Wives, in the same way be submissive to your husbands so that, if any of them do not believe the word, they may be won over without words by the behavior of their wives, when they see the purity and reverence of your lives" (1 Peter 3:1–2).

Do these commands apply only to the male-dominated culture of the ancient world, or are they universal for all husbands and wives throughout all time? That question can be tough to answer. The majority of biblical commands are universal, but there are several commands in the Bible that we consider to be culturally specific, such as Peter's recommendation that women not braid their hair in 3:3. What about the commands listed above about wives and husbands? Scholars have debated for a long time about whether they are universal, and the church has not arrived at a definite answer.

That debate seems unnecessary, however, when you explore the context of the two verses mentioned above. In Ephesians, the verse immediately before Paul's command for wives to submit to their husbands is this: "Submit to one another out of reverence for Christ" (5:21). Paul is talking about submission as a general topic, and then he moves into specifics by saying that wives should submit to their husbands, and then he adds what husbands should do: "Husbands, love your wives, just as Christ loved the church and gave himself up for her to make her holy, cleansing her by the washing with water through the word, and to present her to himself as a radiant church, without stain or wrinkle or any other blemish, but holy and blameless. In this same way, husbands ought to love their wives as their own bodies" (vv. 25–28). In other words, when Paul is already talking about submission, he says that wives should show respect to their husbands by submitting to them, which was culturally required, and that husbands should sacrificially love their wives more than they love themselves, which was not culturally required. The emphasis is actually on the husbands more than the wives.

In the passage from 1 Peter, it's again important to look at what Peter is talking about before he mentions wives and husbands: "Submit yourselves for the Lord's sake to every authority instituted among men: whether to the king, as the supreme authority, or to governors, who are sent by him to punish those who do wrong and to commend those who do right.... Show proper respect to everyone: Love the brotherhood of believers, fear God, honor the king" (1 Peter 2:13–17). Peter is writing to Christians in a world that was persecuting Christians, so he is recommending that believers submit themselves to the authority placed over them instead of rebelling. He talks about everyone submitting to government, about slaves submitting to their masters (2:18–25), and then wives submitting to husbands at the beginning of chapter 3. The goal of this submission is to allow Christians to live out the message of the Gospel rather than trying to break free from earthly authority, which makes sense for wives of that time. A Christian woman would have no way to force her husband into becoming a Christian (which Christian husbands were able to do with their wives), so Peter is recommending that these women serve and submit to their husbands as a vehicle for evangelism.

Question 175. What is the primary message of Paul's letter to the Philippians?

The operative word for the Book of Ephesians is *grace*. For Philippians, it's *joy*. And what makes this theme all the more amazing is that Paul was writing to the Philippians while in chains as a Roman prisoner.

Paul had planted the church at Philippi in AD 50, about ten years before writing this letter. He was dearly loved by the believers there, and the Philippian church was one of only a few that supported him financially over the years. In fact, part of the reason Paul wrote this letter in the first place was to thank the church for a recent financial gift (4:10–18).

Paul's main focus in his letter, though, is on the joy of living as a servant of Jesus Christ. He rejoices that no circumstance in life could shake this joy away from him, including the prospect of death. Paul says, "Yes, and I will continue to rejoice, for I know that through your prayers and the help given by the Spirit of Jesus Christ, what has happened to me will turn out for my deliverance. I eagerly expect and hope that I will in no way be ashamed, but will have sufficient courage so that now as always Christ will be exalted in my body, whether by life or by death. For to me, to live is Christ and to die is gain" (1:18–21). Paul was able to express this joy because of his knowledge that God himself had suffered death to provide a way of salvation for his people (2:5–11).

Paul also had some practical advice for the Philippians, including a warning against false teachers who wanted the church to return to circumcision and a legalistic adherence to the law (3:2–6). Mostly Paul encouraged them to search for the same joy that he had found in Christ. "Rejoice in the Lord always," he told them. "I will say it again: Rejoice!" (4:4).

Question 176. What is the primary message of Paul's letter to the Colossians?

The Book of Colossians was another letter that Paul wrote while he was a prisoner in Rome (AD 60–62). It is very similar in style to Ephesians, although the main subject of the book is different. To the Ephesians, Paul emphasized the importance and vital mission of the church. To the Colossians, however, Paul's letter centers on Christ, who is the head of the church.

This shift in focus happened because false teachers had infiltrated the church at Colossae. They were encouraging the believers there to worship angels (2:18) and strictly follow a legalistic view of the Jewish law (2:20–23), among other things. Paul took time to correct these false ways of thinking and again point the Colossians back to the purity of the Gospel he had first preached to them. He also encouraged and educated them in several practical matters, such as how family members should love each other (4:18–21) and how the Colossian believers could serve Christ through their work (4:22–25).

The main battle that Paul was fighting through this letter was against the ideas of Gnosticism—specifically the belief that Jesus was not God, but only a human being. Paul reminded them, "[Christ] is the image of the invisible God, the firstborn over all creation. For by him all things were created: things in heaven and on earth, visible and invisible, whether thrones or powers or rulers or authorities; all things were created by him and for him" (1:15–16).

Question 177. What was Paul's relationship with the church at Thessalonica?

Thessalonica was a city in Macedonia (modern-day Greece) that Paul visited with Timothy and Silas on his second missionary journey. It was a tumultuous visit to say the least. According to Acts 17, Paul taught for three consecutive Sabbaths in the synagogue, as was his custom, but the Jewish residents of the city stirred up a riot against him, and Paul and his companions were forced to flee to Berea. Paul was only in Thessalonica for three weeks, but he was still able to plant a thriving church.

Paul was concerned for the fledgling flock, so he quickly sent Timothy back to encourage the church leaders and check on their progress. When Timothy returned, he reported that the church was doing surprisingly well, although there were a few items of doctrine that the Thessalonians were confused about, especially Christ's second coming and the resurrection of the dead. In response, Paul sent Timothy back with the letter now referred to as 1 Thessalonians. Paul's second letter to the church followed soon after (what we call 2 Thessalonians) to provide more encouragement and a little more correction.

Question 178. What is the primary message of 1 Thessalonians?

The main focus of 1 Thessalonians is the second coming of Jesus Christ. Since the church was made up mostly of gentiles, they were fascinated by the idea of the Messiah returning to earth. They believed, along with much of the early church, that Christ's return would happen within a matter of years.

This concept made some members of the church nervous. Specifically, many of the believers in Thessalonica were concerned about their friends and loved ones who had passed away. They apparently thought that anyone who had already died would not receive any benefit from the second coming of Jesus Christ. Paul corrects their thinking and encourages them in the second half of chapter 4. "We believe that Jesus died and rose again," he told them, "and so we believe that God will bring with Jesus those who have fallen asleep in him" (v. 14). Paul concludes the letter with several pieces of practical advice for living as a Christian in a secular city, including avoiding immorality (5:4–11) and treating other people with love (5:12–15).

Question 179. What is the primary message of 2 Thessalonians?

In Paul's first letter to the Thessalonians, he assured them that Christ would return to the earth at some point in the future, and that everyone who was or had been part of God's kingdom would spend eternity with him. In Paul's second letter, he reminded the Thessalonians that Christ was indeed going to return, but that they needed to continue working and serving God on earth until that day arrived. Apparently many of the Thessalonian believers had become so heavenly minded that they were less focused on being good on earth.

Paul saw the danger in this line of thinking and was particularly strong in his words: "In the name of the Lord Jesus Christ, we command you, brothers, to keep away from every brother who is idle and does not live according to the teaching you received from us" (3:6). Paul goes on to remind them that he and his companions worked hard to earn their living while in Thessalonica, instead of relying on the charity of the believers there.

Question 180. Who was Timothy?

Timothy grew up as part of a Jewish family living in Lystra, a gentile city found in modern-day Turkey. Tradition says that Timothy's father was Greek, but he left the picture early in Timothy's life, and the young man was raised by his mother, Eunice, and his grandmother, Lois, both followers of Christ.

Timothy and his family likely became Christians through the ministry of the apostle Paul on his first missionary journey, when he and Barnabas visited Lystra. That visit would have made quite an impression on a young man. In the course of two days, Paul healed a beggar who had been crippled at birth, was worshiped as a god by the people of the town, and then was stoned by those same people after Jewish instigators convinced them that Paul and Barnabas were troublemakers (see Acts 14:8–20). Mistaken for dead, Paul was dragged outside of the city after the stoning only to recover and re-enter the city before leaving with Barnabas the next day.

Paul returned to Lystra several years later, and this time Timothy accompanied him when he left. He became Paul's disciple and quickly his good friend as well. In fact, Paul referred to Timothy several times as "my son whom I love" (1 Timothy 4:17, for example). Timothy continued to assist Paul through his second and third missionary journeys, and then Paul left him in charge of the church at Ephesus. Timothy was still serving there when he received the two letters from Paul that we know as 1 and 2 Timothy.

Question 181. What are the primary messages of 1 Timothy?

Along with Titus, the books of 1 and 2 Timothy mark a change in Paul's collection of epistles in the New Testament. Instead of writing to all the believers in a specific church, Paul directed these letters to individuals. The letters were advice and instruction from the apostle specifically written for two of his most trusted coworkers, both of whom were in particularly difficult situations; thus these three books are known today as the "pastoral epistles."

The first letter to Timothy was written soon after Paul was released from prison in Rome, somewhere between AD 63 and 65. The main topic that he discusses is the presence of false teachers and false doctrines in Ephesus and how Timothy should handle them. "As I urged you when I went into Macedonia," Paul wrote, "stay there in Ephesus so that you may command certain men not to teach false doctrines any longer nor to devote themselves to myths and endless genealogies. These promote controversies rather than God's work—which is by faith" (1:3–4). Paul even identified two of these false teachers by name, Hymenaeus and Alexander, whom Paul said he had "handed over to Satan to be taught not to blaspheme" (1:20).

Paul also gave Timothy a good bit of instruction on leading the worship and teaching ministries within the city. He encouraged Timothy to include prayers for the kings and rulers of the world and laid out specific job descriptions and expectations for overseers and deacons (3:1–13). He also gave instructions for various practical ministries led by the church, including the care of widows (5:1–16).

Finally, Paul made sure to encourage his young protégé and to support and equip him in the valuable work he was doing. "Until I come, devote yourself to the public reading of scripture, to preaching and to teaching," Paul wrote. "Do not neglect your gift, which was given you through a prophetic message when the body of elders laid their hands on you" (4:13–14). He even gave Timothy some dietary advice saying, "Stop drinking only water, and use a little wine because of your stomach and your frequent illnesses" (5:23).

Question 182. What do the terms *overseer* and *deacon* mean?

These terms were titles given to different leadership roles within the early church. The Greek word translated as *overseer* meant someone who was in charge of a specific project or person. Paul adapted it to refer to someone in a position of authority within a church. The term translated as *deacon* referred to a servant. These were men charged with assisting the overseers in whatever needed to be done. In today's church, we would think of an overseer as the pastor of a church whose main job is preaching the Word and shepherding the flock. A deacon today is someone who serves the church in a variety of projects and is usually a layperson.

Question 183. What are the primary messages of 2 Timothy?

Paul's first letter to Timothy addressed the outward circumstances that Timothy was facing. Paul encouraged his protégé to protect the message of the Gospel and gave him several pieces of advice on leading the church. Paul's second letter was much more personal and focused primarily on Timothy's own life.

Paul wrote his first letter to Timothy after being set free from his confinement in Rome, but he was arrested again several years later and returned to Rome. This imprisonment occurred suddenly (Paul asks Timothy in the letter to retrieve his scrolls and cloak from Troas [4:13]) and was much harsher than his first confinement. Paul was regarded as a criminal, and he expected to be put to death relatively soon (see 4:6). He was indeed killed soon after writing this letter, which means this letter contains Paul's final written words.

That being the case, Paul eschews a lot of the ministry advice he had given his protégé in the first letter. Instead, Paul encourages Timothy to make the most of his life and talents by serving God to the best of his ability. "What you heard from me," Paul writes, "keep as the pattern of sound teaching, with faith and love in Christ Jesus. Guard the good deposit that was entrusted to you—guard it with the help of the Holy Spirit who lives in us" (1:13–14). Later, he writes: "Do your best to present yourself to God as one approved, a workman who does not need to be ashamed and who correctly handles the word of truth" (2:15).

The apostle ends his letter with a proclamation of his faith in the goodness of God, despite his circumstances: "The Lord will rescue me from every evil attack and will bring me safely to his heavenly kingdom. To him be glory for ever and ever. Amen" (4:18).

Question 184. Who was Titus?

Titus was a gentile who became one of Paul's first companions in ministry. He accompanied Paul and Barnabas on one of their trips to Jerusalem and also tactfully worked at ending a run of conflict and division that was damaging the Corinthian church (2 Corinthians 7:13–16). Paul referred to him in his second letter to the Corinthians as "my partner and fellow worker among you" (8:23).

After his success at Corinth, Paul sent Titus to the island of Crete, off the southern coast of Greece. This assignment was difficult, as both Paul and Titus knew. Chapter 1 of Paul's letter to Titus contains a summary of what Titus was expected to do and why it was not an easy job:

> The reason I left you in Crete was that you might straighten out what was left unfinished and appoint elders in every town, as I directed you.... For there are many rebellious people, mere talkers and deceivers, especially those of the circumcision group. They must be silenced, because they are ruining whole households by teaching things they ought not to teach—and that for the sake of dishonest gain. Even one of their own prophets has said, "Cretans are always liars, evil brutes, lazy gluttons." This testimony is true. Therefore, rebuke them sharply, so that they will be sound in the faith and will pay no attention to Jewish myths or to the commands of those who reject the truth (vv. 5, 10–14).

Paul wrote this letter around the same time that he wrote 1 Timothy—between AD 63 and 65.

Question 185. What was Paul's primary message in his letter to Titus?

As with 1 Timothy, Paul's letter to Titus includes instructions on how to lead the church in Crete in several areas of ministry. He gives specific instructions for different groups of people in chapter 2, including older men, older women, young men, and slaves. These bits of advice are then summarized in 2:11: "For the grace of God that brings salvation has appeared to all men. It teaches us to say 'No' to ungodliness and worldly passions, and to live self-controlled, upright and godly lives in this present age."

Paul concludes in chapter 3 by reminding Titus to encourage the Cretan believers to submit to the authority placed over them and to avoid insults and slander, as well as fruitless arguments over doctrine and points of the law.

Question 186. Who was Philemon?

Like Paul's letters to Timothy and Titus, the Book of Philemon was written to an individual instead of an entire church. Unlike Timothy and Titus, Philemon was not one of Paul's protégés. Instead, he was a wealthy member of the church at Colossae, to which the Book of Colossians was written. Every indication from Paul in the letter suggests that Philemon was an upright citizen and faithful follower of God.

The occasion for Paul's letter is also unique among his epistles. During Paul's first imprisonment in Rome, he had met and been encouraged by a runaway slave named Onesimus. Onesimus had run away from the household of Philemon, so the goal of Paul's letter was to politely ask for Philemon to take Onesimus back into his service and to forgive him for the wrongs he committed.

The primary themes for this letter are forgiveness and grace, and the relationship between Onesimus and Paul becomes a powerful picture of the grace that was given through the death and resurrection of Jesus Christ. "If he has done you any wrong or owes you anything, charge it to me," Paul says. "I, Paul, am writing this with my own hand. I will pay it back" (vv. 17–19).

Chapter 9

THE GENERAL EPISTLES

- Question 187. Who is the author of the Book of Hebrews?
- Question 188. What are the primary messages in the Book of Hebrews?
- Question 189. How does Jesus serve as high priest?
- Question 190. Who was Melchizedek?
- Question 191. Who was James?
- Question 192. What is the primary message of James's epistle?
- Question 193. What is the crown of life?
- Question 194. Should Christians confess their sins to other Christians?
- Question 195. Who was Peter?
- Question 196. What is the primary message of 1 Peter?
- Question 197. Who were the elect that Peter refers to?
- Question 198. What is the primary message of 2 Peter?
- Question 199. What are the primary messages of 1 John?
- Question 200. What is the primary message of 2 John?
- Question 201. What is the primary message of 3 John?
- Question 202. What is the primary message of Jude?

Question 187. Who is the author of the Book of Hebrews?

The author of the Book of Hebrews isn't known for sure, and scholars are quite divided over this question. Many believe that Paul was the author of this letter, and that seems to have been the belief of the early church fathers such as Origen and Clement of Alexandria, although there are several clues that cast doubt upon that theory. For example, Paul includes his name as the first word in every one of the epistles he is known to have authored. "Paul, a servant of Christ Jesus, called to be an apostle and set apart for the gospel of God," he says in the first verse of Romans, but Paul's name is nowhere to be found in the Book of Hebrews.

Other potential authors for Hebrews include Apollos, a well-known preacher during the time of Paul who is described in Acts 18 as "a learned man, with a thorough knowledge of the Scriptures," and Barnabas, who was Paul's companion and coworker during the first missionary journey. The evidence supporting these claims is as tenuous as the evidence supporting the authorship of Paul.

Question 188. What are the primary messages in the Book of Hebrews?

The main theme in Hebrews is a warning to Jewish Christians against returning the rituals and practices of Judaism. It was probably directed first to Jewish believers living in Jerusalem who were experiencing a great deal of persecution and pressure to renounce their faith in Jesus as the Messiah. It is also likely that this letter was copied and distributed to Jewish Christians in other cities as well.

Other epistles had fought the same battle, such as Galatians and Ephesians, and they mostly focused on the superiority of grace over legalism. In Hebrews, however, the author focuses primarily on the superiority of Christ. Throughout the first four chapters of the book, Jesus is lifted up as greater than angels (1:4–2:18), Moses (3:1–19), and Joshua (4:8–11). Furthermore, Jesus is exalted as "the radiance of God's glory and the exact representation of his being, sustaining all things by his powerful word" (1:3).

As the author continues to build his argument for Jesus as the Messiah, the middle chapters of the book reveal the superiority of Jesus as high priest over Aaron, the original high priest for the Israelites. Jesus is proclaimed as high priest "in the order of Melchizedek" (5:10). Melchizedek was a priest of God who received a tribute of submission and honor from Abraham, which means that Melchizedek was of an earlier line of priests than Aaron. The author of Hebrews is claiming that Jesus's priesthood was superior to that of Aaron and the Levites.

In addition, the author emphasizes that the new covenant established by Jesus supersedes the old covenant of the law. It's interesting that he uses a prophetic passage from the Old Testament as proof: "The time is coming, declares the Lord, when I will make a new covenant with the house of Israel and with the house of Judah" (Jeremiah 31:31). Jesus is the personification of this new covenant, the author says. He is the new temple where God and humanity come together (9:1–12), and he is the new sacrifice through which the sins of humanity can be forgiven (10:10–18).

Question 189. How does Jesus serve as high priest?

In the Levitical system described in the Old Testament, the high priest was a kind of mediator between God and humanity. It was the high priest alone who could enter the Holy of Holies, where God manifested his presence through the Ark of the Covenant, and it was the high priest's role to make atonement for the sins of the Israelites. This was a very serious matter and happened only once a year.

But when Jesus died on the cross and rose again, he became the sacrifice that atoned for the sins of all people throughout all of time (the idea of "atonement" refers to washing or making something clean again). Paul talks about this in Romans 3: "For all have sinned and fall short of the glory of God, and are justified freely by his grace through the redemption that came by Christ Jesus. God presented him as a sacrifice of atonement, through faith in his blood" (vv. 23–25). Because Jesus became the mediator between God and humanity, he is now high priest.

Question 190. Who was Melchizedek?

He is one of the more intriguing and mysterious people in the Bible. His name means "King of Salem," or "King of Peace," and he is identified in Genesis 14:18 as "priest of God Most High." Abram offers him a tenth of his plunder as a sign of gratitude to God and submission to Melchizedek, a promise that he will not compete with the king of Salem. On one level, Melchizedek was a powerful and influential Canaanite king who developed an intimate relationship with God, but there is a second level of understanding to this mysterious man.

Hebrews 5 connects Melchizedek with Jesus, although scholars disagree as to the nature of this connection. Some believe that Melchizedek was a type of Christ, a foreshadowing of the high priest and king that would come later to save the descendants of Abram and the rest of the world. Others believe that Melchizedek was a "pre-incarnate Christ," that he was actually Jesus appearing temporarily in human form to Abram to bless the ancestor of God's chosen people.

Question 191. Who was James?

James was an apostle and a leader of the church in Jerusalem, but he was also a son of Mary and Joseph; thus, practically, one of Jesus's brothers. (Mary and Joseph had several natural children after Jesus's supernatural birth—they are mentioned in Matthew 12:45-47.) For that reason, it's interesting to note that James speaks reverently of Jesus in his epistle, even calling himself "a servant of God and of the Lord Jesus Christ" (1:1).

James is relatively unknown today, but he was a key leader at the very beginning of the early church. For example, it was James who gave an important speech in Acts 15:13–21 that persuaded the council of the church not to require gentile believers to adopt Jewish customs. James was also probably active in the council's decision to welcome Paul as an apostle after his dramatic conversion on the road to Damascus.

Question 192. What is the primary message of James's epistle?

The best summary of James's message comes from his own words in 1:22: "Do not merely listen to the word, and so deceive yourselves. Do what it says." James was a no-nonsense kind of guy, and his words are full of practical wisdom for anyone who desires to follow God. As such, this epistle has been called "the Proverbs of the New Testament."

The letter was written to "the twelve tribes scattered among the nations," which is a bit confusing. It could mean James was addressing Jewish men and women who had become Christians, or it could be a symbolic way of addressing the entire church. Either way, James's letter was not meant for one specific city or individual; his instructions are for all Christians.

James was aware that several areas of hypocrisy had infected the church, and he tackled them head on through his letter. He reminded his readers that their words had tremendous power for good and evil, and that followers of God should not speak in a way that reflected the values of world rather than Christ (3:3–12). He also condemned church leaders who had been showing favoritism to the wealthy members of their congregation and ignoring the poor (2:1–13).

But his most scathing words were for wealthy Christians who had continued their practice of oppressing the poor even after becoming Christians. "Weep and wail because of the misery that is coming upon you," he told them. "Look! The wages you failed to pay the workmen who mowed your fields are crying out against you. The cries of the harvesters have reached the ears of the Lord Almighty" (5:1, 4).

Finally, James did take some time to encourage and support the Christians who were undergoing persecution in other cities, something that was becoming more and more common during the time that this letter was written (probably between AD 40 and 50). "Consider it pure joy, my brothers, whenever you face trials of many kinds," he wrote, "because you know that the testing of your faith develops perseverance. Perseverance must finish its work so that you may be mature and complete, not lacking anything" (1:2–4).

Question 193. What is the crown of life?

James referred to salvation for eternity when he said, "Blessed is the man who perseveres under trial, because when he has stood the test, he will receive the crown of life that God has promised to those who love him" (1:12). James used a popular image of the day, the wreath placed on the heads of athletes who competed and won in games like the Olympics, to encourage his readers to continue working diligently in their service to God and his Kingdom.

Question 194. Should Christians confess their sins to other Christians?

There are several places in the Bible where person-to-person confession is highlighted as beneficial. James 5:16 is probably the best example: "Therefore confess your sins to each other and pray for each other so that you may be healed. The prayer of a righteous man is powerful and effective."

Confessing our sins to fellow believers gives them the chance to pray for us, and that is always to our benefit, especially when it comes to resisting temptation and healing from bad choices. Confession is also a necessary element of accountability between believers. When Christians are honest with other Christians about struggles, temptations, and failures, they gain added strength in moving beyond those struggles. Proverbs 27:17 says, "As iron sharpens iron, so one man sharpens another." It works best when an accountability relationship is based on grace and a mutual desire for support and growth, not on one person attempting to "catch" all the hidden sins of another.

Finally, it's important to understand that confessing sins to another Christian does not result in forgiveness for those sins. Only God can grant forgiveness, and he does so freely when Christians come to him and honestly address their shortcomings (1 John 1:9).

Question 195. Who was Peter?

Peter was a disciple of Jesus and was a member of "the twelve," an inner circle of followers that Jesus gave an extra amount of training and attention to. During Jesus's ministry, Peter developed a reputation as a hothead. He was impetuous and often acted before thinking things over. Sometimes this was a good thing. It was Peter, after all, who alone jumped out of the boat on the Sea of Galilee and walked on the water with Jesus (Matthew 14:22–23), but many times Peter's personality got him into trouble. For example, it was Peter who took it on himself to rebuke Jesus when he predicted his coming death, which means it was to Peter that Jesus replied, "Get behind me, Satan!" (Matthew 16:21–23).

After Jesus's death and resurrection, however, Peter matured greatly. In fact, he took on the mantle of leadership for the early church when he preached a powerful sermon on the Day of Pentecost after he and the other disciples had received the Holy Spirit. This sermon led to about three thousand new believers, which became the bedrock of the church (see Acts 2:14–41). And it was Peter who welcomed the first gentiles into the church after receiving a vision from God making it clear that Jesus's sacrifice and resurrection were meant for the whole world, not just for the Jews (see Acts 10).

Peter remained the focal point of the church in Jerusalem for many years, and the early chapters of Acts record his word and deeds before switching to highlight Paul's missionary journeys in chapter 11.

Question 196. What is the primary message of 1 Peter?

Peter's first epistle covers two major themes: hope and suffering. This letter was written when Peter was in Rome sometime between AD 60 and 64 and was intended to be read in all the churches scattered throughout Asia Minor (present-day Turkey). Like Paul, Peter was not visiting the city on vacation, but was under arrest for leading a religious movement that was disturbing the peace of the Roman

Empire. Tradition says that Peter was executed by the order of Roman Emperor Nero shortly after Peter wrote his two epistles.

Peter was not the only follower of Christ experiencing persecution at the time. Jewish leaders had started the persecution of Christians in Jerusalem, forcing many believers to flee the city and scatter to other regions of the known world, which ultimately helped spread the church and the good news of the Gospel. With the Romans actively persecuting Christians, many believers were losing heart and losing faith, thinking that God had abandoned them.

Peter does not ignore those problems in his letter. He acknowledges right in the beginning that the Christians reading his words "have had to suffer grief in all kinds of trials" (1:6). He urges them to focus on the reality of Christ and the hope they have been given of eternal life as children of God (1:1–5). He believed that such a focus would change their perception of their current suffering: "These [trials] have come so that your faith—of greater worth than gold, which perishes even though refined by fire—may be proved genuine and may result in praise, glory and honor when Jesus Christ is revealed" (1:7). Peter repeats this pattern throughout his letter, saying, "Yes, you are suffering and in pain right now. But remember that Christ also suffered on this earth before being reunited with his Father in heaven, and it will be the same for us" (see 4:12–13, for example).

Question 197. Who were the elect that Peter refers to?

This is one of the ways that Peter refers to all those who believe in Jesus and have given control of their lives over to him. In other words, it's another way of talking about Christians. What is interesting here is that Peter was writing to Christians scattered throughout the various regions of Asia Minor, and they were mostly on the low end of society. They were not "elect" by the standards of the world, but they had been chosen by God from the beginning of time.

Question 198. What is the primary message of 2 Peter?

Peter's first letter to the churches in Asia Minor was one of encouragement and consolation in response to threats from outside the church. He wanted them to get a proper perspective on the persecution they were experiencing and hold strong because of the hope they had in Jesus Christ. Peter's second letter, however, is a warning about several dangers that were threatening believers from inside the church.

Peter calls attention to the presence of false teachers who had already infiltrated the church and who would continue to do so (chapter 2). These teachers usually tried to convince new Christians that Jesus was not really human or not really God. More importantly, though, Peter feared what would happen if the leaders and members of the church failed to grow spiritually. He reminds them that God had already given them "everything we need for life and godliness through our knowledge of him who called us by his own glory and goodness" (1:3)—but they had to take hold of those gifts through action. "For this very reason," he writes, "make every effort to add to your faith goodness; and to goodness, knowledge; and to knowledge, self-control; and to self-control, perseverance; and to perseverance, godliness; and to godliness, brotherly kindness; and to brotherly kindness, love. For if you possess these qualities in increasing measure, they will keep you from being ineffective and unproductive in your knowledge of our Lord Jesus Christ" (1:5–8).

Peter also urged his readers to continue reading the scriptures and to keep in mind that they are the words of God, not of men (1:12–21). He concludes his letter by reminding them that Christ would return, and that they should continue to hope in that (chapter 3).

Question 199. What are the primary messages of 1 John?

John wrote this letter mainly to encourage and strengthen the various communities of believers that had been established around Ephesus, in what is now the western half of Turkey. He wrote the letter around AD 90, which means that the period of heavy persecution under Roman Emperor Nero had come and gone. Thousands of Christians had perished in that wave, including all of the apostles except for John, but new churches had continued to spring up and thrive.

John was writing to those churches, and he seems to have had four primary goals. First, he wanted to help the people understand what it means to have joy in this life (chapter 1). Second, he wanted to help the believers avoid sin and live as children of God (chapter 2). Third, he wanted to warn the churches against false teachers and false doctrines (2:18–27). And fourth, he wanted to help the believers know and understand that they have eternal life and that they should live like it (chapter 5).

This epistle is also famous for giving seven "tests" that can help believers evaluate themselves as followers of God. They are as follows:

1. Walk in the light: "If we claim to have fellowship with him yet walk in the darkness, we lie and do not live by the truth" (1:6).
2. Admit you are a sinner: "If we claim to be without sin, we deceive ourselves and the truth is not in us" (1:8).
3. Obey God's will: "The man who says, 'I know him,' but does not do what he commands is a liar, and the truth is not in him" (2:4).
4. Imitate Christ: "Whoever claims to live in him must walk as Jesus did" (2:6).
5. Love others: "Anyone who claims to be in the light but hates his brother is still in the darkness" (2:9).
6. Relationship to the world: "Do not love the world or anything in the world. If anyone loves the world, the love of the Father is not in him" (2:15).
7. Prove Christ is righteous by your life: "If you know that he is righteous, you know that everyone who does what is right has been born of him." (2:29).

Question 200. What is the primary message of 2 John?

This letter is the only epistle in the Bible addressed specifically to a woman (although some believe the "lady" described is a symbolic phrase for a specific church), and it was probably written less than a year after John's first epistle. The letter has two main themes, and they are connected to each other: love and truth.

First, John emphasizes that followers of Christ need to live a life that is based on love, and that we do that by obeying God and following his commands (vv. 4–6). Second, John wanted to expose the agenda of false teachers and encourage his reader to remain grounded in the doctrines he had previously taught her: "Anyone who runs ahead and does not continue in the teaching of Christ does not have God; whoever continues in the teaching has both the Father and the Son" (v. 9).

Question 201. What is the primary message of 3 John?

John's third epistle is also a personal one, written to a "dear friend" named Gaius, who had been housing and caring for the traveling preachers sent by John to support and equip local churches. John encourages Gaius to continue his good work, even though he was being opposed by a strong-willed church leader named Diotrephes.

In fact, the letter serves as a juxtaposition of those two men, Gaius and Diotrephes. Gaius was faithful in his hospitality and effective in his work. Diotrephes was the kind of man who "loves to be first" and was working against John by refusing to let the traveling preachers speak in the church or even receive hospitality in his town, despite a personal warning from John.

The letter gives all who read it a clear choice: you can either choose to faithfully follow what God is doing in his church in the world or can seek out your own agenda. "Do not imitate what is evil but what is good," John concludes. "Anyone who does what is good is from God. Anyone who does what is evil has not seen God."

Question 202. What is the primary message of Jude?

Like the apostle James, Jude was a brother of Jesus Christ. Like James, Jude does not flaunt his kinship with Jesus, but rather shows humility by calling himself "Jude, a servant of Jesus Christ and a brother of James" (1:1). Jude was also a good friend of the apostle Peter, and the language and themes of Jude's short epistle are similar to the book known as 2 Peter. They were even written around the same time, probably AD 65.

The main thrust of Jude's letter is to warn church leaders against false teachers that were entering the ranks of believers. These were "godless men who change the grace of our God into a license for immorality and deny Jesus Christ our only Sovereign and Lord." In other words, these false teachers were claiming that Christians could engage in whatever behaviors they wanted. As long as they had been forgiven by God, they could sin to their heart's content.

After condemning these men and their false beliefs, Jude concludes his brief letter by urging believers to remain firm in what they know to be true: "But you, dear friends, build yourselves up in your most holy faith and pray in the Holy Spirit. Keep yourselves in God's love as you wait for the mercy of our Lord Jesus Christ to bring you to eternal life."

Chapter 10

APOCALYPTIC BOOKS

Question 203. What is apocalyptic literature?

There is no official definition of apocalyptic literature, and scholars today still debate about the elements of what makes something "apocalyptic," but there is agreement on several key identifiers, including the following:

- **Heavenly revelation** The authors of apocalyptic literature usually claim to be passing on mysterious visions and revelations that they received from spiritual beings, usually angels.
- **Layers of meaning** Apocalyptic visions are typically meant to be interpreted at several levels. They can refer to events that belong to the present world, but at the same time have meaning for the future. They can look back to the past as well.
- **A breakthrough** Apocalyptic visions usually look to a time in the future when the heavenly kingdom breaks through the boundaries of our earthly world. This breakthrough usually involves a big contrast. In Revelation, John contrasts the current persecution of the church with the future victory of God's kingdom breaking into our world. This "breaking in" is different from prophecy, because prophecy usually involves future events that will come about through natural processes such as Micah's prophecy of the Messiah being born in Bethlehem.
- **Visually intense** Apocalyptic literature includes powerful symbols and visual representations to portray what will happen when the heavenly kingdom breaks through into our earthly world. These images are always complex and packed with meaning.

It should be pointed out that no book in the Bible is made up entirely of apocalyptic literature. Even Revelation, which contains the highest percentage of apocalyptic content, also contains elements of prophecy and sections that are best described as an epistle from John to various churches. Similarly, there are several books in the Bible that contain bits and pieces of apocalyptic literature. Ezekiel has several apocalyptic visions, for example, as does Isaiah. The biblical books with the highest concentration of apocalyptic content are Revelation and Daniel.

DANIEL
Question 204. What historical events occurred in the ancient Middle East during the time period written about in Daniel?

After breaking free from Assyrian rule around 600 BC, the Babylonians took over the Assyrians' role as conquerors of the known world. Babylonian King Nebuchadnezzar focused his attention on the southern kingdom of Judah during three military campaigns. (Israel, the northern kingdom, had been conquered and dispersed by the Assyrians about one hundred years earlier.) During the first two attacks, Nebuchadnezzar took most of Judah's wealth back to Babylon, along with the best and brightest of Jerusalem's nobles and tradesmen. In the third attack (586 BC), Jerusalem was destroyed.

Question 205. Who was Daniel?

Daniel belonged to a family of high rank in Jerusalem, which means he was taken as a captive back to Babylon after the first invasion of Judah (605 BC). He was probably around sixteen years old when this event occurred, and he spent the rest of his life as a citizen of Babylon.

The most important thing to know about Daniel is that he was a faithful servant of God, even through his long life in the city of Babylon. He was given a Babylonian name (Belteshazzar) and forced to adopt several Babylonian customs, but he continued to actively worship Yahweh as the one true God. As a result, Daniel was blessed in many ways by God, and everyone who encountered him knew it, even Nebuchadnezzar (see 2:46–47).

Daniel was such a valuable asset that he remained a key advisor through the reign of four kings. Nebuchadnezzar was succeeded on the throne of Babylon by his son Belshazzar, and when the Medes and Persians conquered Babylon in 539 BC, Darius the Mede kept Daniel in a high place of authority, eventually identifying the Israelite as his most trusted advisor. When Cyrus the Persian issued the proclamation that allowed the captive Jews to return to their home in Jerusalem, Daniel was still serving the king. He was well over ninety years old at this point, however, and too old to make the journey back home.

Question 206. Did the events of Nebuchadnezzar's dream come true?

Yes, they did, and they can be verified in history. Nebuchadnezzar dreamed of a great statue made of several materials—the head was made of gold, the trunk and arms were silver, the belly and thighs were brass, the legs were iron, and the feet were iron mixed with clay. While the king was watching this statue in his dream, a rock was cut out by divine hands that smashed the statue completely to pieces and then turned into a mountain that filled the whole earth (2:31–35).

According to Daniel's interpretation, each section of the statue represented a future kingdom that would gain dominance in the known world. Looking back at history, we can identify those kingdoms:

- **Head of gold** This was Babylon, which was the dominant world power from 626–539 BC.
- **Chest and arms of silver** This was the Medo-Persian Empire, which conquered Babylon in 539 BC and remained prominent until 330 BC.
- **Belly and thighs of bronze** This was the Grecian Empire, which swept across the known world in 330 BC under the leadership of Alexander the Great. The Greeks remained in power until 146 BC.
- **Legs of iron/feet of iron and clay** This was the Roman Empire, which gained dominance in 146 BC and remained a world power until AD 476.

Up until this point, Nebuchadnezzar's dream seems like a straightforward prophecy of how nations would rise and fall in the coming centuries, but then came the rock, which represents Jesus Christ, the Messiah. Apocalyptic literature is known for showing how the heavenly kingdom will "break through" into the physical world, which is represented in a striking way as Jesus, the rock, comes out of nowhere to utterly destroy all the kingdoms of the earth. This was not a literal destruction, of course, but a show of dominance. The mightiest kingdoms and rulers of this world are shattered to pieces when compared to Jesus, the king of the heavenly realms.

Notice that there are several other indicators that reveal Nebuchadnezzar's dream to be an apocalypse. There is the striking visual imagery, of course, but there is also the curious phrase that Daniel speaks in 2:29: "As you were lying there, O king, your mind turned to things to come, and the revealer of mysteries showed you what is going to happen." Remember that most apocalyptic visions claim to be mysteries revealed by messengers from the heavenly realms.

Question 207. Did King Nebuchadnezzar become a follower of God?

Many who read Daniel come under the impression that the Babylonian king experienced a conversion to Judaism because of all the statements he makes in praise of Daniel's God. "Surely your God is the God of gods and the Lord of kings and a revealer of mysteries," he says in 2:47. He also wrote the following as the greeting of a letter recorded in 4:2–3: "It is my pleasure to tell you about the miraculous signs and wonders that the Most High God has performed for me. How great are his signs, how mighty his wonders! His kingdom is an eternal kingdom; his dominion endures from generation to generation."

It is highly unlikely, however, that Nebuchadnezzar rejected the gods of his Babylonian heritage and became a faithful follower of Yahweh, because Nebuchadnezzar, along with the rest of the ancient world, had no concept of monotheism. Every culture except the Israelites believed that there were many gods in the world and that those gods were usually attached to specific regions of land and societal functions.

For that reason, Nebuchadnezzar had no compunction against recognizing the power and ability of Daniel's God when it came to interpreting dreams. Nor did he fear that his praise of Yahweh would offend the Babylonian gods. That wasn't how the system worked. By praising Daniel's God in such ways, Nebuchadnezzar was simply continuing his practice of staying on the good side of all the gods he came in contact with that had demonstrated some form of power or ability to influence the world.

Question 208. What messages can be found in Daniel's vision of the different beasts?

Chapter 7 of Daniel's book gives another view of apocalyptic literature, although the visions and symbols represent the rise and fall of the same kingdoms from Nebuchadnezzar's dream in chapter 2. The lion represents Babylon. The bear represents the Medo-Persian alliance. The leopard represents Greece and Alexander the Great, who conquered the known world in less than three years. The leopard's four heads predicted the division of the Grecian Empire into four regions after Alexander's death, and the terrifying beast with iron teeth represents Rome.

There are several messages in these two apocalyptic visions. First, it becomes clear that God is in control of human history. Reliable sources trace the Book of Daniel back to 530 BC, several centuries before most of the major historical events that it predicts. We can also learn something about the limits of apocalyptic literature from these visions. They accurately foretold the future, including God's breakthrough into our world, but the people of Daniel's time had no chance to predict how the events would unfold. In other words, Daniel's visions show that apocalyptic literature and prophecies are meant to build faith after the predicted events come to pass, not to give humans the ability to see the future.

Question 209. How should Gabriel's revelation to Daniel about the "seventy weeks" be interpreted?

Many scholars believe that Gabriel's proclamation can be used to map out a large section of recorded history between Daniel's time and the birth of Jesus. They believe that the seventy "weeks" actually refers to seventy periods of seven years each, or a total time of 490 years.

In this interpretation, the first seven weeks, or forty-nine years, that Gabriel mentions began at the command from God to rebuild the temple. So that time period applies to the rebuilding of the temple and the restoration of Jerusalem. The next sixty-two weeks, or 434 years, spans from the rebuilding of Jerusalem's wall to the death of Jesus Christ, which is when "the Anointed One will be cut off and will have nothing" (9:26). In this interpretation, the final week, or period of seven years, has not occurred yet. It has been delayed while the Gentiles rule the Earth and it will finally come about during the judgment of God on the world and the Great Tribulation, which may be referenced by Daniel in 12:1.

Is this the correct interpretation of Gabriel's revelation to Daniel? We certainly can't say for sure. The numbers do match up pretty well when converted to periods of seven years, but the tricky thing about apocalyptic literature is that it has so many layers. We just don't know what the future may hold. Thankfully, the message of Daniel is clear that we don't have to worry about the future. God has it under control.

REVELATION
Question 210. What are the main themes in the Book of Revelation?

Many people who encounter the Book of Revelation find it strange and overwhelming—and for good reason. To the modern reader, Revelation is a confusing mix of epistles, images, numbers, symbols, and crazy animals. It's hard to understand how everything fits together, and even when the different events occurred (or will occur).

But at the core of Revelation stand two main themes that serve as the foundation for all of the whirling activity on its surface. When we keep these broad ideas in mind, they help us make sense of the specific imagery and confusion that are present in Apocalyptic literature (see question 203 for more information).

First and foremost, the Book of Revelation is a vision of the glorified Christ. John encounters Jesus early on in his vision, and it is a Jesus unlike anything we encountered in the Gospels: "His head and hair were white like wool, as white as snow, and his eyes were like blazing fire. His feet were like bronze glowing in a furnace, and his voice was like the sound of rushing waters. In his right hand he held seven stars, and out of his mouth came a sharp double-edged sword. His face was like the sun shining in all its brilliance" (1:14–16).

This description is filled with complex symbolism, and it would be confusing and frustrating to try to parse what each symbol represents. The reality is we don't have to. What John is mostly communicating through this imagery is one overarching impression: Jesus is awesome. He is powerful. He is glorious to behold. This impression is confirmed in another picture of Christ, this time in chapter 19: "I saw heaven standing open and there before me was a white horse, whose rider is called Faithful and True. With justice he judges and makes war. His eyes are like blazing fire, and on his head are many crowns. He has a name written on him that no one knows but he himself. He is dressed in a robe dipped in blood, and his name is the Word of God" (vv. 11–13).

The other major theme in the Book of Revelation is that God will be victorious over evil. This is the umbrella under which we experience John's vision of judgment and seven bowls and four horseman and locusts with heads like a lion; all of it points to the end of the story and the conclusion that God wins.

Really, that's the Book of Revelation in a clear, concise nutshell: Jesus Christ is glorious and awesome, and at the end of the story he will be victorious over evil and injustice and suffering and all that is wrong in the world.

Question 211. Is Revelation an example of apocalyptic literature?

Every chapter in Revelation is not apocalyptic literature—the letters to the seven churches are epistles, for example—but Revelation does include several large and complicated apocalyptic visions. We know that these visions are apocalyptic instead of prophetic because they meet the criteria listed earlier in this chapter:

- **Heavenly revelation** John is guided through his visions by Christ himself at the beginning, and then by an angel.
- **Layers of meaning** The visions in Revelation certainly contain at least two layers of meaning. The first was the present-day persecution of the church by Roman Emperor Domitian. The second is the future battle between the forces of good and evil that would result in Christ being exalted as the victor and judgment poured out on evil.
- **A breakthrough** Revelation highlights two future breakthroughs of the supernatural realm into the natural. The first involves the powers of evil and the antichrist; the second involves Christ as the Conquering King and the reshaping of heaven and earth.
- **Visually intense** Revelation is full of symbols and powerful visual images. These can be difficult to decipher or make sense of individually, but taken together they point to God's ultimate victory of good over evil.

Question 212. What is the rapture?

It has been well documented that the word *rapture* is never used in scripture, but it has become a topic of popular fiction and intense curiosity in recent years. The main ideas about the rapture do not come from Revelation, but from references included in the epistles. One source is 1 Thessalonians 5:1–2: "Now, brothers, about times and dates we do not need to write to you, for you know very well that the day of the Lord will come like a thief in the night." Another is Jesus's words from Luke 17:34–35: "I tell you, on that night two people will be in one bed; one will be taken and the other left. Two women will be grinding grain together; one will be taken and the other left." The theory is that all of the Christians alive on earth will instantly be transported to heaven (1 Thessalonians 4:17 is another important passage for this view).

It is not possible to say whether the idea of the rapture is correct or incorrect. The Bible just doesn't give enough evidence to make any certain predictions about what the future will bring, and the predictions that do exist contain the possibility of extra layers of meaning that aren't fully understood.

For those who do believe a rapture will occur to separate all the Christians from the non-Christians on the Day of Judgment, there is another question that makes them turn to the Book of Revelation for answers: Will the rapture happen before the Great Tribulation or after?

Again, people are divided in their beliefs, and no one can say for sure, because the Bible doesn't say for sure. Some believe that the rapture will occur before the Great Tribulation, which means that all living Christians will be spared from its troubles. This is called pre-tribulationalism. Another view is that rapture will occur after the tribulation; this is the post-tribulationalism view. A third view states that rapture will occur in the middle of the Tribulation, before things get really bad for Christians. This is the mid-tribulationalism view.

Regardless of when we are called up to heaven, the Bible makes it clear that "whoever believes in [Jesus] shall not perish but have eternal life" (John 3:16).

Question 213. What is the Great Tribulation?

This refers to a time when Christians will be persecuted on earth for their faith in Jesus Christ. The main scriptural roots of this idea come from Daniel 12:1: "At that time Michael, the great prince who protects your people, will arise. There will be a time of distress such as has not happened from the beginning of nations until then. But at that time your people—everyone whose name is found written in the book—will be delivered." Revelation 7:14 also speaks of a multitude of believers who had come out of a great tribulation.

Some scholars believe these verses are pointing to a specific time in the future when the world will be in terrible chaos, Christians will be severely persecuted, and the antichrist will rule the world. Others believe that the Great Tribulation refers to all times in human history when believers undergo suffering and persecution because of their faith in Jesus Christ. This topic has been debated for centuries and will continue to be debated for years to come without a definite solution. The Bible simply doesn't give us enough information to know what will happen.

Regardless of whether the tribulation is a future period of seven years or the current suffering of every persecuted believer, the end message of Daniel and Revelation is the same: Everyone who follows God will experience suffering and trials in this world, but we can be thankful that this world is not our home. We are on the way to a better place.

Question 214. How should numbers in the Book of Revelation be interpreted?

Most of the numbers in Revelation are symbolic, and they are treated much differently from how numbers are treated today. For example, the most famous number from Revelation is 666, but there is no reason to believe that people will be forced to brand that specific number on their forehead or right hand. Rather, the ancient scholars linked numbers to the letters of the alphabet, and the letters in the name Nero Caesar add up to 666. This certainly makes sense, given that Nero was the first Roman emperor to openly persecute Christians. Also, seven was considered to be the perfect number by the ancient Israelites, which meant that it was God's number; it symbolized his perfections. That being the case, the number 666 might represent eternally falling short of God's perfection.

Other numbers have symbolic importance in Revelation. Twelve is used several times in the book, and it also refers to completeness or perfection. Thus, everything about the New Jerusalem is measured in units of twelve. There are twelve gates, twelve foundations, twelve thousand stadia, 144 cubits, twelve angels, and twelve tribes (21:9–21). These are not literal measurements; rather, they are symbols of perfection.

Question 215. What will heaven be like?

More than any other book, Revelation gives a glimpse of the future in heaven, but because John's vision is recorded as apocalyptic literature, it cannot be interpreted as a literal drawing of what heaven will be like. There may not, in actuality, be streets paved with gold or even pearly gates.

Revelation does offer some overall impressions of what heaven will be like. For example, it is known for sure that heaven will be a place where God is universally recognized as King (4:1–3). Heaven will offer rewards and rest for followers of God who remained faithful during their time on earth (2:7; 3:21). Heaven will be a place where God is worshiped and praised (19:1–7). And heaven will be a place for "every nation, tribe, people, and language" (7:9).

Most importantly, heaven will be the completion of God's plan to redeem human beings from their sin. It will be a return to the relationship God originally intended for Adam and Eve before they separated themselves from him by becoming impure. The results of that fall were devastating, separation from God plus pain and death, but in the end, God will restore what was lost: "And I heard a loud voice from the throne saying, 'Now the dwelling of God is with men, and he will live with them. They will be his people, and God himself will be with them and be their God. He will wipe every tear from their eyes. There will be no more death or mourning or crying or pain, for the old order of things has passed away'" (21:3–4).

APPLICATION

Now that you've explored the historical background of the Bible and examined its different books and authors, this final section answers an obvious and sometimes difficult question: How should the Bible be applied to modern times?

Chapter 11

THE BIBLE AND JUDEO-CHRISTIAN DOCTRINE

- Question 216. What does the Bible say about the Trinity?
- Question 217. What does the Bible say about the nature of God?
- Question 218. What does the Bible say about the character of God?
- Question 219. What does the Bible say about angels?
- Question 220. Who is Satan, and how does he affect the world?
- Question 221. What does the Bible say about the nature of human beings?
- Question 222. What is sin, and how does it affect us?
- Question 223. How do we experience forgiveness for our sin?
- Question 224. Why was death a necessary response to sin?
- Question 225. What does it mean to experience salvation?
- Question 226. Is it arrogant to say that Jesus is the only way to be saved?
- Question 227. What happens to those who die before ever hearing about Jesus?
- Question 228. What is the relationship between faith and salvation?
- Question 229. What does justification mean?
- Question 230. What is sanctification?
- Question 231. What is glorification?
- Question 232. What happens to the people who die without becoming saved?
- Question 233. Is it possible for Christians to lose their salvation?
- Question 234. How do I know if I'm a Christian?
- Question 235. What is the purpose of baptism?
- Question 236. How does the Bible define the church?
- Question 237. Does the New Testament say that women should not have leadership roles in the church?
- Question 238. Does the Bible require Christians to tithe?
- Question 239. Why does the Old Testament include so many dietary restrictions?
- Question 240. Should Christians today keep kosher?

Question 216. What does the Bible say about the Trinity?

The Trinity is one of the fundamental doctrines of the Bible and the church, yet it is also one of the most frustrating. Many people have created different analogies and pictures to explain what the Trinity is and how the Trinity works—an egg (shell, white, and yolk), water existing in three phases, a family, a clover, and so on. But all of these comparisons break down because of one major stumbling block: The Bible does not explain the Trinity for us. The Bible doesn't even make an attempt to explain; it just allows the Trinity to operate as a mystery.

With that in mind, there are two specific things that the Bible teaches us about the Trinity. First, there is only one God. Deuteronomy 6:4, a famous passage for both Jews and Christians, says: "Hear, O Israel: The LORD our God, the LORD is one." Romans 3:29–30 says: "Is God the God of Jews only? Is he not the God of gentiles too? Yes, of gentiles too, since there is only one God, who will justify the circumcised by faith and the uncircumcised through that same faith."

The second thing we know from scripture is that God exists as three distinct "persons" (Father, Son, and Holy Spirit) that are somehow all part of the same being. The Bible never openly identifies that God contains these three persons, but it does speak of each person as God on several occasions. For example, Jesus says the following in Matthew 6:26: "Look at the birds of the air; they do not sow or reap or store away in barns, and yet your heavenly Father feeds them." He speaks of "your heavenly Father" as something different from himself. Other parts of scripture make it clear that Jesus is indeed God. In the Gospel of John, Jesus says, "I and the Father are one" (10:30). Hebrews 1:3 says "The Son is the radiance of God's glory and the exact representation of his being, sustaining all things by his powerful word." Finally, the scriptures make it clear in several places that the Holy Spirit is also distinct from the Father and Son, but also God. In Acts 5:3–4, for example, the author clearly states that lying to the Holy Spirit (v. 3) is the same as lying to God (v. 4).

To summarize, it can be said for sure that there is only one God and that the Bible clearly describes God as Father, Son, and Holy Spirit. How those three elements fit together is simply a mystery.

Question 217. What does the Bible say about the nature of God?

First, the Bible makes it clear that God is a unique being in the universe; there is only one God (Deuteronomy 6:4), and he exists in three persons known as the

Trinity (see the first question of this chapter for more). These are the most important facts regarding the nature of God, but the Bible also says much more.

For example, the Bible makes it clear that God is omnipotent (all-powerful). This means that God can do anything in the universe that can be done. Luke 1:37 states it clearly: "For nothing is impossible with God." Some people attempt to challenge the nature of God by coming up with scenarios that seem to undercut his omnipotence, such as the question, "Can God create a rock so big he can't lift it?" or "Can God sin?" These questions misinterpret what it means for God to be all-powerful. God's omnipotence means that if he says something will happen, he has the power to make it happen.

In addition, the Bible says that God possesses all knowledge. He is omniscient, which means that God knows all things that can possibly be known, including the past, present, and future. Psalm 147:5 says, "Great is our Lord and mighty in power; his understanding has no limit."

The Bible also states that God is omnipresent; he is not limited by time or space, and he actually exists everywhere at the same time. "'Am I only a God nearby,' declares the LORD, 'and not a God far away? Can anyone hide in secret places so that I cannot see him?' declares the LORD. 'Do not I fill heaven and earth?'" (Jeremiah 23:23–24).

Finally, the Bible identifies God's physical makeup: He is not made of flesh and blood, but of spirit. He is a supernatural being in the most literal sense of the word. He sustains the natural world, which means he goes beyond the natural world. As such he is invisible (1 Timothy 1:17), but he can manifest himself to us in visible ways. He is immaterial (with a body or mass), but he created the physical world and influences it as he pleases. And he is eternal; he is the creator of time and therefore is not bound by time, as we are (Revelation 1:8).

Question 218. What does the Bible say about the character of God?

The Bible teaches that God is the source of everything that is good (James 1:17), which means his character contains everything that is good. Thus, God is wise, noble, humble, kind, and so on. That also means that God does not possess any evil qualities; he is not petty or cruel, and he does not lie. These distinctions go beyond saying "God is good" or "God is not bad." Rather, God is the definition of all things good, and something is bad if it reflects something different from God's character.

The Bible specifically identifies several positive attributes of God's character. For example, 1 John 4:16 makes it clear that God is loving: "And so we know and rely on the love God has for us. God is love. Whoever lives in love lives in God, and God in him." Again, this means more than saying God demonstrates love to us; it is saying that God is the source of love. God is also holy and righteous. He is set apart from the world, and there is no part of him that is evil or wrong; he is pure (see Habakkuk 1:13 and Isaiah 6:3). God is also merciful (Numbers 14:18), faithful (2 Timothy 2:13), and truthful (Titus 1:2).

The Bible also identifies several attributes of God that many people don't consider to be positive, although they are certainly necessary. For example, God is just and the source of all justice. "Yet the LORD longs to be gracious to you," writes Isaiah, "he rises to show you compassion. For the LORD is a God of justice. Blessed are all who wait for him!" (Isaiah 30:18). God is also jealous (Exodus 20:5), which means he is not willing to tolerate a divided loyalty from those he has ransomed. Finally, anger and wrath are part of God's character (Romans 1:18). These are not spontaneous and uncontrolled, like human wrath and anger. Rather, they are the extension of God's justice and his intolerance of sin.

Question 219. What does the Bible say about angels?

The Bible mentions several types of beings that all fit under the category of "angels." The first is cherubim ("winged beings"), which are mentioned in Genesis 3:23 and Ezekiel 10, among other places. Then there are seraphim ("burning ones"), which are mentioned in Isaiah 6:3, Revelation 4, and elsewhere. Many of the angels mentioned in the Bible are simply called messengers, as in Genesis 16:17–11, Matthew 1:20–24, and so on.

The most important thing to know about angels is that they are spiritual beings. They live and operate in a spiritual dimension that God created alongside the physical world in which humans live and operate, but they are usually unseen and unfelt by people. There are times when angels interact with the physical world and human beings, however, as the Bible makes clear—most often as messengers from God to people. It was an angel, for example, that told Mary she would give birth to the Messiah.

Angels also play a role in spiritual warfare—fighting against the spiritual forces of evil in the spiritual dimension—although we have little information from the Bible about how that actually works. Daniel chapter 10 gives us the best window into those battles: "Since the first day that you set your mind to gain understanding and to humble yourself before your God, your words were heard, and I have come in response to them. But the prince of the Persian kingdom resisted me twenty-one days. Then Michael, one of the chief princes, came to help me, because I was detained there with the king of Persia. Now I have come to explain to you what will happen to your people in the future, for the vision concerns a time yet to come" (vv. 12–14). Here an angel was sent to give a message to Daniel, but apparently he was resisted by a demonic being (the "prince of the Persian kingdom") for three weeks before help came from Michael, the archangel.

Question 220. Who is Satan, and how does he affect the world?

Satan is a spiritual being who pops up in many places throughout the Bible, yet surprisingly, there is very little that can be said about him in certain terms. It isn't known for sure where Satan came from. Church tradition has said that Satan was the most powerful angel who became jealous of God's status in heaven, led a rebellion, and was thrown down. This is based largely in the text of Isaiah 14, which contains verses like "How you have fallen from heaven, O morning star, son of the dawn! You have been cast down to the earth, you who once laid low the nations!" (v. 12) However, the immediate context of those verses describes the rise and fall of the nation of Babylon, and it is not certain whether they contain a secondary link to Satan. Jesus seems to add a little light in Luke 10:18 when he says, "I saw Satan fall like lightning from heaven." Again, though, the immediate context of that verse is the disciples' encounter with spiritual warfare, and it is not clear whether Jesus was talking about a physical fall by Satan out of heaven.

There are several things that the Bible does confirm about Satan and how he interacts with Christians and the world.

- **Satan is a created being** Satan is not the opposite of God. He is a spiritual being that was created by God, which means he is far less than God. As a created being, Satan is limited to being in one place at one time, does not know everything, and is not all powerful.
- **Satan is the enemy of God's people** Several portions of scripture do confirm that Satan actively works against people who follow God, including 1 Peter 5:8: "Be

self-controlled and alert. Your enemy the devil prowls around like a roaring lion looking for someone to devour."

- **Satan is not alone** Although Satan is not omnipresent and omniscient, he does control a network of spiritual beings that are also working for evil and against God's will for the world. These creatures are commonly called demons, and their existence is supported by numerous texts in the Old and New Testaments (including Psalm 106:37, Matthew 8, Luke 8, James 2:19, and others).
- **Satan and his followers have already been defeated** It is true that Satan and his followers are fighting against God's plans for the universe, but in the Book of Revelation the Bible shows us how that fight ends: "And the devil, who deceived them, was thrown into the lake of burning sulfur, where the beast and the false prophet had been thrown. They will be tormented day and night for ever and ever" (20:10).

Question 221. What does the Bible say about the nature of human beings?

The first thing the Bible says about human beings is that we, along with everything else in the universe, were created by God. Whether that means humans were created in seven literal days seven thousand years ago or evolved over millions of years or anything else, the important thing to know is that humanity is not a random occurrence; we are part of God's creation.

In addition, human beings are a combination of material and immaterial pieces. We have a body and a soul. (Some believe we also possess a spirit that is separate from the soul, but that is mostly a debate about words.) This immaterial element is what separates human beings from the other animals throughout God's creation. Our bodies are complex and miraculous, but also temporary. Our souls are just as real, and they are the eternal essence of what makes someone a "person." In other words, your soul is what makes you "you."

Finally, human beings possess free will, which means we have the ability to choose between right actions and wrong actions. God is sovereign over the universe that he created and has the ability to control everything in it. The fact that humanity has free will means that God does not exert his control over us. He allows us to act in ways that we desire, whether or not those ways are what he wants us to do. Of course, this also means that human beings receive the consequences of the choices they make.

Question 222. What is sin, and how does it affect us?

At its most basic level, sin is separation from God. A sinful act is any choice or way of thinking that contrasts with God's character. For example, a lie is a sin because God is always truthful. Sin also involves a state of being that is separate from God. When Adam and Eve committed the first acts of sin, they did not merely go down the wrong path for a while; they completely separated themselves from God with no way of getting back.

The same is true for every person who has ever lived. "For all have sinned and fall short of the glory of God," says Paul in Romans 3:23. Isaiah 59:2 says, "But your iniquities have separated you from your God; your sins have hidden his face from you, so that he will not hear." We are all separated from God at birth because of the sinful state of all human beings, and we all commit our own acts of sin that confirm our separation.

This reality of sin affects all of creation in many different ways. Things like hatred, racism, violence, and greed are rooted in the presence of sin; so are guilt, fear, pride, and loneliness. All these things are present in society because of our separation from God. Even the natural world has been infected by sin, resulting in hurricanes, tornados, predators, extinction, and so on. Paul writes in Romans 8:22 that "the whole creation has been groaning as in the pains of childbirth right up to the present time."

Question 223. How do we experience forgiveness for our sin?

The Bible makes it clear that human beings cannot achieve forgiveness for their sins through any action or effort on our part. We are separated from God at birth because of the way sin has infected all people (Psalm 51:5). We exist in a state of sinfulness, and no amount of good decisions or actions can undo that separation. Indeed, Isaiah 64:6 says that "all of us have become like one who is unclean, and all our righteous acts are like filthy rags."

But the Bible also makes it clear that forgiveness is possible. "Come now, let us reason together," the Lord says in Isaiah 1:18, "though your sins are like scarlet, they shall be as white as snow; though they are red as crimson, they shall be like wool." Romans 4:7 says, "Blessed are they whose transgressions are forgiven, whose sins are covered."

What is surprising for many people is that the vehicle through which God grants our forgiveness is the shedding of blood. Indeed, the author of Hebrews writes that "without the shedding of blood there is no forgiveness" (9:22). In the Law of the Old Testament, this was accomplished through animal sacrifice. The Israelites would place their hand on the animal about to be killed as a symbolic identification with the animal and transfer of sin from one living creature to another. The blood of that animal, representing its life, washed away both individual and corporate sin. There was nothing magical about this ceremony, nor was there anything magical about the blood; it was still God granting forgiveness to his people. The sacrifices helped the Israelites understand the seriousness of their sin and that they were being spared from physical and spiritual death because of their connection with God.

This theme is continued in the New Testament through the sacrifice of Jesus Christ on the cross. Jesus told his disciples the following during the Last Supper: "This is my blood of the covenant, which is poured out for many for the forgiveness of sins" (Matthew 26:28). The idea is that the sins of all people were transferred to Jesus during his time on the cross and he paid the penalty of death for those sins when he literally died. We have the chance to be forgiven because he allowed his blood to be shed.

Question 224. Why was death a necessary response to sin?

Most people believe that death came about as a punishment for sin. That seems to be what the Bible says, as well, at first glance, at least. In Genesis 2:17, we learn that God told Adam and Eve, "You must not eat from the tree of the knowledge of good and evil, for when you eat of it you will surely die." In Romans 5:12, Paul writes that "sin entered the world through one man, and death through sin, and in this way death came to all men, because all sinned."

The message seems to be that people have to die as a punishment for their sin. In some ways that is true. Death was not a part of God's original plan for human beings, as far as we can tell, and death is certainly a consequence of Adam and Eve's decision to separate themselves from God through an act of sin.

Can we say for sure that death is a punishment? Was God acting in anger or justice when he sentenced the physical bodies of his creations to break down and perish, or is it possible that God's pronouncement of death was an act of grace? Think about that for a moment. If God's original plan was that the physical bodies of human beings would not die, then imagine what it would be like if we continued to live forever on this earth after sin entered the world. Would it be a blessing to have eternal life if we were eternally separated from a pure relationship with God because of our infection of sin, or would that be hell?

Seen in that light, the death of our physical bodies is best viewed as an escape hatch for the human soul. Death is God's Plan B that sets us free from an eternal life of physical sin and instead gives us the opportunity to experience eternal life in a restored relationship with God and a new physical body, in heaven.

Question 225. What does it mean to experience salvation?

The doctrine of salvation includes the forgiveness of sin we have been offered through the sacrifice of Jesus Christ, but also more. It addresses both our current situation in this world and our eternal future in the world to come.

The first question we need to ask when we think about salvation is this: What are we being saved from? According to the Bible, we are saved from the infection of sin that causes us to be separated from God. As mentioned in the questions above, all human beings exist in a state of sinfulness, and all human beings participate in that sinfulness by committing acts of sin. When we experience salvation, we are removed from the state of sinfulness, what Paul refers to as our "sinful nature" (see Romans 7). We are no longer separated from God, and we can enjoy a relationship with him once again. Since we were born with our sinful nature, Jesus referred to this experience of salvation as being "born again" (John 3:3). The technical term for this instant restoration of our relationship with God is *justification* (see questions 229 and 230 on justification and sanctification).

The second question we need to ask about salvation is this: What are we saved for? The answer, of course, is heaven, but heaven is more than sitting on clouds with harps or walking along streets of gold. It is a restoration of what God originally intended when he created Adam and Eve in the Garden of Eden, complete with work, social interaction, and an intimate relationship with God.

Question 226. Is it arrogant to say that Jesus is the only way to be saved?

It may or may not be an arrogant statement, but it is at least a logical statement according to the Bible. Every religious system in the world is exclusive at its core meaning; all religions claim to be the "only way." That being the case, people only have two choices when it comes to learning about God and salvation—either one religion is correct and all of the others are wrong, or all of them are wrong.

People don't have to make a blind decision, though. Religious systems are testable, just like anything else. The holy books of each religion can be tested to see which one is most accurate when it comes to history and science. Those books can also be tested with regard to historical integrity and reliability. People can do research to identify similarities and differences when it comes to the core beliefs and doctrines of a religious system, as well as the results when those beliefs and doctrines are applied.

When people make those kinds of comparisons, they find that Christianity stands out. The Bible is the most reliable ancient book ever written when it comes to historical accuracy and integrity. Jesus Christ has been confirmed as a historical figure, and his death and resurrection are well documented. Christianity is also the only religious system that is based on the idea of grace, rather than asking people to earn their way into paradise. Again, these statements are considered arrogant by some, but that does not make them any less true.

Christians do need to be careful, however, when they say that "Jesus is the only way." Because when they say that, they usually mean that their understanding of how Jesus works in peoples' lives to bring forgiveness is the only way that it can happen. In other words, Christians can sometimes put Jesus in a box when it comes to salvation. This is a mistake. The Bible is clear that Jesus is the only door through which a person can experience reconciliation with God (John 14:6), but it does not say that Jesus is limited to one specific prayer or someone using phrases like "born again." To say that Jesus is the "only way" means that he alone brings us salvation, but he is free to offer that salvation in any way he chooses and to anyone he chooses.

Question 227. What happens to those who die before ever hearing about Jesus?

This is a question that cannot be answered for certain, because it addresses the mind and thoughts of God, but there are several clear principles of scripture that can help us better understand this issue.

First of all, the Bible does make it clear that Jesus is the only door that leads to salvation. In John 14:6, Jesus himself says, "I am the way and the truth and the life. No one comes to the Father except through me." Acts 4:12 confirms that Jesus really meant what he said: "Salvation is found in no one else, for there is no other name under heaven given to men by which we must be saved."

The fact that Jesus is the one who offers salvation does not mean that he always offers it in the way we expect, though. There is no magic formula when it comes to God's grace and our salvation, no set of words that a person has to say in a certain prayer, for salvation to be granted. Salvation is something that is between Jesus Christ and the soul of every individual, and God may very well have ways of working with those who are not exposed to the Gospel that we don't understand. One example is the phenomenon of Jesus appearing in the dreams of people from other cultures, particularly those living in Muslim nations. Jesus is considered a prophet by Islam, of course, but there have been numerous stories from all over the world in recent years of Muslim men and women meeting Jesus in their dreams and being called to follow him.

One other thing that can be said for sure is that God does not intentionally push people away when it comes to salvation. He does not hide himself from any nations or cultures or people groups. Timothy 2:1–4 makes this clear: "I urge, then, first of all, that requests, prayers, intercession and thanksgiving be made for everyone—for kings and all those in authority, that we may live peaceful and quiet lives in all godliness and holiness. This is good, and pleases God our Savior, who wants all men to be saved and to come to a knowledge of the truth." Also see 2 Peter 3:9: "The Lord is not slow in keeping his promise, as some understand slowness. He is patient with you, not wanting anyone to perish, but everyone to come to repentance."

Jesus may be the only way for human beings to experience salvation, but God is also able to speak to people around the world and call them in ways we are not aware.

Question 228. What is the relationship between faith and salvation?

At its most basic, faith is simply trusting God. It is believing in what God has said through his creation, through the life of Jesus, through the Bible, and through the work of the Holy Spirit in our hearts. And not just believing, but responding in a way that demonstrates our trust in what God has promised and our intention to obey God's will.

Hebrews 11:1 says that faith "is being sure of what we hope for and certain of what we do not see." It doesn't mean that faith is blind. We don't have faith in anything that is random or undefined. Rather, we have faith in the things God has specifically promised will come true. When it comes to salvation, for example, we place our faith in the Bible's promise that Jesus died on the cross as a sacrifice for our sins, that he conquered death and rose again, and that we can have an eternal relationship with God. Having faith means we live our lives as if these things are true, even though we did not see them with our own eyes.

Fortunately, we don't have to scrape up faith to access God's gift of salvation. Faith itself is another gift from God. Ephesians 2:8 says, "For it is by grace you have been saved, through faith—and this not from yourselves, it is the gift of God." Salvation is a gift, and so is the initial burst of faith that is necessary for us to access that salvation. After we experience salvation, it's important to continue exercising our faith by living as though what the Bible says is true. It's like a muscle; the more we boldly take action based on our faith in God, the more our faith increases.

Question 229. What does justification mean?

Justification means to be "made right," and the term refers to the instant a person accepts God's gift of salvation through Jesus Christ. In that moment, all of that person's sins—past, present, and future—are forgiven, and he or she is restored to a functioning relationship with God. It is important to remember that human beings can do nothing to earn or achieve justification. Because we exist in a state of sinfulness, we cannot restore our relationship with God. We can only accept the gift of salvation (and justification) that was made possible by Jesus's death and resurrection.

It is true that the word *justification* is used often in the New Testament, but the principle is contained in the Old Testament as well. In fact, the prophet Zechariah paints a vivid picture of what it means to be justified: "Now Joshua was dressed in filthy clothes as he stood before the angel. The angel said to those who were standing before him, 'Take off his filthy clothes.' Then he said to Joshua, 'See, I have taken away your sin, and I will put rich garments on you.' Then I said, 'Put a clean turban on his head.' So they put a clean turban on his head and clothed him, while the angel of the LORD stood by" (3:3–5). Joshua is used here as a representation of all God's people, but the image is the same for everyone. When we accept God's gift of salvation, the filth and dirt of our sinful nature is covered up with the perfect and sinless nature of Jesus. That way, when God looks at us, he no longer sees the sins we have committed and instead sees the righteousness of Jesus. That is the essence of justification.

Question 230. What is sanctification?

While justification happens the moment we accept God's gift of salvation, sanctification is a process. In fact, sanctification includes everything that happens in our lives between the moment we are saved and the moment we die.

Remember that when we experience justification, we experience forgiveness for all of our sins. We also receive the righteousness of Jesus Christ that covers over our sinful nature, like a pure white coat covering our dirty old jacket. That doesn't mean we are sinless, like Jesus, though. Justification doesn't mean that we no longer sin. Rather, our sins are forgiven, and the "new nature" of Jesus Christ covers up our "old nature," which means our relationship with God can be restored.

Sanctification is the process where we gradually eliminate the sinful nature from who we really are. It is a lifelong process of resisting temptation and obeying God, and the result is that we become more and more like Jesus. We become the person that God made us to be. It's important to realize that we never accomplish this during our lifetime on earth. There is no Christian who is completely good.

Question 231. What is glorification?

Glorification is the final stage of sanctification. When a person is "glorified," he or she has been completely stripped of the sinful nature that all human beings are infected with on earth. We become the people that God originally intended for us to be. Of course, this doesn't happen on earth. Glorification happens only when we begin our eternal life with God in heaven.

Romans 8 has a good summary of the salvation process, from justification to glorification: "For those God foreknew he also predestined to be conformed to the likeness of his Son, that he might be the firstborn among many brothers. And those he predestined, he also called; those he called, he also justified; those he justified, he also glorified" (vv. 29–30).

Question 232. What happens to the people who die without becoming saved?

The Bible is clear about some things concerning the afterlife and vague about others. The fate of those who die physically without being reconciled to God fits into the vague category.

There are some things we know for sure, of course. The most important thing is that no person who has rejected the forgiveness offered by Jesus Christ will spend eternity with God in heaven. Those people are still mired in their sinful nature; they are still separated from God and therefore cannot enjoy the perfect relationship with him that exists in heaven. Instead, people who reject a relationship with God will spend eternity in a place of separation from God, a reality we refer to as hell.

Contrary to popular belief, the Bible is not very specific on what hell is like. In the Old Testament, the word used to describe the afterlife is *Sheol*, which is the place of the dead. This word is translated differently in various verses—*grave*, *pit*, and *depths* are the most common translations—but they all refer to the same place. In the ancient world, the place of the dead is where all people went after they died, whether good or bad. Surprisingly, the Old Testament writers didn't make much of a differentiation between heaven and hell. David, for example, regularly references Sheol as his destination after he died. "What gain is there in my destruction," he cried out in Psalm 39:9, "in my going down into the pit? Will the dust praise you? Will it proclaim your faithfulness?"

The separation of heaven and hell is very present in the New Testament, however, and begins with Jesus. In John 14:2, Jesus is clearly describing heaven when he says, "In my Father's house are many rooms; if it were not so, I would have told you. I am going there to prepare a place for you." And he is clearly describing a different place in verses like Matthew 25:41, where he says, "Then he will say to those on his left, 'Depart from me, you who are cursed, into the eternal fire prepared for the devil and his angels.'" The word Jesus uses to describe hell is *Gehenna*, which was an actual location in Jesus's day. It was a valley where human sacrifices to the god Molech had been conducted for many years, and in the time of Jesus it was used as a trash dump. The valley was continually kept burning as a means of consuming the trash, and that seems to be the image Jesus was referencing when he speaks of hell.

Is hell consistent with the images that are usually connected to it—fire and brimstone and little devils running around with pitchforks? Probably not. Fire is typically used in the New Testament as a symbol for refinement, not punishment. Since the New Testament describes hell as both a place of eternal fire and eternal darkness, we can be certain that those are not literal, physical descriptions of hell as a place. Unfortunately, we can also be sure that hell does exist as a place of separation from God, and that people who choose to maintain that separation by rejecting God's forgiveness will experience it.

Question 233. Is it possible for Christians to lose their salvation?

Theologians have debated back and forth on the possible answer to this question for centuries. One of the main reasons that Christians haven't come to a consensus on this question is that different Bible verses seem to support different answers.

For example, Paul seems to say in 2 Corinthians that people become completely changed when they experience salvation: "Therefore, if anyone is in Christ, he is a new creation; the old has gone, the new has come!" (5:17). When Jesus talks about his sheep in John 10:38, he says, "I give them eternal life, and they shall never perish; no one can snatch them out of my hand." On the other hand, several New Testament writers spend time warning Christians to pay attention to their walk with God so that they don't fall away. Hebrews 6:4–6 is a good example: "It is impossible for those who have once been enlightened, who have tasted the heavenly gift, who have shared in the Holy Spirit, who have tasted the goodness of the word of God and the powers of the coming age, if they fall away, to be brought back to repentance, because to their loss they are crucifying the Son of God all over again and subjecting him to public disgrace." And Jesus seems to identify levels of salvation in the Parable of the Sower (Luke 8:1–15). Verses 13 and 14 are especially applicable to this discussion: "Those on the rock are the ones who receive the word with joy when they hear it, but they have no root. They believe for a while, but in the time of testing they fall away. The seed that fell among thorns stands for those who hear, but as they go on their way they are choked by life's worries, riches and pleasures, and they do not mature."

Scholars are at a stalemate regarding this issue. Those who believe Christians can never lose their salvation are advocates of eternal security, and there seems to be biblical support for that idea. Those who believe it is possible for Christians to lose their salvation are advocates of conditional security, and there seems to be biblical support for that idea as well.

Fortunately, the practical applications of eternal security and conditional security are pretty much the same. Nobody can deny that some people claim to be Christians for a while—including attending church, witnessing, praying, and so on—but then deny their faith later on. For those who advocate conditional security, those people were genuine Christians who fell away. For those who advocate eternal security, those people were never really Christians in the first place. The practical result is the same: Those who deny Jesus Christ are lost and in need of God's grace, whether or not they were Christians for a time. The same is true for people who are currently Christians. Those who advocate eternal security would say you can never lose your salvation, while those who advocate conditional security think it is possible to fall away. Practically, however, both camps understand that the best thing to do is continue obeying God and living to fulfill his plan for your life.

Question 234. How do I know if I'm a Christian?

Many Christians experience a measure of doubt regarding whether or not they have really given their lives over to God and are saved. This is a natural concern, simply because the stakes are so high. We want to be sure.

The first thing that should be understood is that there is no magic formula or initiation that confirms that a person is a Christian. Saying a certain prayer doesn't guarantee that you're a Christian. Going to church every time the door is open doesn't guarantee that you're a Christian. Even reading the Bible and praying every day doesn't guarantee anything.

Put simply, you can know for certain you are a Christian if you have a relationship with God, and if you are working to serve him with your life. Having an actual relationship with God is important because of the situation we are saved from. In our sinful state without the forgiveness offered by Jesus Christ, we were unable to have a working relationship with God; therefore, the first sign of salvation is that our relationship with God becomes restored. This manifests itself in several ways. Do you experience God regularly? Do you talk with him? Do you listen to him? Do you feel nudges from the Holy Spirit every now and then as you contemplate decisions or review the events of your day? When you do encounter God, are you moved to thankfulness and worship? These are all evidence of a living, growing relationship with God.

The second item mentioned above is also important: Are you working to serve God with your life? The Bible is clear that good works cannot earn salvation (Ephesians 2:8–9), but it is also clear that good works are strong evidence that we are operating as servants of God. When Jesus talked to his disciples about distinguishing between false prophets and true Christians, he said: "Likewise every good tree bears good fruit, but a bad tree bears bad fruit. A good tree cannot bear bad fruit, and a bad tree cannot bear good fruit. Every tree that does not bear good fruit is cut down and thrown into the fire. Thus, by their fruit you will recognize them" (Matthew 7:17–20). God is working in the world, and those who serve God as Christians should be visibly contributing to that work.

Of course, that raises another question: What kinds of fruit should Christians produce? There are two sections of scripture that speak to this issue best. The first is from Galatians 5:22–23: "But the fruit of the Spirit is love, joy, peace, patience, kindness, goodness, faithfulness, gentleness and self-control." The second comes from Jesus in Matthew 25:

> *Then the King will say to those on his right, "Come, you who are blessed by my Father; take your inheritance, the kingdom prepared for you since the creation of the world. For I was hungry and you gave me something to eat, I was thirsty and you gave me something to drink, I was a stranger and you invited me in, I needed clothes and you clothed me, I was sick and you looked after me, I was in prison and you came to visit me.... I tell you the truth, whatever you did for one of the least of these brothers of mine, you did for me" (vv. 34–40).*

These are the kinds of actions that correspond with God's work in the world.

Question 235. What is the purpose of baptism?

Baptism is best described as a recommended step in the process of turning one's life over to God. Its primary purpose is to allow new Christians to publically announce their intention to follow Jesus in all things. It is a chance for them to boldly declare that they have joined Jesus's kingdom and are submitting to his rule. The ritual of immersion in water is also a proclamation and reminder of how salvation was made possible through Jesus Christ. He experienced death on the cross (was covered in our sin and went down into the grave) but then rose up again in a burst of new life. As it was with Jesus, so it is with those who put their trust in him.

It is important to point out that the church has viewed baptism as an important step in the salvation process for centuries. Jesus himself made it a high priority in the Great Commission: "Therefore go and make disciples of all nations, baptizing them in the name of the Father and of the Son and of the Holy Spirit, and teaching them to obey everything I have commanded you. And surely I am with you always, to the very end of the age" (Matthew 28:19–20). But baptism is not a required step. It is not necessary for salvation, nor is it necessary for receiving the Holy Spirit as a proof of salvation, as some believe.

Question 236. How does the Bible define the church?

The best definition of the church comes from 1 Corinthians 12, where Paul talks about the body of Christ. "The body is a unit, though it is made up of many parts," he writes, "and though all its parts are many, they form one body. So it is with Christ. For we were all baptized by one Spirit into one body—whether Jews or Greeks, slave or free—and we were all given the one Spirit to drink" (vv. 12–13). In verse 27, he tells the church, "Now you are the body of Christ, and each one of you is a part of it."

To understand this a little better, look back at something Jesus told his disciples in John 14. He had been talking about the miracles he had performed, and he said, "Believe me when I say that I am in the Father and the Father is in me; or at least believe on the evidence of the miracles themselves. I tell you the truth, anyone who has faith in me will do what I have been doing. He will do even greater things than these, because I am going to the Father" (vv. 11–12).

The disciples didn't understand this statement, and many who read it today don't understand it, either. How can anyone do greater things than Jesus? He was Jesus! But that's actually the point. What Jesus meant was that his collected followers across the world and across time (the church, in other words) would do greater things than he did when he had a physical body on Earth. When you think about it, he was right. Jesus's ministry was limited to a very small geographical area, and he personally influenced a very small number of people, but the church has spread across the world and literally influenced billions of people throughout the centuries.

Question 237. Does the New Testament say that women should not have leadership roles in the church?

This is another question that church leaders have not been able to agree on over the centuries, because there are verses in the Bible that seem to support arguments both for and against women serving in leadership roles in the church.

Here's what Paul says in 1 Timothy 2: "A woman should learn in quietness and full submission. I do not permit a woman to teach or to have authority over a man; she must be silent. For Adam was formed first, then Eve. And Adam was not the one deceived; it was the woman who was deceived and became a sinner. But women will be saved through childbearing—if they continue in faith, love and holiness with propriety" (1 Timothy 2:11–15). That seems straightforward, but we have to wonder if these instructions were culturally limited. In other words, was

Paul giving these commands to women in one specific time and city, or was he giving them to all women of all cultures?

This point gets confusing because there are sections of scripture that seem to make a different argument, like this one, which was also written by Paul: "You are all sons of God through faith in Christ Jesus, for all of you who were baptized into Christ have clothed yourselves with Christ. There is neither Jew nor Greek, slave nor free, male nor female, for you are all one in Christ Jesus. If you belong to Christ, then you are Abraham's seed, and heirs according to the promise" (Galatians 3:26–29). If we are all equal because of our faith in Jesus, than why not allow women to teach men?

To answer this question, move beyond identifying isolated verses that support one side or another, and instead try to look at the broader movements of scripture. For example, it is clear from the New Testament that all believers are given spiritual gifts that should be used in the church (see 1 Corinthians 12). It's also clear that many women throughout history and today have been blessed with the gift of teaching.

What is more, there is a strong inclination to elevate women in the ministry of Jesus and the leaders of the early church. In those days, women truly were viewed as second-class citizens. They had very few rights, were rarely educated in any way, and were expected primarily to stay at home. Jesus and the leaders of the church shrugged off many of these conventions, however. Jesus himself taught women on several occasions, including his good friends Mary and Martha (see Luke 10). Jesus also had many women followers, both as financial contributors and learners. Paul, too, mentioned several women who were instrumental to the workings of the early church, including Priscilla, Phoebe, Mary, and many others.

So it would not be accurate to say that the New Testament commands women not to take leadership roles within the church. On the contrary, the teaching of Jesus and the leaders of the early church move in the direction of a countercultural elevation of women and an encouragement for both women and men to use their gifts within the church.

Question 238. Does the Bible require Christians to tithe?

God commanded a tithe—offering 10 percent of each harvest or profit—for the nation of Israel as a way to finance the priests and Levites who served in the Temple and in the towns throughout Israel. Leviticus 27:30 says: "A tithe of everything from the land, whether grain from the soil or fruit from the trees, belongs to the LORD; it is holy to the LORD." When Jesus died and rose again as a sacrifice for all people, he removed the need for a Levitical priesthood, though; thus he removed the need for a tithe.

The New Testament has a lot to say on the subject of giving. For example, Jesus makes it clear that Christians should give generously to people who are in need: "Give to everyone who asks you, and if anyone takes what belongs to you, do not demand it back. Do to others as you would have them do to you" (Luke 6:30–31). Both Jesus (Luke 10:7) and Paul (1 Timothy 5:18) make it clear that the people who are served by a local church should support that church financially.

Mainly, though, the message about money and giving in the New Testament is that Christians should not hoard their money or spend it on pleasure, but instead use it as a tool to advance God's kingdom. That means we should give cheerfully, first and foremost: "Remember this: Whoever sows sparingly will also reap sparingly, and whoever sows generously will also reap generously. Each man should give what he has decided in his heart to give, not reluctantly or under compulsion, for God loves a cheerful giver" (2 Corinthians 9:6–7). Instead of asking, "How much am I supposed to give for God's work?" we should be asking, "How much can I give right now, and how can I manage my finances in order to give more?"

Question 239. Why does the Old Testament include so many dietary restrictions?

There were several purposes for the many laws and restrictions laid out in the Old Testament. Some were to prevent sin, while others were to provide forgiveness after sin. Some laws were given to protect the innocent and punish the guilty, and a large portion of God's laws and commands for the Israelites were designed to accomplish something completely different: separation and purity.

When God selected the Israelites as his chosen people, his goal was to build a nation that would provide an example of godliness to the rest of the world and eventually provide blessings to the world and pave the way for everyone to have fellowship with God (see Genesis 17). To accomplish that goal, one of the first things that God commanded of the Israelites was that they be holy, which means "set apart." The Israelites had to live and behave differently from the sinful world around them so that the people of that world would see that the Israelites were holy, and eventually learn about God. That is part of the reason why the Israelites needed to abstain from sinful behavior and why they needed to be cleansed when they did sin. They were supposed to be holy, set apart, and pure.

God also wanted this holiness to be reflected in the Israelites' everyday lives, so he set up laws and commands that focused on purity as a way to remind the Israelites of their need for holiness. For example, here's what God commanded in Leviticus 19:19: "Keep my decrees. Do not mate different kinds of animals. Do not plant your field with two kinds of seed. Do not wear clothing woven of two kinds of material." This does not mean that making clothes from two different kinds of fabrics was evil; instead, the command was designed to help the Israelites continually think about purity and holiness.

This same design carries over for the dietary laws established in Leviticus. Genesis 1 established several purebred categories of animals: birds that fly in the air, fish that swim in water, and land animals that walk on the earth. In Leviticus 11 and other places, the Israelites are forbidden from eating the flesh of animals that seem to violate those categories, things like water creatures that didn't have fins or scales (11:10) or creatures that crawled or slithered on land rather than walked (11:41–43). In addition, the dietary laws seem to lift up certain animals as the most pure of their category, including sheep and goats for land animals. Therefore, animals that operated differently from sheep and goats (those that didn't have a split hoof completely divided and that didn't chew the cud) were considered unclean.

The Bible does not assert that any of the unclean animals were inherently wrong, and the dietary laws weren't established to promote health or prevent disease, as some have speculated. The restrictions on food were designed to promote holiness and purity, and the Israelites understood them as such.

Question 240. Should Christians today keep kosher?

No, Christians today are not required to follow the dietary laws of the Old Testament. The reason is that God specifically lifted those restrictions after the death and resurrection of Jesus paved the way for all people to become holy in God's eyes. This happened through a vision given to the apostle Peter: "He saw heaven opened and something like a large sheet being let down to earth by its four corners. It contained all kinds of four-footed animals, as well as reptiles of the earth and birds of the air. Then a voice told him, 'Get up, Peter. Kill and eat.' 'Surely not, Lord!' Peter replied. 'I have never eaten anything impure or unclean.' The voice spoke to him a second time, 'Do not call anything impure that God has made clean.' This happened three times, and immediately the sheet was taken back to heaven" (Acts 10:11–16).

Peter's vision had a larger purpose, paving the way for the early Jewish Christians to begin witnessing to gentiles as well. A secondary effect was that the early Christians recognized that gentiles did not have to abide by most of the Jewish "holiness restrictions." In fact, the council of the early church sent a letter to all gentile believers some time later to address the issue of whether gentile Christians needed to be circumcised and follow the Old Testament restrictions. Here are the items they recommended the gentiles observe: "You are to abstain from food sacrificed to idols, from blood, from the meat of strangled animals and from sexual immorality. You will do well to avoid these things. Farewell" (Acts 15:29). The dietary regulations were not included and have not been considered necessary for gentile Christians since.

Chapter 12

THE BIBLE AND MODERN ETHICS

Question 241. What does the Bible say about divorce?

The Bible says several things about divorce, but none of them are favorable. God is clear in Genesis that his intent for marriage and human sexuality is permanent, that man and woman join together to form "one flesh" (2:24). For that reason, God responds with anger in the Bible when people take advantage of that union or dissolve it completely. In fact, here's what God had to say on the subject from Malachi 2:

> *You weep and wail because he no longer pays attention to your offerings or accepts them with pleasure from your hands. You ask, "Why?" It is because the LORD is acting as the witness between you and the wife of your youth, because you have broken faith with her, though she is your partner, the wife of your marriage covenant. Has not the LORD made them one? In flesh and spirit they are his. And why one? Because he was seeking godly offspring. So guard yourself in your spirit, and do not break faith with the wife of your youth. "I hate divorce," says the LORD God of Israel (vv. 13–16).*

Jesus confirmed this stance when he was asked about divorce in Matthew 19. "'Haven't you read,' he replied, 'that at the beginning the Creator "made them male and female," and said, "For this reason a man will leave his father and mother and be united to his wife, and the two will become one flesh"? So they are no longer two, but one. Therefore what God has joined together, let man not separate'" (vv. 4–6).

Divorce had become a common element of the Israelite culture because of a law from Deuteronomy 24 that required a man to provide a certificate of divorce for a wife that he found indecent. This law was put in place to protect the women of Moses's time, not to allow frivolous divorce. Men of Moses's time had a habit of kicking their wives out of the house in order to make room for new women. But because the older wives were not officially divorced, they could not support themselves or remarry, which left them destitute. Jesus corrected that line of thinking in vv. 8–9: "Moses permitted you to divorce your wives because your hearts were hard. But it was not this way from the beginning. I tell you that anyone who divorces his wife, except for marital unfaithfulness, and marries another woman commits adultery."

The phrase "except for marital unfaithfulness" represents one of the exceptions in the Bible concerning the prohibition of divorce. The other comes from Paul in 1 Corinthians 7: "If any brother has a wife who is not a believer and she is willing to live with him, he must not divorce her. And if a woman has a husband who is not a believer and he is willing to live with her, she must not divorce him…. But if the unbeliever leaves, let him do so. A believing man or woman is not bound in such circumstances; God has called us to live in peace" (vv. 12–15). In other words, if one spouse becomes a Christian and the other spouse abandons the marriage, divorce is an acceptable option.

The Bible is clear that divorce and remarriage do not constitute adultery in instances of marital unfaithfulness and abandonment by an unbelieving spouse. With divorce in other situations, however, the words of Jesus don't leave a lot of wiggle room: "I tell you that anyone who divorces his wife, except for marital unfaithfulness, and marries another woman commits adultery" (Matthew 19:9). These words are harsh, and they were meant to be taken that way. Jesus was speaking during a time when divorce was viewed casually, as it is in our culture today. In Jesus's time, however, the terms of a divorce all favored the male spouse completely and usually left the woman abandoned financially and stigmatized culturally, so at least some of Jesus's harshness is probably aimed against this double standard. But we can't get away from the fact that Jesus did not view divorce as a casual matter at all.

God takes marriage seriously, and he does not look favorably on those who casually enter into that union and then casually break it. His ideal is for a husband and wife to unite in marriage for a lifetime, but when we fall short of his ideal on any subject, we can still come to him for forgiveness (1 John 1:9).

Question 242. Does the Bible advocate spanking children?

The Bible advocates discipline for children as a measure of correction and growth. The main verses that most people quote in connection with this issue come from the Book of Proverbs. "Discipline your son, for in that there is hope; do not be a willing party to his death" (19:18) is the first one. But the most famous verse is Proverbs 13:24, which says, "He who spares the rod hates his son, but he who loves him is careful to discipline him."

Many Christians over the years have taken these verses to mean that spanking is the preferred method of discipline in the Bible, but that is stretching the meaning of the text beyond reason. The Bible advocates discipline and correction to train children in the proper way of living, but it never says that parents must physically strike their children. Of course, the Bible does not say that parents should avoid physically striking their children, either. Christian parenting experts today recommend that parents use whatever form of discipline works best with their children.

Question 243. Does the Bible say that the practice of homo-sexuality is wrong?

Yes. Whenever the Bible brings up the topic of homosexual practices, they are referenced as sinful behavior. Leviticus 18:22, for example, makes things fairly clear: "Do not lie with a man as one lies with a woman; that is detestable." The writers of the New Testament echo this idea, including the apostle Paul: "Do not be deceived: Neither the sexually immoral nor idolaters nor adulterers nor male prostitutes nor homosexual offenders nor thieves nor the greedy nor drunkards nor slanderers nor swindlers will inherit the kingdom of God" (1 Corinthians 6:9–10).

Christians need to keep a proper balance in mind when it comes to the current debate around homosexuality, though. The reason that homosexuality is labeled as "wrong" in the Bible is that it represents a distortion of God's intentions for marriage and sexuality. God says in Genesis 2:24, "For this reason a man will leave his father and mother and be united to his wife, and they will become one flesh."

Homosexuality is only one outcome of that distortion. Premarital sex (whether heterosexual or homosexual) is another major distortion of God's intentions; so is adultery, divorce, and physical and emotional abuse in the context of marriage. All these behaviors go against God's plans for sexuality, which means that all of them are equally wrong. Many Christians today seem to view homosexuality as disgusting and vulgar, while divorce and premarital sex are viewed as normal. That is a poor reflection of the Bible's stance on the issue of homosexuality and a poor reflection of Jesus's instructions for us to "love your neighbor as yourself."

Question 244. Does the Bible say that having a homosexual orientation is wrong?

The scriptures clearly prohibit people from engaging in homosexual practices, as mentioned in the question above, but does it mean nonpracticing homosexuals need to change the way they think and feel? In other words, is it the presence of romantic feelings for a person of the same gender that is wrong, or only the consummation of those feelings?

The Bible does not answer this question directly. There are no passages of scripture that specifically label homosexual feelings as sinful, nor does any part of the Bible explain whether people are born with homosexual tendencies or nurtured toward those tendencies later in life. What the Bible does make clear is God's original intent for sexuality:

But for Adam no suitable helper was found. So the LORD God caused the man to fall into a deep sleep; and while he was sleeping, he took one of the man's ribs and closed up the place with flesh. Then the LORD God made a woman from the rib he had taken out of the man, and he brought her to the man. The man said, "This is now bone of my bones and flesh of my flesh; she shall be called 'woman,' for she was taken out of man." For this reason a man will leave his father and mother and be united to his wife, and they will become one flesh (Genesis 2:20–24).

God's original intentions for sexuality were that romantic feelings be experienced by a man and a woman in the context of marriage, which means that romantic feelings between two people of the same gender were not part of God's plan, but neither were sexual feelings between heterosexuals who are not married, nor sexual feelings that go beyond a person's spouse. Such feelings are referred to as temptation, and to give in to these feelings is called lust.

The church has taught for centuries that resisting temptation and avoiding lust is a proper response to any sexual feelings that are not part of God's original plan. The church applauds a young couple that abstains from sexuality until marriage, for example, as well as single people who never marry and resist the temptation to lust. The same standard should be applied to those who experience romantic and sexual feelings for people of the same gender. Resisting lust, whether heterosexual or homosexual, is a vital step in resisting the practice of sexual immorality and should be commended.

Question 245. Is it wrong for Christians to use contraception?

To answer this question, you need to first reflect on what the Bible says about many other questions. For example, is reproduction the only purpose for human sexuality? If so, then contraception would clearly be wrong. But Genesis 2 connects sexuality with human companionship (especially verses 19–25), and Song of Solomon certainly focuses on the pleasure and joy of marital sex without mentioning children at all, so the Bible does not limit sexual activity to reproduction.

There's a second question that deeply affects the issue of contraception. When does a human life begin? If human life begins at the moment of conception, than any method of contraception that involves eliminating a fertilized egg would be ending a human life, which is clearly prohibited in scripture. Unfortunately, the Bible does not say whether a fertilized egg is a human being, or at what point in the process of development it becomes one. Some scholars have used David's words in Psalm 51:5 as evidence that life begins at conception: "Surely I was sinful at birth, sinful from the time my mother conceived me." But to make this connection is to place literal value on a poetic expression, which is a poor way to interpret any text.

Still there's a third question that needs to be answered when addressing the issue of contraception: Do parents have the right to plan out how many children they want in their family and when they will be conceived? Some believe the Bible answers this question with a no. They believe that children are a gift from God and should come through his timing, not ours. For support, they point to verses like Psalm 127:3–5: "Sons are a heritage from the LORD, children a reward from him. Like arrows in the hands of a warrior are sons born in one's youth. Blessed is the man whose quiver is full of them." Bible scholars disagree on the modern application of these verses, though.

With all that in mind, it is difficult to say what the Bible's view is concerning modern-day contraception. The best thing for couples to do as they think about this issue is study, research, and work with the Holy Spirit to find answers to the questions above.

Question 246. What does the Bible say about masturbation?

This is a topic that the Bible does not address directly. There are no verses in scripture that even mention the practice of masturbation. The Bible does speak to the larger issues of lust and temptation surrounding masturbation, though, and those verses provide direction.

There is one particular biblical story that often comes up with this topic. In Genesis 38, there is a woman named Tamar who was married to a man named Er, who passed away. As a result of Er's death, Tamar became the wife of Er's brother, Onan. This was an important custom for the Israelites, the idea being that any children born from Tamar and Onan's union would legally belong to Er, so that his family line would not die out. Here's what happened next: "But Onan knew that the offspring would not be his; so whenever he lay with his brother's wife, he spilled his semen on the ground to keep from producing offspring for his brother. What he did was wicked in the LORD's sight; so he put him to death also" (vv. 9–10). Many people over the years have used this story and Onan's death to label masturbation as sinful, but that is not a correct interpretation. What Onan did that aroused God's anger was refuse to fulfill his obligation to his brother by providing Tamar with a son.

The bigger issue surrounding masturbation is its connection with lust. Jesus spoke against lustful thoughts in Matthew 5:27: "You have heard that it was said, 'Do not commit adultery.' But I tell you that anyone who looks at a woman lustfully has already committed adultery with her in his heart." Similarly, Colossians 3:5 commands us to "Put to death, therefore, whatever belongs to your earthly nature: sexual immorality, impurity, lust, evil desires and greed, which is idolatry."

Masturbation is almost never a purely mechanical process. It requires stimulation, either from visual images or mental pictures and sexual thoughts, and if a person habitually gives in to lustful thoughts and converts them into actions, he or she is in danger of establishing a lifestyle that treats sexuality as an itch to be scratched, rather than what God created it to be: a powerful and intimate connection between husband and wife.

Question 247. Does the Bible prohibit Christians from drinking alcohol?

The Bible never says that followers of God should not drink alcohol. In fact, the Bible records many heroes of the faith drinking wine on many occasions, including Jesus (Matthew 26:27–29). The apostle Paul commanded Timothy, a young pastor, to "stop drinking only water, and use a little wine because of your stomach and your frequent illnesses" (1 Timothy 5:23).

At the same time, the Bible does prohibit drunkenness. Ephesians 5:18 says, "Do not get drunk on wine, which leads to debauchery. Instead, be filled with the Spirit." Is the Bible's position on alcohol that anyone can drink as much as they want, as long they we don't cross the line separating buzzed from drunk? Not quite. There are other things to consider as well.

For one thing, alcohol does have a lot of potential for causing harm, and sometimes consumption can affect other people. If Christians ever find themselves in a situation where drinking could cause damage to another person or serve as a bad example, they should abstain. "Do not destroy the work of God for the sake of food," Paul writes in Romans 14:20. "All food is clean, but it is wrong for a man to eat anything that causes someone else to stumble." In a similar way, Christians should remember that their bodies are temples for the Holy Spirit (1 Corinthians 6:19), which means they need to treat their physical selves in a way that honors God.

Question 248. What does the Bible say about immigration?

The Bible has a great deal to say about immigration, especially in the Pentateuch and the Levitical Law. In Exodus 22:21, God commanded the Israelites to not actively mistreat any immigrants among them: "Do not mistreat an alien or oppress him, for you were aliens in Egypt." God then takes things a step further in Leviticus 19:34: "The alien living with you must be treated as one of your native-born. Love him as yourself, for you were aliens in Egypt. I am the LORD your God."

It can be difficult to apply these commandments to the political debate surrounding immigration in the twenty-first century, though. The commands in God's Law were given to the Israelites, who were God's chosen people on earth. They had been set aside by God as the vehicle through which he wanted to bless all the nations of the world (Genesis 18:18). Welcoming immigrants from other nations was a natural step in that process. But the situation is different in places like America today. The United States is not a theocracy (a nation led exclusively by God) as the nation of Israel was. The United States is a democracy, which means its leaders must factor in things like national security, the economy, labor laws, and so on, when drafting laws and policies. In other words, God's commands in Leviticus should not be considered a political mandate for every nation on earth.

God's laws do, however, set up a clear moral mandate for the church. The church is governed exclusively by God, with Christ as its head, and Christians throughout the world have inherited the calling of Abraham to bless all the nations of the earth. In other words, the Bible makes it clear that the church is responsible to love and care for the immigrants it encounters, and it certainly should not oppress them in any way. Beyond the commands mentioned above, Christians need to remember that several key figures in the Bible were immigrants at one time or another. Abraham, for example, was an immigrant from Ur. Moses fled Egypt and resided in the land of Midian. David fled from Saul and lived as in immigrant among the Philistines, and Jesus experienced life as an immigrant when Mary and Joseph fled the wrath of Herod and went to Egypt.

These stories, coupled with Jesus's command to "love your neighbor as yourself," make it clear that caring for immigrants and wanderers should be a high priority of the church.

Question 249. Does the Bible condemn or approve of war?

This is another issue where it's important to distinguish between God's commands to the nation of Israel—a theocracy—and the role of the church after the death and resurrection of Jesus. It is clear that God commanded the Israelites to make war against several nations and groups of people. Joshua was charged to wipe out the Canaanites from the Promised Land; God commanded King Saul to completely annihilate the Amalekites; and David's wars against the enemies of Israel, including the Philistines, were conducted in obedience to God.

That fact certainly does not mean that the church should seek to engage in warfare or violence against people and nations that do not follow God. Looking back in history, the Inquisition and military campaigns like the Crusades were major mistakes on the part of church leaders. Those mistakes were often made because Christians were focused on power and wealth, not on living as servants of God.

How should Christians think about wars today? Again it is important to remember that there is a difference between the governments and political structures of countries and the church spread throughout the entire world. Governments need to make decisions based on the needs and safety of their respective nations, and the early verses of Romans 13 indicate that those governments "bear the sword" through the authority of God.

The church is another matter, however. The New Testament makes it clear that God's people on earth are charged to be advocates of peace. In Romans 12:18, for example, the apostle Paul writes, "If it is possible, as far as it depends on you, live at peace with everyone." Yes, the Book of Revelation makes it clear that the future holds a final battle between God and the forces of evil, but from now until then, God's church should work to bring peace wherever possible.

Question 250. Does the Bible support capital punishment?

The Old Testament certainly advocates capital punishment. In fact, several of the laws within the Pentateuch actively command the death penalty to be enforced for certain crimes. Take Exodus 21:12, for example: "Anyone who strikes a man and kills him shall surely be put to death." Exodus 22:19 says, "Anyone who has sexual relations with an animal must be put to death." Leviticus 24:16 says, "Anyone who blasphemes the name of the LORD must be put to death. The entire assembly must stone him. Whether an alien or native-born, when he blasphemes the Name, he must be put to death." In total, the Law lists eighteen crimes for which the offender could be put to death.

Once again, keep in mind that these laws were written for the nation of Israel as a theocracy, a country under the direct rule of God. When punishments like the ones mentioned above were carried out, they were considered the judgment of God, not of men, upon the guilty parties. Obviously modern countries like America do not operate the same way as Israel, nor do they have the same mandate to act on behalf of God. How then do we determine what the Bible has to say about the death penalty in modern times?

There are two key ideas in the Bible that speak to this issue. First, the Bible makes it clear that any person can be rehabilitated through the transforming power of the Holy Spirit. In other words, no people are so evil that they cannot repent of their sin, experience salvation, and turn their lives around. The classic example is the thief who was crucified next to Jesus. With his dying breaths, he expressed faith in Jesus as Lord and was told by the Savior, "Today you will be with me in paradise" (see Luke 23:39–43).

The second key idea from the Bible is that all our actions have consequences. Galatians 6:17 says, "Do not be deceived: God cannot be mocked. A man reaps what he sows." Those consequences come about in eternity through the judgment of God, but they can also be reaped during our time on earth, and local government is one of the systems to which God has given authority for carrying out those consequences. "Everyone must submit himself to the governing authorities, for there is no authority except that which God has established. The authorities that exist have been established by God. Consequently, he who rebels against the authority is rebelling against what God has instituted, and those who do so will bring judgment on themselves" (Romans 13:1–42).

In summary, then, the Bible supports local governments making and enforcing laws to protect the innocent of society and to punish those who do wrong. There is no prohibition in the Bible against capital punishment being included in those laws. Therefore, it cannot be said that the Bible speaks out against capital punishment, although, in a democratic country like America, Christians should certainly feel free to exercise their rights when it comes to influencing or changing those laws. What can be said for sure is that the church has a mandate from God to work for the salvation and rehabilitation of all people, including those who have been sentenced to death.

Question 251. Does the Bible forbid suicide?

Yes, the Bible does forbid the act of suicide by making it clear that killing a human being is wrong. There are exceptions, of course. The Old Testament does command capital punishment as a consequence for several crimes (see the previous question), but that was viewed as a direct judgment of God. The Bible also does not shy away from the reality of war, which seems to exempt soldiers from the charge of murder when they carry out their duty. But there is no passage of scripture that allows a person to end his or her own life, which means the sixth commandment holds the precedent: "You shall not murder."

At the same time, it's important to point out that the Bible does not call for a curse on or special punishment for those who do commit suicide. Such an action is not an unforgiveable sin. Several people are actually recorded in scripture as committing suicide. Many of these events occurred when the people in question were in the middle of a battle, including Saul (1 Samuel 31:4–6), Samson (Judges 16:29–30), and Zimri (1 Kings 16:15–20). Other people committed suicide because of deep shame or grief, including Ahithophel (2 Samuel 29:1–17) and Judas Iscariot (Matthew 27:5). In all these situations, the suicide is described as a historical event alongside several other historical events, without any kind of moral or ethical note to mark the act of suicide as especially grievous.

In fact, the Bible specifically mentions that there is only one unforgivable sin, which is the rejection of the Holy Spirit (see Mark 3:29, for example).

Question 252. Does the Bible forbid euthanasia?

As with the topic of suicide, the Bible does not specifically address the moral implications of assisted suicide. There is as least one event of assisted suicide in the Bible, and it comes in Judges 9 after a woman dropped a millstone on Abimelech's head and cracked his skull: "Hurriedly he called to his armor-bearer, 'Draw your sword and kill me, so that they can't say, "A woman killed him."' So his servant ran him through, and he died" (v. 54).

Again, this is mentioned as a historical event, with no moral footnote included to say whether the armor bearer's action was right or wrong. Therefore Christians must fall back on what the Bible clearly does say about ending a human life: "You shall not murder" (Exodus 20:13).

Question 253. Does the Bible forbid "pulling the plug" and allowing someone to die?

As mentioned in previous questions, the act of suicide and the act of assisted suicide are not given a specific moral judgment in the Bible, which means they fall under the prohibition against taking human life found in Exodus 20:13. The same cannot be said of "pulling the plug," because doing so does not actively end a human life.

The Bible does relay several key themes that speak to end of life issues and situations, however. First, the Bible makes it clear that physical death is not something that followers of God should be afraid of. "For to me, to live is Christ and to die is gain," wrote the apostle Paul. "If I am to go on living in the body, this will mean fruitful labor for me. Yet what shall I choose? I do not know! I am torn between the two: I desire to depart and be with Christ, which is better by far; but it is more necessary for you that I remain in the body" (Philippians 1:21–24). Human life is just a breath in comparison to eternity (James 4:14), and death is unavoidable (Hebrews 9:27), so there is no reason for Christians to be afraid of the transition for themselves or for their loved ones.

At the same time, the Bible makes it clear that life is a gift from God, and that God alone understands the span of each person's days. Psalm 139:15–16 says this: "My frame was not hidden from you when I was made in the secret place. When I was woven together in the depths of the earth, your eyes saw my unformed body. All the days ordained for me were written in your book before one of them came to be."

These biblical principles provide a couple of practical guidelines to follow. First, because God alone knows when someone's last moment of life is, removing a person from life support and allowing him or her to die of natural causes does not violate any of the Bible's commands. It may even be an act of love. Medical history, however, makes it clear that miracle recoveries do happen. For that reason, "pulling the plug" should be done only through the guidance of the Holy Spirit, who knows the measure of each person's days.

Question 254. Does the Bible encourage Christians to take care of the environment?

Yes it does and almost from the very beginning. Here are God's instructions to humanity during the creating account of Genesis 1: "God blessed them and said to them, 'Be fruitful and increase in number; fill the earth and subdue it. Rule over the fish of the sea and the birds of the air and over every living creature that moves on the ground'" (v. 28). The word translated *subdue* carries the idea of "ruling over" something—of supporting and caring for it, as a king rules over his kingdom. God emphasizes this responsibility in Genesis 2: "The Lord God took the man and put him in the Garden of Eden to work it and take care of it" (v. 15). Before sin distorted both humanity and the natural world, God intended for people to enjoy the earth and care for it.

We have the same commands now, even though sin has infected both people and nature. That's because God is working to restore the perfection of the natural world, just as he will cleanse us completely from sin when we meet him in heaven. Isaiah 65:17 says: "Behold, I will create new heavens and a new earth. The former things will not be remembered, nor will they come to mind." The apostle Peter confirms this future in his epistles (see 2 Peter 3:13) and John mentions the coming "new earth" in his vision from God recorded in the Book of Revelation (21:1). So, just as we work with God to fight against the effects of sin in our own hearts—looking forward to the time when we will be made whole—we should work to take care of this world as a reminder of the world that is yet to come.

Question 255. Why doesn't the Bible condemn slavery?

This is a hard question to address for many Christians. Not only does the Bible fall short of condemning slavery, it actively recommends the practice. Here's a command from God in Leviticus 25:44–45: "Your male and female slaves are to come from the nations around you; from them you may buy slaves. You may also buy some of the temporary residents living among you and members of their clans born in your country, and they will become your property." Here's what the apostle Paul adds in Ephesians 6:5–9: "Slaves, obey your earthly masters with respect and fear, and with sincerity of heart, just as you would obey Christ…. And masters, treat your slaves in the same way. Do not threaten them, since you know that he who is both their Master and yours is in heaven, and there is no favoritism with him."

How should these verses be interpreted today with the advances the world has made in recent centuries to abolish slavery? The answer is that the slavery discussed in the Bible is a far cry from the slavery opposed by people like Abraham Lincoln and William Wilberforce.

In the ancient world, slavery was very often voluntary. Becoming a slave to a farmer or merchant was just another way to find a job. These slaves were treated fairly, usually paid a wage, and were allowed to return to freedom after their period of service had ended. For the Israelites, slavery was also an accepted system through which a person could repay debts. The people of the ancient world had no savings accounts to speak of and no real system of currency. For that reason, a household could be devastated if a drought hit or a farmer's livestock died suddenly. In those situations, there was no way for a family to eat other than to borrow from others and accrue large debts; thus slavery became a dignified way to repay those debts. It allowed Israelites to earn what they needed instead of relying on the charity of their neighbors.

In short, slavery for the ancient world was mostly a social structure that helped ease the burden of debt and human need. For the Israelites especially, it did not involve the capture and forced labor of unwilling men, women, and children.

Chapter 13

How Can I Use the Bible in Everyday Life?

Question 256. What do Christians mean when they talk about "doing their devotions"?

From the earliest days of Christianity, church leaders have recommended that Christians interact with God on a regular basis. In modern times, this interaction is often labeled a devotion or a quiet time. This devotional time usually consists of two main elements, reading the Bible and prayer.

Prayer is best understood as having an ongoing, lifelong conversation with God. And as with any good conversation, praying to God should involve both talking and listening. We talk to express our gratitude and praise to God as well as to tell him what is currently on our minds and hearts, but we also need times of silence where we let go of our own concerns and focus on what God is saying back to us through the quiet, nudging voice of the Holy Spirit.

Here's what 2 Timothy 3:16–17 says about the Bible: "All Scripture is God-breathed and is useful for teaching, rebuking, correcting and training in righteousness, so that the man of God may be thoroughly equipped for every good work." That is the goal for Christians when they read God's Word, to allow the Holy Spirit to equip them with what they need to serve God each day. It happens intellectually, meaning Christians learn through prayer and devotional reading what is right and wrong and how God wants them to behave. It is also a gradual process of transformation. As Christians interact with the words of the Bible on a consistent basis, the Holy Spirit actually changes who they are and makes them more like the people God originally designed them to be.

The Bible has been described as "God's instruction manual" and "a personal letter from God to you," and those are both good ways to think about it. Another good analogy comes from the author of Hebrews, who writes, "We have much to say about this, but it is hard to explain because you are slow to learn. In fact, though by this time you ought to be teachers, you need someone to teach you the elementary truths of God's word all over again. You need milk, not solid food! Anyone who lives on milk, being still an infant, is not acquainted with the teaching about righteousness. But solid food is for the mature, who by constant use have trained themselves to distinguish good from evil" (5:11–14). This passage was written as a rebuke for Jewish Christians who had begun to slide in their faith, but the word picture is a good one for how the Bible relates to Christians. It provides them with spiritual nourishment and is a part of the food that gives the fuel needed to live the Christian life.

Question 257. Are Christians required to read the Bible every day?

Having a daily devotional time is not a necessary element of Christianity. People will not lose their relationship with God or automatically fall into sinful patterns if they fail to experience God's Word each and every day. Reading the Bible every day, however, is certainly a good idea and one that was modeled by the leaders of the early church.

Several authors of the New Testament used food as an analogy to recommend regular experiences with God to their readers. Peter wrote the following to several churches in Asia Minor, which were filled with recent converts to Christianity: "Therefore, rid yourselves of all malice and all deceit, hypocrisy, envy, and slander of every kind. Like newborn babies, crave pure spiritual milk, so that by it you may grow up in your salvation, now that you have tasted that the Lord is good" (1 Peter 2:1–3). This was not a random connection. Peter intended to teach that just as humans need physical nourishment on a regular basis (and preferably every day), they also grow best spiritually when they have a healthy diet of prayer and interaction with God's Word.

The apostle Paul used the metaphor of an athlete training for a competition as a way to describe the benefits of interacting with the Bible daily. "Everyone who competes in the games goes into strict training," he wrote to the church at Corinth. "They do it to get a crown that will not last; but we do it to get a crown that will last forever. Therefore I do not run like a man running aimlessly; I do not fight like a man beating the air. No, I beat my body and make it my slave so that after I have preached to others, I myself will not be disqualified for the prize" (1 Corinthians 9:25–27). To Timothy, for whom Paul was a mentor, he wrote, "Have nothing to do with godless myths and old wives' tales; rather, train yourself to be godly. For physical training is of some value, but godliness has value for all things, holding promise for both the present life and the life to come" (1 Timothy 4:7–8). Paul's point in using this word picture is clear. Just as an athlete requires regular physical training to compete well in a race, so do Christians require regular spiritual exercise to grow strong and accomplish the tasks God has put before them.

Question 258. What is the best way for a Christian to approach reading the Bible?

There's no right or wrong answer when it comes to what portions of the Bible a Christian should read on a given day. There are a few guidelines that can help people approach the text in a way that is most beneficial, though.

First, Christians should allow themselves to experience the entire Bible instead of limiting themselves to portions of the New Testament, Psalms, and Proverbs. The apostle Paul makes it clear that "all Scripture is God-breathed and is useful for teaching, rebuking, correcting and training in righteousness, so that the man of God may be thoroughly equipped for every good work" (2 Timothy 3:16–17). For that reason, Christians should make an effort to read and meditate on every verse of the Bible throughout the course of their lives.

Second, different books of the Bible should be approached in different ways. Take the epistles of the New Testament, for example. They were originally composed as letters, and the authors usually intended for them to be read out loud in one hearing to a gathering of people. For that reason, those who approach the epistles today are best served when they get started by reading the entire book through in one setting and then go back and spend days or weeks meditating on individual chapters and verses.

Many books of the Bible are much too large for readers to realistically take that approach, however. When you study books like Exodus, Job, Isaiah, or Matthew, try to skim through the text on the first day and look for natural divisions in the story line. Genesis 1–11 covers the creation of the world and its later judgments through the flood and the tower of Babel, for example, while the rest of Genesis concentrates on the story of Abraham and his descendants. It works well to read through those eleven chapters and then go back and study individual sections of those chapters for a few weeks and then move on to the story of Abraham and repeat the process. This method is a great way to keep the larger context of the text in mind as you read individual pieces and stories.

Finally, Psalms and Proverbs are collections of material that was written over time, so they are ideally suited to be read in bite-sized chunks. You don't have to worry about context if you read just Psalm 139 or several proverbs from chapter 20, for example. Those books are meant to be read devotionally and with more of a shotgun approach.

Question 259. Does it matter what translation is used when studying the Bible?

It does matter which Bible translation Christians use for their regular study of God's Word, but only up to a point. The most important factor in any Bible translation is that it be as accurate as possible when compared to the text in its original languages.

That means you want a translation that was put together by a respected and qualified team of scholars. Most of the main Bible translations currently for sale today are considered to be very accurate, including the New International Version (NIV), New American Standard Bible (NASB), King James Version, New King James Version, English Standard Version (ESV), New Revised Standard Version (NRSV), and the New Living Translation (NLT).

The other important factor when choosing a Bible translation is readability. You want to be studying a Bible that is as easy for you to understand as possible. There is a bit of tension between a translation being as accurate as possible and still easy to understand, which is why there are so many Bible translations currently available. The NRSV and NASB are viewed as very literal translations, which means they translate the text on a word-for-word basis. These version can be a little more difficult to read. The NIV and the NLT are on the other end of the spectrum. They are based on phrase-by-phrase translations, which makes them easier to read but also slightly less accurate. As it was originally translated in 1611, the King James Version also suffers in the area of readability.

Question 260. Can paraphrases be used when studying the Bible?

A Bible paraphrase is a retelling of the scripture texts in today's language. It is different from a translation, in that it does not seek to have a word-for-word or phrase-for-phrase connection to the original manuscripts of the Bible. Rather, the author of a paraphrase takes the ideas of sections of the text and rewrites them in his or her own words, focusing on the language of the day, more than literal translation.

Paraphrases can be very useful supplements to traditional Bible study. Because they are written in today's language—including modern slang and word pictures—they can provide helpful insights and clarity for sections of the Bible that are difficult to process or understand. *The Message* is a particularly popular paraphrase available today, and its author, Eugene Peterson, is a talented and respected teacher of the Bible.

Most church leaders do not recommend using a paraphrase as your primary method of studying the Bible. Paraphrases do prioritize readability over textual accuracy, which sometimes causes problems, and paraphrases are usually written by one person, which means they can lack the diverse range of opinions and experience usually found among Bible translation teams.

Question 261. What other books or resources are good aids for Bible study?

The opportunities are almost limitless when it comes to purchasing supplementary material that claims to help Christians understand and apply God's Word. There are a great many tools that are genuinely useful.

The first is a good study Bible. A study Bible is a copy of God's Word that includes a variety of helpful notes, tips, maps, definitions, cross references, and other tools. The added information is usually included right on the page with the biblical text, which can really enhance your experience during regular study times. Study Bibles come in many translations, so you don't have to limit yourself, and they are generally affordable. The *Life Application Study Bible* has been a popular choice for many years.

Another recommended tool is some kind of biblical commentary, which may sound daunting, but you don't have to go out and get the sixty- or seventy-volume commentaries that pastors often use to prepare their sermons. There are a variety of commentary sets that include only a few volumes, and some individual books that provide just about everything you need in a single copy. *What the Bible is All About* by Henrietta Mears is a good example of the latter. The value of a good commentary is that it goes a couple levels beyond study notes to provide you with cultural context, explanations of terms, debates and questions surrounding passages, and more. Commentaries are also great at connecting individual books of the Bible with the rest of the canon, which allows you to keep the entire context of the Bible in mind as you study its parts.

Lastly, a daily devotional guide, which can be several different things, is an excellent Bible study tool to have on hand. Some devotional guides map out a yearly study plan that mixes in specific parts of the Bible to be studied each day, although most study Bibles include several of these types of plan within their pages. Other devotional guides provide a brief outside commentary on a specific passage of scripture, along with thoughts for application and questions for reflection or discussion. *Daily Bread* is a good example of this kind of devotional, as is *My Utmost for His Highest,* by Oswald Chambers.

Question 262. What is *lectio divina?*

Lectio divina is an ancient method of studying the scriptures that was adopted by the early church fathers and used for several centuries in the church. Translated as "sacred reading," *lectio divina* involves meditating on smaller passages of scripture and attempting to connect with the Holy Spirit in regard to what is being read. The process of *lectio divina* involves multiple stages. Through these steps, Christians contemplate the Word of God slowly and deliberately, working with the Holy Spirit to unlock the deeper meanings of the text and its application to the life of the believer.

The stages of lectio divina vary depending on the method, but here are four steps that are widely accepted:

- **Lectio** This is the initial reading of the text, and it is intentionally slow and deliberate. The goal of this stage is to pay attention to the nudging of the Holy Spirit as you read and see if any word, phrase, or idea from the text stands out. It is often helpful to read the text out loud during this stage.
- **Meditatio** This stage involves an extended rumination on the text. You think deeply about what it says and what it means for your life, especially in regard to any words or passages that stood out for you during the lectio phase.
- **Oratio** This stage involves an extended prayer to God. Talk with him about the text you have been contemplating, what you think it means, and how you think it connects to your world. Don't be afraid to talk with him about other issues during this stage as well. If requests or notions of praise interrupt your mind, release them to God by telling him about them.
- **Contemplatio** The final stage of lectio divina involves contemplation. This is where you do nothing but be silent and listen for the still, small voice of God. Achieving this kind of silence of the mind is difficult for many people in our noise-cluttered culture, so give it time. Again, if distractions continually enter your mind and keep you from listening, offer them to God as little prayers and then get back to the business at hand.

Question 263. What does it mean to pray through the scriptures?

This is a method of Bible study that intentionally connects reading the text of the Bible with prayer. When you pray through a specific passage of scripture, you let that passage of scripture shape and direct your prayer to God, including elements of praise, thanksgiving, and requests.

Take a look at the first two verses from Psalm 1: "Blessed is the man who does not walk in the counsel of the wicked or stand in the way of sinners or sit in the seat of mockers. But his delight is in the law of the LORD, and on his law he meditates day and night." If you were to pray through these verses, you might say something like this: "Father God, thank you so much for removing me from the counsel of the wicked. Thank you for my family and for my friends who give me such good advice. Father, I know that I still stand in the way of sinners sometimes, and I pray that you would please forgive me. Help me resist temptation, and please help me keep avoiding the seat of mockers. I do delight in your law, God. Thank you for your Word, and please help me keep meditating on it day and night."

The idea is simple, and there are two main benefits to praying through scripture. The first is that it helps you process what you are reading in a new and more active way. Like working out a puzzle through a model in your hands rather than thinking of it in your head, you get a better grasp of scripture you're reading when you pray through each line. The other main benefit is that you stop feeling like you are praying the same thing over and over again every time you try to talk with God. Praying through the scriptures brings a wonderful sense of variety to those conversations. This method works best with the Psalms and other lyrical passages of scripture, but can also work surprisingly well with many sections of the New Testament epistles and also with narrative passages throughout the Bible.

Question 264. What are the spiritual disciplines?

A spiritual discipline is any habitual practice that helps a person connect with God. Although spiritual disciplines do not automatically earn you a quicker, more personal relationship with God when you practice them, they do allow God to draw you closer to him and help you grow. Reading the Bible and praying are good examples of spiritual disciplines, and there are several more. Here are a few of the main ones:

• **Fasting** The practice of abstaining from food for an extended period of time (usually one meal or a day's worth of food) is very common in the Bible and can be transformational when practiced regularly. Fasting goes beyond not eating, however. When you fast, your body sends out many signals, reminding you that you are hungry and need to eat. The goal of fasting is to use those signals as a reminder to connect with God and pray, instead.

- **Solitude** The practice of solitude is also abstaining, but from the company of people instead of food. When alone for several hours, or even an entire day, you give yourself an opportunity to think deeply about what is happening in your heart, what is happening with God, and what behaviors may need to change to fix any problems with the first two.
- **Silence** Solitude is often paired with silence in practice. Christians have been intentionally moving away from noise and distractions for centuries to focus better on God, but the discipline of silence is especially valuable in today's noise-obsessed culture. To practice silence, simply move away from as much noise as possible (this can be anywhere from a remote location away from city noise to a quiet room in your own home) for an extended period of time and allow yourself to think. Also, allow yourself to listen to what the Holy Spirit may be trying to say, once you can hear him.
- **Worship** The practice of worship goes way beyond singing songs on Sunday morning, though singing to God can be an excellent expression of the discipline of worship. The essence of worship is thinking about God and who he is, thinking about what he has done for us, and then allowing yourself to respond appropriately through praise. This can be through song, spoken prayers of gratitude and praise, written psalms, art, or anything that allows you to express your worship to God.
- **Sabbath** This important discipline is one of the few that is commanded in the Bible. Practicing the Sabbath requires abstaining from work for an entire day each week and thus showing your faith that God can be more productive with six days than you can with seven. It doesn't have to be Sunday, but it's best if you mark your Sabbath on the same day each week, as much as possible. While you rest, be sure to praise the God who is in control of the universe, so that you don't have to be.

Question 265. How do Christians identify their spiritual gifts?

There are two important things to know about spiritual gifts right off the bat: 1) There are many kinds of gifts, and 2) everybody has some. Here's what Paul wrote in 1 Corinthians 12: "Now to each one the manifestation of the Spirit is given for the common good. To one there is given through the Spirit the message of wisdom, to another the message of knowledge by means of the same Spirit, to another faith by the same Spirit, to another gifts of healing by that one Spirit, to another miraculous powers, to another prophecy, to another distinguishing between spirits, to another speaking in different kinds of tongues, and to still another the interpretation of tongues. All these are the work of one and the same Spirit, and he gives them to each one, just as he determines" (vv. 7–11).

The next question is this: How do I find out what my spiritual gifts are? There are several ways to go about it. One is to read through the sets of gifts listed in the Bible and see which ones seem to fit. The most relevant passages for this exercise, in addition to the verses listed above, are Romans 12:6–8, Ephesians 4:11–12, and 1 Peter 4:10–11. There are "spiritual gifts assessments" that can help with this process, and it's also a good idea to talk with the people who know you best and ask what ministry strengths they see in you.

The other option is to work with the Holy Spirit himself to find your gifts. Make this question a regular part of your prayer life, and ask the Spirit to reveal your gifts and how best to use them. You can even request that the Spirit bless you with gifts that you think you need. Even better, start serving in different areas of ministry and see what happens. If you don't feel a pull when you serve in one area—if there isn't a connection and a confirmation from the Holy Spirit—try to serve in other ways. You certainly can't go wrong with that approach!

Question 266. Should Christians try "putting out a fleece" to figure out God's will?

The idea of putting out a fleece goes back to the story of Gideon from Judges 6. Gideon had been approached by the angel of the Lord and commanded to lead an army against the Midianites, who had been oppressing God's people. Gideon was afraid, however, and he apparently wanted extra confirmation from God that everything would be okay. Gideon put a fleece on the ground one night and asked God to make the fleece wet with dew and the ground around it dry as a sign that he would actually be able to defeat the Midianites. God answered Gideon's request, but Gideon still wasn't satisfied, and he asked that the reverse happen the next morning—that the fleece be dry but the ground all around be wet. Once again, God answered his request, and the fleece was dry.

Gideon's fleece tests revealed his lack of faith. He had already been visited by the angel of the Lord and promised that everything would go well, but his requests for further confirmation showed that his fear was getting the better of his faith. God was not angry with Gideon for this lack of faith, however, and graciously gave Gideon all the signs he needed until he was ready to obey.

Is this a practice that should be used today? According to the New Testament and subsequent church history, probably not, or at least not very often. Christians today possess several resources for finding God's will that Gideon and the people of his time lacked. The first is the scriptures. Through the Bible, we have a clear picture of the kind of people God wants us to be and the kinds of things he wants us to do. Christians also have the Holy Spirit living inside them as a counselor and guide. It is much better to work with God through prayer and listen for the nudging of the Holy Spirit than to set up tests and try to force God into responding.

In certain situations, however, a fleece may be a good idea. Specifically, if you think you have been given a direction from God but are uncertain, a fleece can be helpful in confirming that you correctly understand what God wants you to do, but this confirmation should be handled only in submission, through diligent prayer. It is always a bad idea to try to force God to respond to our desires and whims.

Question 267. Does doing what the Bible says guarantee a successful life?

The answer depends on your definition of success. You are certainly not guaranteed fame, fortune, and extended good health. Those who preach about the so-called prosperity Gospel focus on a few verses from scripture but ignore the overall statement made by the Bible about what's in store for those who follow God.

Jesus makes it clear on several occasions, what may be in store for those who follow him. In John 16: 33 Jesus says, "In this world you will have trouble. But take heart! I have overcome the world" (John 16:33). The lives of his apostles bore out his statement—the vast majority of them were persecuted, imprisoned, and martyred for their faith. It doesn't mean that all Christians are guaranteed to have horrible, painful lives, but it certainly does mean that they aren't guaranteed easy, comfortable lives, either., Christians are guaranteed one thing, however: a place with God in heaven when their time on earth is finished.

Index

importance of, 64

Book of Numbers, 38–40
  author of, 38–39
Book of Obadiah, 92
  message of, 92
Book of Philemon, 137
Book of Proverbs, 74–76
  on cosigning on loan, 75
  purpose behind, 74–76
Book of Psalms, 71–74. *see also* psalm(s)
  authors of, 71
  repetition in, 72–73
Book of Revelation, 155–159
  numbers in, interpretation of, 158
  themes in, 155
Book of Romans, themes of, 122
Book of Ruth, 50–51
  author of, 50
  themes of, 50–51
Book of Song of Songs, 77–78
  plot of, 78
Book of Zechariah, 98–99
  message of, 99
Book of Zephaniah, 97
  message of, 97
Book(s) 1 and 2 Chronicles, 61–63
  accuracy of numbers described in, 61–62
  author of, 61
  similarity to books 1 and 2 Kings, 61
Book(s) 1 and 2 Kings, 56–60
  similarity to book(s) 1 and 2 Chronicles, 61
Book(s) 1 and 2 Samuel, 52–56
breakthrough
  in apocalyptic literature, 150

in Book of Revelation, 156
bronze, belly and thighs of, 152
Bronze Age, 3–4
  Noah in, 3
"burnt offering," 36

C

Caesar, Julius, 20–22
Cain, wife of, 28
calendar
  Israelites', connection with our modern calendar, 41–42
  modern, Israelites' calendar's connection with, 41–42
Canaan
  conquest of, 46–48
  Israelites destroying people in, necessity of, 40–41
Canaanites, in Middle East, during time of Old Testament, 2
capital punishment, Bible on, 191–192
casting lots, as method of identifying God's will, 54
Chambers, Oswald, 202
chest and arms of silver, 152
children, spanking of, Bible on, 185
Christians
  alcohol use by, Bible on, 189
  Bible reading by
    approach to, 199–200
    daily, 199
  confessing sins to other Christians, 143–144
  contraceptive use by, Bible on, 187–188
  dependence on wisdom literature of Bible, 74–75

Tower of Babel, building of, negative
consequences of, 29–30
translation(s), of Bible, 200–201
Tree of the Knowledge of Good and
Evil, 28
Trinity, Bible on, 162
trust, in Bible, 13–23

U
unclean, meaning of, 39–40
universe, age of, in Bible, 26
Urim, 53–54

V
viciousness, of David, in writing, 73
victory at Gibeon, 47, 48
vision of beasts, in Book of Daniel, 153
visually intense
in apocalyptic literature, 150
in Book of Revelation, 156

W
wandering for forty years, by Israelites,
reasons for, 39
war, Bible on, 191
Western world, modern, vs. ancient
Middle East, 5
whale, Jonah swallowed by, 93
What the Bible is All About (Mears),
202
wife(ves)
men with more than one, in Old
Testament, 52–53
submitting to husbands by, Bible's
instruction on, 129–130

will, God's, casting lots as method of
identifying, 54
wisdom
books of, 67–78
psalms, 72
wisdom literature, of Bible, Christians'
dependence on, 74–75
women, not having leadership in
church, New Testament on, 178–179
world, Satan's effect on, 165–166
"worldly," meaning of being, 124
worship, 205
ancient culture and, 9–12
wrestling match, between Jacob and
God, 31–32

Z
Zechariah, book of, 98–99
Zephaniah, book of, 97
ziggurats, 29–30

About the Authors

James Stuart Bell is the owner of Whitestone Communications, a literary development agency. He has received inside or cover credit on over one hundred books. He has written for The Complete Idiot's Guide series as well as A Cup of Comfort series.

Sam O'Neal lives with his wife, Jessica, and their two young children in suburban Chicago. By day Sam is the managing editor of SmallGroups.com for Christianity Today International. By night he is a writer, freelance editor, and raving fan of the Chicago Bears.